The Zulu Aftermath

IBADAN HISTORY SERIES

Editor Dr. K. O. Dike
Vice-Chancellor, University of Ibadan

The Zulu Aftermath

A Nineteenth-Century Revolution in Bantu Africa

J. D. Omer-Cooper

Northwestern University Press
Evanston 1966

First published 1966

Library of Congress Catalog Card Number: 66–19147

Printed in Great Britain

Acknowledgements

In preparing the book I owed much to the encouragement and inspiration of Dr. K. O. Dike, Vice-Chancellor of the University of Ibadan and Editor of this series of studies in African history. I am also deeply indebted for many ideas to my colleagues in the History Department at Ibadan and to the many students whose questions have set me onto new tracks. I would like to extend my thanks to the Methodist Missionary Society for permission to use material from their archives and for the help given me by their library staff. I am also most grateful to the authorities and staff of the Archivo Historico Ultramarina in Lisbon, to M. Kruger and his staff in the library of the Société des Missions Évangéliques de Paris; to the Librarian, Deputy Librarian and staff of the University of Ibadan Library, and to the Librarian and staff of the Royal Commonwealth Society Library, London. I would particularly like to thank Professor I. Schapera of the London School of Economics for reading the text and for his many invaluable suggestions.

Abbreviations

M.M.S. Methodist Missionary Archives, London.
A.H.U. Archivo Historico Ultramarina, Lisbon.

Contents

List of Maps

List of Illustrations

Introduction to the Ibadan History Series

THE *Ibadan History Series* grew out of the efforts of some members of the Department of History, Ibadan University, Nigeria, to evolve a balanced and scholarly study of the history of African peoples south of the Sahara. In the years before the Second World War, the study of African history was retarded, and to some extent vitiated, by the assumption of many scholars that lack of written records in some areas of Africa meant also the absence of history. Documentary evidence had become so overwhelmingly important for the European scholar that he tended to equate written documents with history, and to take the absence of documents to mean the absence of events worthy of historical study. As a result in the nineteenth century, when Europe occupied Africa, her scholars did not attempt to understand or to build on the historical traditions in existence there; they sought instead to challenge and to supplant them. The history of European traders, missionaries, explorers, conquerors and rulers constituted, in their view, the sum total of African history.

Fortunately for the historian of today, African historical consciousness remained alive throughout the period of colonial rule: that tradition was too much a part of the African way of life to succumb to the attacks of the European scholar. Even in the heyday of white supremacy some educated Africans of the period were sufficiently dominated by their past to feel impelled to commit to writing the laws, customs, proverbs, sayings and historical traditions of their own communities. Notable among these may be mentioned James Africanus Horton of Sierra Leone, Reindorf and Sarbah of Ghana, Otomba Payne and Samuel Johnson of Nigeria, Apolo Kagwa of Uganda, to name but a few. The published works they left behind have become important sources of African history today; but they were swimming against the current of their time and made little impression on contemporaries. Historians continued to write as if Africans were not active participants in the great events that shaped their continent.

The decided change towards a new African historiography came with the movement towards independence. African nationalists rejected the European appraisal of their past. They demanded a new orientation and improved educational facilities to effect this reappraisal. With the establishment of new universities in Africa, it was inevitable that the teaching of history and the training of African historians would receive a new impetus. For obvious reasons the changeover was slow in coming. Even in the new universities the old theories for a time prevailed: besides European history, there were courses only on 'European activities in Africa' at the undergraduate level, and at the postgraduate level research was generally on British and French policy towards their African territories.

By the late 1940's, however, African research students were insisting that African history must be the history of Africans, not of Europeans *per se* in Africa; that local records and historical traditions must be used to supplement European metropolitan archives; in short, that Oral Tradition must be accepted as valid material for historical reconstruction. No doubt the validity of non-written sources for historical research had been pointed out before, but it was new for university departments of history to accept it, especially in relation to African Oral Tradition. Even then not everyone was happy about it. Anthropologists replied cautiously that Oral Tradition, even when seemingly factual, was not history and could only be interpreted in terms of its functions in society and within the particular culture. But this did not destroy its validity as material for history; it only argued for a return to the link between history and sociology advocated in the fourteenth century by the famous Tunisian historian, Ibn Khaldum.

Even in studies of European impact on African societies and cultures, where European archival material still remains our major source, this source should be checked and supplemented by Oral Tradition, material artefacts and other sources of history in Africa. The achievement of the present position in the study of African history has been the result of individual and co-operative efforts of many scholars in different parts of the world, but I think it is fair to say that the Universities in Africa, and Ibadan in particular, have played and are playing their part in this pioneering work.

The History Department here has always tried to reflect the new approach to African history. It has pioneered some of the recent studies into African indigenous history and culture. These include the scheme for the Study of Benin History and Culture and two other schemes now in progress, concerned with the cultural history of the peoples of Northern and Eastern Nigeria. Our staff now include the largest concentration of trained African historians to be found anywhere in a single institution. Our postgraduate school is also expanding.

Hitherto, the fruits of our research have been published largely in articles in the *Journal of the Historical Society of Nigeria*. The aim of the Ibadan History Series is to facilitate the publication in book form of some of the major works which are beginning to emerge from the Ibadan School of History and to make available to a growing public, with the minimum of delay, the results of the latest contributions to our knowledge of the African past.

K. ONWUKA DIKE

Ibadan, Nigeria, *18th January, 1965*

Introduction

THE nineteenth century was one of turmoil and violent change in African history. This was largely the result of external influences. The Industrial Revolution brought with it a suddenly increased demand for raw materials and markets. European activities which over most of the continent had been confined to the coast and exercised no more than a marginal and indirect influence on African societies, assumed a new intensity. At first the growing demand for raw materials led to a dramatic increase in the traditional form of European exploitation of Africa—the transportation of manpower to the New World to be employed in the production of sugar and coffee. Later, under the combined impact of changing economic circumstances and philanthropic enthusiasm, the Slave Trade gave way to the attempt to tap the productive capacities of the continent directly to provide raw materials for the insatiable factories and customers for the ever-increasing flood of goods. European interest expanded from the coast into the hinterland, spreading an economic revolution. At the same time the great missionary societies sent dedicated men and women to every part of the continent determined to affect a spiritual and cultural revolution in African society. Europe now began to influence Africa in a manner never attempted after the failure of the Portuguese Congo Experiment: directly through missionaries working within societies and attempting to instil new beliefs, moral standards and aptitudes rather than externally through trade contact. The combined process culminated in the 'Scramble for Africa' and the establishment of colonial rule. In this period of transformation which established the outlines of the modern physiognomy of the continent, Africa was not mere passive material moulded by external forces. The development of European activities themselves was a matter of reciprocal action and reaction with indigenous African societies. Their nature, direction and extent and their permanent significance for African history all depended on the African reaction to them. But in the very century when external influences were to assume dramatically increased importance for the development of Africa, internal forces which had been gathering strength over centuries were to bring about far-reaching changes over wide areas of the continent. These great movements were independent of European influence in origin, though as they developed they interlocked with expanding European activity affecting and being affected by it. They brought about changes in African societies and African demography which are of no less significance for an understanding of modern Africa than those resulting from external influences.

One of these great movements was the spread of Islamic reforming fervour in the Western Sudan, resulting in the series of Jihads which not only permanently transformed much of the western sudanic belt but also spread their effects deep into the forest, as in Yorubaland, where they combined with internal forces in the Oyo empire and European influences to produce the present pattern in Western Nigeria. A second, which is the subject of this work, began in South Africa and spread through Central Africa as far as the southern shores of Lake Victoria.

The grestest movement in African history is undoubtedly the long and mainly unrecorded process of expansion and colonization which brought the Bantu from their original home, probably in West Africa, to occupy most of the continent south of the Sahara. This long expansive movement can only be explained by a steady growth of population over the centuries, leading to the urge to occupy and settle new lands, and by superior weapons and/or economic techniques and patterns of social organization which gave the Bantu the advantage over earlier peoples. The movement as a whole was probably extremely complex, marked by conflicting currents, backwashes, eddies and whirlpools as well as calm stretches of even flow.

In African prehistory the southern sub-continent seems usually to have evolved at a slower pace than the rest; providing a last refuge for peoples and cultures that had disappeared elsewhere. It was the last area to be settled by the expanding Bantu and as late as the nineteenth century Bantu colonization was still incomplete. South of the Fish and Orange rivers and west of the Kalahari the indigenous population still consisted of the stone-age hunting and food-gathering Bushmen, and their pastoral cousins, the Hottentots, though by this time the community of white immigrants expanding from the Cape had deprived these peoples of ownership of most of their lands and was in direct contact with the advance guard of the Bantu.

North and east of these lines, however, a Bantu population had been established for several centuries. The period of colonization was over and as population continued to increase a local centre of high pressure developed in Zululand, producing a violent eddy which sent ripples scudding over most of Southern and Central Africa.

The beginnings of this development in Zululand can be traced to the eighteenth century when under pressure of land hunger and more severe intertribal conflict, the small tribe of the first settlement phase (little more than an expanded clan) began to give way to large multitribal blocs which competed for the allegiance of the remaining independent tribes. As this took place a process of institutional change also began, probably facilitated by contact between tribes belonging to the two major divisions of the Southern Bantu (Sotho and Nguni). Conflict between the new groupings increased the pace of change still further and between 1818 and 1828 it reached a revolutionary climax in the Zulu kingdom of Shaka.

The immediate stimulus to this development was military conflict and the logic of the process can be found in the adaptation of existing institutions along militarist lines and with a view to the incorporation of tribal aliens in an expanded fighting force. It resulted in the emergence of a large kingdom, with subjects drawn from many different original tribes, rigidly organized on military lines and with a tremendous concentration of power in the hands of the monarch: a system radically different in structure and spirit from the prototypes from which it had grown.

This process by its very nature could not be confined to its original centre of origin. It was accompanied by warfare on a scale hitherto unknown amongst the Southern Bantu which sent defeated tribes fleeing from the storm centre, their cattle and grain stores abandoned to the victors, to fall as ravenous hordes of pillagers upon others, starting a chain reaction which spread its effects over thousands of miles.

As the tempo of conflict mounted in Zululand one of the original tribal blocs was pushed out to the north-east. There under its chief, Sobhuza, it consolidated its authority over numerous alien tribes and laid the foundations of the modern Swazi state. Then, as the Zulu triumphed over all opposition, defeated tribes were driven out of the area to the north, west and south. Two great peoples, the Ngoni (consisting of two independent sections) and the Shangana, took the northward direction. In a violent reversal of the age-old Bantu trend to the south, they carried Southern Bantu cultural conceptions to the areas of modern Mozambique, Malawi, Zambia and Tanganyika.

Westward across the Drakensberg two powerful groups, the Ngwane and the Hlubi, fled onto the interior plateau throwing the peaceable tribes of the highveld into turmoil and confusion. In a similar direction but further to the north Mzilikazi, Shaka's rebellious general, led a break-away section of the Zulu themselves, founding a kingdom in the Transvaal on the wreckage of numerous earlier tribes, till under pressure of conflict with the Zulu and the Boers of the Great Trek, he took his people north again to establish the Ndebele (Matabele) kingdom in Matabeleland.

The anarchic conditions amongst the highveld peoples resulting from these sudden invasions produced several important consequences. The pattern of population distribution in Transorangia and the Transvaal was radically altered. Wide areas were almost deserted; others became centres of dense population. Many tribal fragments came together under Moshesh to form the Basuto nation. Other tribes which survived the storm tended to expand by absorbing weaker groups. One powerful people, the Kololo, was driven to abandon its homeland and undertook a prolonged migration to the upper Zambesi, establishing an empire in Barotseland which in turn had offshoots in the Shire valley of modern Malawi.

To the south of Zululand the once-dense population of Natal was devastated by the passage of hordes of refugees fleeing from the Zulu and then by Zulu armies themselves. Natal was almost deserted and its population piled up in a confused jumble of tribes on the borders of Pondoland. Many of these refugees penetrated into the Transkei and threw themselves on the mercy of the Thembu and Xhosa. They were allowed to settle down as Mfengu and became an unassimilated minority which further complicated the tangled politics of the Cape's eastern frontier.

These migrations all sprang from a single source, they overlapped in time and often influenced one another directly. Though their effects were felt in widely separate areas they are really aspects of a single process which, in scale alone, must be regarded as one of the great formative events of African history. It far exceeds other comparable movements such as the sixteenth-century migrations of the Zimba and Jagas and it positively dwarfs the Boer Great Trek.

This colossal upheaval was accompanied by carnage and destruction on an appalling scale. Whole tribes were massacred and even more died in the famine and anarchy which followed in the wake of the desolating hordes. Still greater numbers abandoned their ancestral lands and sought refuge in difficult mountain country or elsewhere, where geographical features held out hope of asylum. The pattern of population distribution in South Africa (and to a lesser extent in Central Africa) was radically changed. Instead of a fairly even scatter of tribes with population density varying according to the advantages of water and soil, great agglomerations of peoples emerged, often centred on relatively inhospitable terrain and separated from one another by considerable tracts of virtually empty land.

This in turn directly influenced the expansion of the South African white community. Population pressure and angry feelings against the philanthropic leanings of the British Government found a vent in mass emigration into the vacuum created by the preceding Bantu movements. The line of Boer advance, deflected from its natural route up the east coast by the Xhosa resistance, turned northward and poured into the gaps newly created in the Bantu settlement pattern. The new white states which arose out of the Trek were each centred on areas particularly heavily devastated by the *Mfecane*[1] while the areas of continuing Bantu occupation (Basutoland, the Transkei, Zululand, Swaziland, Bechuanaland) were those which had been spared in the upheaval.

In Central Africa also the intrusion of the militarist Ngoni amongst the peoples of modern Malawi, Zambia and Tanganyika combined with the devastations attendant on the expansion of the Slave Trade to produce conditions of chaos and desolation which invited European intervention.

This is to look mainly at the negative consequences of what was in essence a process of positive evolution. In Zululand a new type of state had emerged, the large centralized kingdom replacing the small clan-based tribe, and as the turbulence created by this transformation radiated outwards it spread the process of socio-political change. Some of the peoples who fled from the Zulu had learnt the essentials of their political and military organization from them (one group, the Ndebele, was in fact a break-away section of the Zulu state). As they moved they carried the essentials of this system, modifying them in a number of ways to suit the exigencies of the circumstances in which they found themselves. Others whose lives were disrupted by the chain of disturbances had no direct contact with Zulu methods but in reaction to conditions of chaotic insecurity they clustered together in large supra-tribal communities, developing their own methods of governing and maintaining the coherence of their new socio-political units. The Basuto kingdom of Moshesh was by far the most important of the states formed in this way but the Bhaca of the Transkei were created by an analogous process and many other groups in South and Central Africa exhibited the same tendency to varying degrees. The wars and migrations of the Mfecane were the by-products of a socio-political revolution towards

1 The term *Mfecane* is an Nguni word used for the wars and disturbances which accompanied the rise of the Zulu. It has previously been used by Walker in his *History of Southern Africa*. The Sotho term *Lifaqane* often used to describe the disturbances in the area of Sotho occupation is derived from the Nguni word.

larger communities and wider loyalties. It was a genuine process of nation-building, though in the course of its development it destroyed old unities as well as creating new ones. The venerable Momomatapa empire, which had survived three centuries of Portuguese contact and had reached its peak in the eighteenth century under the Rozwi dynasty of Shangamire, was irreparably shattered and the unity of the Maravi peoples gravely impaired.

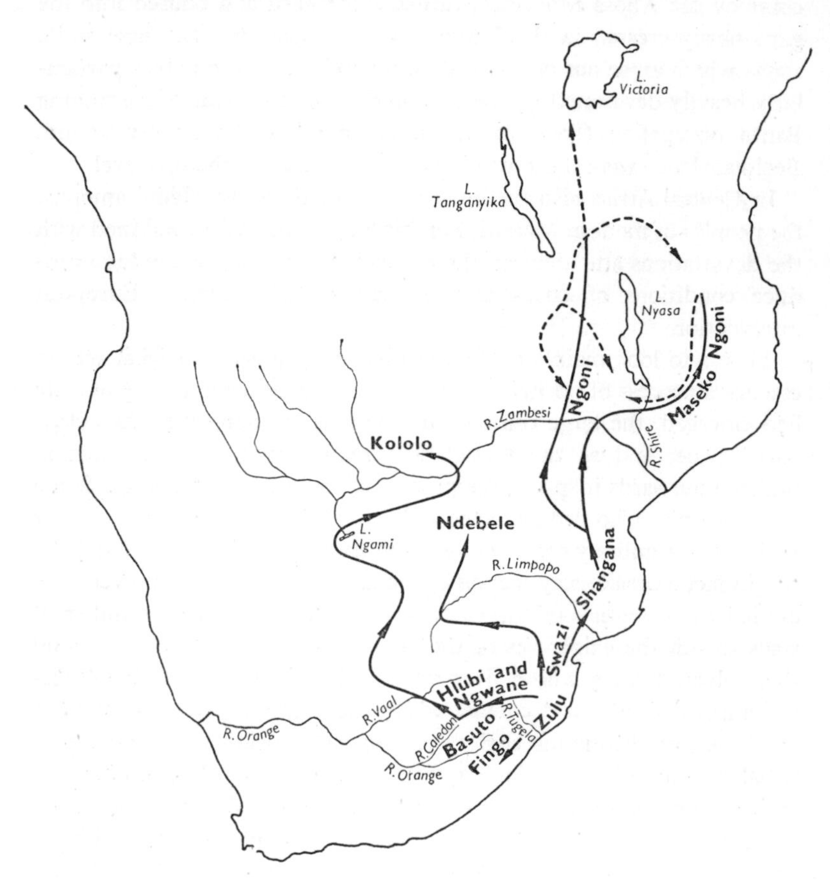

General direction of the main movements of the Mfecane

In the agony of war and insecurity attendant on this revolution, leadership was all-important and the Bantu produced a galaxy of great leaders who deserve to be considered among the outstanding architects of African history—Shaka, the military and political genius of the Zulu; Moshesh, the creator of the Basuto nation and one of South Africa's greatest statesmen; Zwangendaba, who led the Ngoni on their tremendous migration from northern Zululand to modern Tanganyika; Faku, the Pondo chief, who prevented the tide of war sweeping over the Transkei—to mention only a few.

The significance of the Mfecane does not lie solely in the past. The socio-political communities which it brought into existence have in many cases survived into modern times. Two of them, the Basuto and Swazi kingdoms, have remained as distinct political entities and are on the point of entering the community of independent African states. Others, though incorporated in the still-wider units imposed by colonialism, persist as cultural units and powerful foci of loyalty. The events of the Mfecane have moreover impressed themselves indelibly on the consciousness of subsequent generations. The memories and traditions of this period serve to maintain the sense of identity of peoples who were vitally affected by it, influencing attitudes within and between groups in many complex ways. In the context of white rule, this heritage has helped many peoples to keep alive a sense of pride and independence of spirit. Together with other factors it has contributed to that great reservoir of largely inarticulate feelings and attitudes which underlies the emergence of modern African political movements.

The purpose of the present work is to give an analysis of the movement as a whole; to relate the great chain of wars and migrations to the underlying processes of socio-political change and to attempt an assessment of the significance of the Mfecane in the history of Southern and Central Africa, the way it affected later developments and its enduring importance for an understanding of the contemporary situation. In painting on so large a canvas I have inevitably had to sacrifice a certain degree of depth and detail in the treatment of particular movements in order to preserve a picture of the coherence and interconnectedness of the whole vast process and bring out its essential character as the spread of a revolutionary process of change from a single centre. My purpose is basically synthetic and interpretive. I have examined the Archives of the Methodist Missionary Society, the Société des Missions Évangéliques de Paris, and the Portuguese Archivo Historico Ultramarina for material which might throw new light on different aspects of the process. My main task has, however, been the attempt to bring together the existing published material—source material, in the form of travellers' and missionaries' accounts and compilations of oral tradition; secondary matter in the form of historical works and anthropological studies—to form an hypothetical reconstruction of the nature of process and the way that it developed as it spread out from its original centre. The most important lacuna in my investigations of which I am conscious is the unpublished material in German on the Ngoni of Tanganyika which might be discovered in the East German Archives. I would also have liked to have been able to consult the administrative records of Tanganyika, Malawi, Zambia and Southern Rhodesia though these would be more directly relevant to the colonial period than to the present study.

One of the difficulties which I encountered in preparing this work calls for special mention. It was the question of when to end accounts of the development of the various African societies involved in the Mfecane. Though the upheaval was in origin independent of external influences, the story of the peoples involved later becomes entangled with the history of colonial expansion and gradually merges into the general history of the various colonial territories. The process of internal change with Bantu societies which started in the Mfecane continued long after contact with Europeans had begun. My problem was to avoid being drawn into a general treatment of the establishment of colonial rule while at the same time not truncating the history of Bantu political societies. In order to assess the historical importance of the Mfecane, it also seemed necessary to carry the story of some of the more important states right down to modern times. I have therefore not followed any absolute rule with regard to terminal dates but attempted to let the nature of each situation determine the matter. In general I have concentrated on the formative precolonial period and where necessary provided a skeleton outline of subsequent developments.

1 Bantu South Africa before the Mfecane

SOUTH AFRICA is the southern continuation of the great African plateau which extends northward into the Sahara. Changes in sea level in remote times and erosion by rivers eating away at the plateau edge have produced a coastal strip which runs right round the sub-continent and rises to an escarpment marking the rim of the plateau. This escarpment is most clearly marked on the east coast where the Drakensberg range constitutes a formidable barrier to human movement and the most important watershed in South Africa. At its northern end in Zululand the hard rock of the Drakensberg range gives way to softer material and the escarpment loses its character as a sharp divide. This area forms a natural meeting-place for peoples and cultures. Further north again the edge of the plateau recedes to a great distance inland giving way to the great coastal plain of Southern Mozambique and the Transvaal lowveld. At the southern end of the Drakensberg range the escarpment breaks up into a series of ranges until near the Cape the pattern is complicated by the fold mountains of the Cape series. Along the west coast the escarpment appears again and can be traced northward past a gap produced by the Orange River to the Benguela Highlands of Angola.

The plateau as a whole has a very gentle westward tilt. Though much of it is remarkably flat (platteland) it is relieved of complete monotony by mountain ranges like the Magaliesberg and the Zoutpansberg as well as by the ubiquitous isolated flat-topped hills (koppies) which are such a striking feature of South African scenery.

This general structural pattern determines the climate and vegetation and has influenced the history of South African peoples in many ways. In summer, winds from the Indian Ocean bring rains which precipitate first along the coastal strip and the eastern escarpment and gradually diminish westward towards the Atlantic. A cold current running down the western shores of South Africa prevents the same phenomenon occurring on that side, and the Atlantic winds precipitate their moisture out at sea leaving the western coastlands parched and arid. (In the immediate vicinity of the Cape the mountains of the Cape series radically alter this pattern. The summer rainfall régime gives way to a 'Mediterranean' climate with winter rains and behind the mountains the semi-desert Karroo is shielded from rain-bearing winds.)

Along the east coast numerous rivers flow down from the escarpment to the Indian Ocean and have served as historic frontiers. As they have relatively small catchment areas, they are, however, generally easily fordable, except in times of flood. They did not constitute permanent obstacles to human movement. The greatest rivers of South Africa rise on the eastern edge of the plateau and flow westward towards the Atlantic. The Orange and the Caledon rise in the Basutoland massif. Uniting their waters in the plains of Transorangia, they are joined further west by the Vaal and the combined waters flow on westward to the ocean.

In accordance with the rainfall pattern the vegetation is densest in the bushveld of the eastern coastal strip and gives way to open grasslands on the interior plateau. These become more sparse to the west until they are replaced by the scattered tree scrub of Bechuanaland and the Kalahari. In South Africa as a whole permanent sources of water are relatively scarce. They are more common in the east and almost disappear in the Kalahari. The cold southern winter prevents the spread of tsetse fly or malaria and provides a healthy environment for men and cattle, but even in the most favoured areas prolonged droughts can drastically reduce the carrying capacity of the land from time to time.

The Southern Bantu, who occupy most of modern Southern Rhodesia, the southern provinces of Mozambique and South Africa, belong to a great family of peoples which spread out from an original centre, possibly in the region of the Cross River, and gradually occupied most of sub-Saharan Africa south of a line from the Bight of Benin to the Horn of Somaliland.[1] During the long process of expansion the Bantu intermingled with, and gradually absorbed or expelled, the previous populations. The latter are now known largely from the remains of their rock-paintings and stone implements and from the survival of traces of their languages. In East and South Africa they probably consisted of hunting and food-gathering peoples belonging to the Bushman group, while in the Congo Basin the Pygmies probably constituted the aboriginal population. In East Africa the Bantu also came in contact with the Nilotic peoples and with Arab traders.

In course of time the Bantu divided into many different groups with very different languages and cultures. Some developed elaborate political

1 This hypothesis is based largely on linguistic evidence. See Greenberg: *The Languages of Africa*. Though still not universally accepted, it is receiving increasing support.

systems like the Monomatapa kingdom which created the great complex of stone buildings at Zimbabwe, while others adhered to a family/village organization. Two characteristics distinguish the Southern Bantu from their northern neighbours, the Central Bantu, who settled in a belt across the continent from the Congo to Mozambique. They all trace descent patrilineally (from father to son) while the Central Bantu for the most part accept the matrilineal (mother's brother to sister's son) descent pattern. They are also cattle-keepers while the Central Bantu tend to rely exclusively upon agriculture. These traits suggest a probable

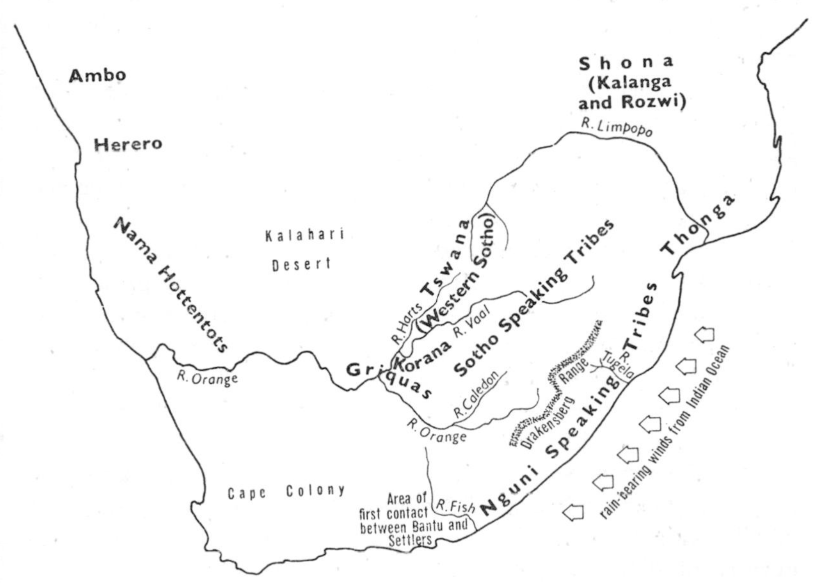

Outline distribution of peoples at the beginning of the nineteenth century

relationship between the Southern Bantu and the patrilineal Bantu of Tanganyika and Uganda who are in contact with cattle-keeping Nilotic peoples.[1]

In South Africa the Bantu were relatively recent immigrants. Though the lateness of their arrival has been much exaggerated[2] it is unlikely

1 The historical relationship between the Bantu and the Nilotic peoples of East Africa is still very unclear.

2 Thus Murdock makes the wholly unjustified statement that the Sotho did not enter Bechuanaland until 1720. *Africa, Its Peoples and Their Culture History*, p. 386.

that they were south of the Limpopo in any considerable numbers before the twelfth century A.D. at the earliest.[1] Though by the eighteenth century they had been established in much of South Africa for a considerable period, expansion was still actively continuing into territory as yet unsettled. Before their coming the land had been occupied by two closely related peoples, the Hottentots and Bushmen. Both belonged to a single racial stock with the distinctive characteristics of yellowish-brown skin colour, short stature, chamaeocephalic skull shape and tendency to pronounced steatopygy. These characteristics are clearest in the Bushmen. The Hottentots may have been the result of racial mixture. Both peoples spoke related languages characterized by click sounds.[2] In their religious beliefs and rituals they also had much in common but in their economic life they were widely different.

The Bushmen lived entirely by hunting and food-gathering. They lived in small tightly knit hunting bands peregrinating around a jealously guarded hunting territory. They slept in temporary shelters or in caves which they adorned with representations of animals, men and hunting scenes. By disposition a mild and peaceful people, they would resist intrusion on their hunting grounds to the death, attacking the enemy directly with their poisoned arrows and indirectly by surprise raids on their cattle. The Hottentots were pastoral people who subsisted mainly on their cattle and sheep. They practised no agriculture and enriched their diet by hunting and food-gathering like the Bushmen. Their distribution was largely confined to the coastal areas from South-west Africa round the Cape and up the east coast of South Africa as far as the Kei River at least. Their more developed economy enabled the Hottentots to live in larger socio-political groups. They were associated in tribes each made up of a number of related clans. These tribes frequently sub-divided as population and herds increased.

As the Bantu advanced these earlier peoples were gradually expelled or absorbed. Often relations were hostile but there was a good deal of intermarriage and the Bantu adopted some of the click sounds from the languages of their predecessors. Sometimes Bushmen communities were associated with Bantu tribes in a vassal relationship (a situation which still persists in some parts of the Bechuanaland Protectorate). Else-

1 Al Masudi writing *circa* A.D. 943 stated that Sofala was then the limit of settlement of the Zanj. Further south lived the Wak-Wak who kept no cattle, went naked and spoke in unintelligible whistles. In spite of much learned controversy it is reasonable to assume that the Wak-Wak were Bushmen. See de Meynard and de Courteille, transl.: *Les Prairies d'Or et Mines de Diamants.*

2 The Khoisan languages, as the tongues of the Bushmen and Hottentots are called, use five click sounds which are unique to them and to languages known to have been influenced by them.

where, pockets of the earlier inhabitants survived in relatively inhospitable localities within territory long occupied by the Bantu.[1]

The pattern of Bantu settlement in South Africa was strongly influenced by geographical factors. The coastal corridor stretching along the east coast from Zululand and Natal to the borders of the Cape Colony was the home of numerous tribes belonging to a distinct language group, the Nguni. The tribes of this group speak what can be regarded as dialects of a single language. They are all mutually intelligible though difference of pronunciation and vocabulary exist particularly between the most northerly and most southerly tribes of the group. Because they had advanced further to the south than any other Bantu people and had traversed relatively well-watered country which may be assumed to have had a comparatively dense pre-Bantu population, the Nguni adopted more of the click sounds, typical of Khoisan speech, than other Southern Bantu.[2] In culture the Nguni tribes were also closely related to one another.

Accounts of Portuguese sailors shipwrecked on the east coast, together with oral tradition, have made it possible to form a rough picture of the timing of Bantu colonization in this area. From these sources it has been calculated that the Xhosa, vanguard of the Nguni group, were settled near the upper Umzimvubu by 1300 and possibly considerably earlier and that by 1593 they had reached as far south as the Umtata River.[3] By the eighteenth century they had reached the Fish River and were beginning intensive settlement still further west when they encountered the first Boer farmers moving up the coast in search of grazing land.[4]

On the interior plateau another language group, the Sotho, was settled. They had entered South Africa in three separate migrations into the area of modern Bechuanaland. From there they spread out southward and eastward over most of the plateau nearly as far south as the Orange River. Westward movement was prevented by the Kalahari though one tribe, the Tawana, penetrated to Lake Ngami and settled on its shores. More heterogeneous than the Nguni, the Sotho divided into three main sub-groupings. The westernmost tribes are known as the Tswana (Bechuana); those of Transorangia and Basutoland as the

1 See I. Schapera: *The Khoisan Peoples of South Africa*. It has been estimated that as many as 50,000 Bushmen survive to this day, the majority in association with Bantu in Bechuanaland, South-west Africa, and Angola. See P. Tobias: 'Bushmen of the Kalahari', *Man*, March 1957, pp. 132–9.

2 The Nguni use three of the Khoisan clicks now represented alphabetically by c, q, and x. In the Sotho languages they are very little used.

3 M. Wilson: 'Early History of the Transkei and Ciskei', *African Studies*, vol. 18, no. 4, 1959, pp. 167–79.

4 See J. Marais: *Maynier and the First Boer Republic*, pp. 1–15.

Southern Sotho; and the tribes of central and northern Transvaal as the Northern Sotho. In this last area two other smaller immigrant groups had settled. These were the Venda and the Lemba who are believed to be offshoots of the Kalanga people of Southern Rhodesia.[1] The dates of the Sotho migrations cannot be established with the same certainty as those of the Nguni. The first migration may have entered Bechuanaland in the thirteenth or fourteenth century, and the ancestors of the present Tswana peoples were settled near their present habitat by about 1600.[2]

Though these two language groups were separated from one another by the coastal escarpment the separation was by no means absolute. Some Nguni groups filtered across the central Drakensberg into what is now Basutoland. It was, however, at the northern end of the range, where the escarpment ceases to be an important barrier, that overlapping was most considerable. Some Nguni (the Transvaal Ndebele) had penetrated from the coast onto the plateau, while in northern Zululand and Swaziland Sotho tribes lived alongside Nguni.

The Kalahari remained a refuge for a sparse population of Bushmen hunting groups and west of it Hottentots still occupied the land as far north as modern Windhoek. North of this a third language group, consisting of the Herero and the Ambo, were gradually moving south. These peoples, however, were not directly involved in the Mfecane.

In spite of differences of language and custom the Nguni and Sotho hared a basically common culture. Both were cattle-keepers and cattle meant far more to them than a mere source of food and clothing. Cattle were the only currency in which the dowry validating a marriage could be paid. They were the only acceptable sacrifice on important ritual occasions and their possession was the sign of social status. The cattle enclosure (kraal) was the centre of every settlement not merely in the physical but also in the social sense. In this area, ritually taboo to women, the men would gather to discuss questions of policy or law. In addition to their herds, however, the two groups also practised agriculture. Millet, the staple crop, with the later addition of maize, was planted mainly by the women, and corn not needed for immediate consumption was stored in covered pits beneath the surface of the cattle enclosure. It was this mixed economy which enabled the Bantu to maintain relatively high population densities and to develop more complex social and political institutions than their predecessors.

The basic family unit often consisted of a considerable number of persons closely related in the male line. A single family head would

1 See I. Schapera, ed: *The Bantu-speaking Tribes of South Africa*, pp. 63–6.
2 I. Schapera: *The Ethnic Composition of Tswana Tribes*, pp. 5–7.

adjudicate over minor disputes. Members of the family lived near to one another, their huts forming either an isolated rural hamlet or a family compound within a larger settlement. The distribution of family settlements was determined by geographical as well as social considerations. On the east coast, where permanent sources of water were comparatively numerous, families formed isolated hamlets scattered fairly evenly over the land. On the interior plateau, the Sotho tended to live in more concentrated village settlements and near the fringes of the Kalahari, where permanent waterholes were very scarce, the Tswana lived in substantial towns around them, keeping their cattle at outposts which might be some distance from the central settlement. Marriage was commonly polygamous and the wives of a polygamous husband were divided into a number of households with a fixed order of prestige and different rights to the inheritance of property. Amongst the Nguni, for example, households were distinguished as 'right hand' or 'left hand' according to the position they occupied in relation to the central cattle enclosure. Persons who traced descent from a common ancestor constituted a clan. They shared a common name and might not intermarry until, with the passing of generations, a clan split and intermarriage was legalized. This often happened when a chief wanted to marry within his own clan.[1]

Southern Bantu political organization was of a form natural to a people in the process of actively colonizing new territory. The tribe, the unit of political life, though larger than that of the Hottentots, still usually consisted of only a few thousand members. The principle of family relationship was very important and to some extent the tribe of this period could be regarded as a clan enlarged by the adhesion of a certain number of members who did not belong to the central stock. From other points of view, however, it had developed beyond the stage of a kinship group and must be regarded as a simple type of state.[2] At the core of every tribe was a central lineage. The chief was always a member of this and his close relatives often held subordinate offices or were members of his council. All possessed a certain aristocratic status, though this might not imply any political or economic privilege.

In addition to members of the central clan most tribes contained families who belonged to other clans. These commoner families associated themselves with the traditions of the royal clan to a considerable extent. The ancestors of the chief were regarded as guardian spirits of the whole community and the tribal name was taken either from that

1 The range of prohibited unions was considerably wider among the Nguni than the Sotho.

2 See I. Schapera: *Government and Politics in Tribal Societies.*

of an outstanding ruler (as among the Nguni) or from the totem animal of the royal clan (as among the Sotho). But commoner families retained their own clan identities and members of the same clan might be divided between several different tribes. In times of war, however, political loyalty superseded the bonds of clan membership. The tribe was thus a genuine political society rather than a group based on blood relationship. Families might even leave an unpopular chief and transfer their membership to another tribe. This was regarded as treason by the deserted chief but welcomed as a means of increasing his strength by the ruler to whom they fled. Through this process the relative strength of tribes might vary considerably from time to time and the danger of finding his following wasted away by desertion was a powerful sanction restraining a ruler from acting in the face of public opinion.[1]

In other respects also the Bantu tribe displayed the characteristics of a state system. Each tribe laid claim to a definite territory even though its boundaries might not be accurately defined. Rights to the use of land within this area were controlled by the chief in the name of the tribe as a whole. Permanent private ownership of land was not recognized, but where a family had broken new ground for planting it was usually considered to have a right to its use unless deprived of it for some grave offence. A chief could allow other communities to make use of tribal land in return for a payment in recognition of his authority. The grant of such privileges never implied a permanent transfer of ownership nor could it exclude the members of the owning tribe from making use of the land together with the newcomers.

It is perhaps in relation to law that the political nature of the Bantu tribal community can be seen most clearly. The conception of private justice had been almost completely superseded. A man was regarded primarily as a member of the political community rather than of his clan. Murder was a crime against the chief to be punished in his court and not a family matter to be settled by a blood feud. Even when a man died of natural causes his family might have to give a beast to the chief to compensate him for the loss of a follower. This principle did not only apply to cases of death. All disputes or crimes outside the circle of the immediate family were dealt with through the hierarchy of public courts where the accused could summon witnesses to refute his accusers in an open trial.

Constituting as he did the focus of political loyalty and the symbol of tribal unity, the chief's position was of the greatest importance. He was at one and the same time civil, military, judicial and religious head of his people. His court was the supreme court of appeal from all inferior

1 See, e.g., W. Shaw: *The Story of My Mission*, pp. 440–2.

tribunals and his decision was theoretically final in all political matters. As the living link between the community and its ancestors he was the chief celebrant in many important rituals and even such specialist activities as the detection of sorcerers or the magical summoning of rain, which often fell outside his competence, were undertaken under his authority and control. In some tribes it was forbidden to partake of the new crop until the chief had formally authorized it in annual first-fruit ceremonies.

The chief's position was, however, far from absolute for he was expected to rule with the advice of the leading men and in accordance with custom and the general consensus of opinion. In day-to-day matters he would be assisted by an inner council of confidential advisers. On more important occasions a wider council of all important subordinate chiefs would be held before decisions were taken. Amongst the Sotho, whose closer pattern of settlement made it practicable, vital matters of policy were discussed in a general assembly open to all adult males and known as the *pitso*. In these assemblies anyone interested could speak his mind and even criticize the chief severely. Decisions were not taken by a formal vote. The chief would pronounce his own conclusion but he generally did so in the light of the mood of the meeting. (Amongst the Nguni, public assemblies were only held at the annual first-fruit ceremonies and lacked the political significance of the *pitso*.) Though the chief always had the last word and could theoretically override the sentiments of any of these councils and assemblies, public opinion was supported by the sanctions of assassination, civil war or secession.

Administrative authority in the tribe was distributed between the chief and a hierarchy of subordinates. Depending on its size, the tribal territory was divided into a number of sub-divisions, provinces and districts. Each of these was under the authority of a sub-chief and where the tribe was large there might be a two-tier system. At the base of the pyramid the family head was the ultimate unit of authority. All the important subordinate chieftaincies were normally held by close relatives of the chief. Exceptions to this might arise when break-away groups from other tribes were incorporated but even in such cases their leaders generally affiliated themselves to the royal family by marriage. In this system the royal households played an important role. Chiefs' wives were divided into households like those of commoners but on a much larger scale. Each household of a powerful tribal chief constituted a village in itself and they were often situated in different parts of the tribal territory. In some tribes it was customary to affiliate districts to one or other of the royal homesteads. These became the administrative headquarters of the areas in which they were established and the local rallying points for the tribal army.

To assist him further in the exercise of his office, the tribal ruler was served by at least one, and sometimes several, permanent officials, *induna*. The title was applied to every state official, whether a leader appointed to a military command or a simple messenger, but there was always a chief *induna*. His duties were multifarious. He was expected to be the 'eyes and ears' of the chief, to keep him informed of the state of public opinion and guard against conspiracies. He could deputize for the chief at judicial proceedings and issue instructions in his name. Chief *indunas* were generally chosen from commoner families to prevent them using their powerful position to usurp the chieftaincy.

Subordinate chieftaincies were organized on the same lines as the central one. The sub-chief would conduct business with the advice of men of local importance. He would have an *induna* of his own and would hold his own court. The main difference between his position and that of the tribal ruler lay in the fact that he acted under the ultimate authority of his overlord and might have appeals against judgement in his court referred to the higher tribunal.

Both Nguni and Sotho tribes practised a system of initiation into manhood. The rite consisted of circumcision followed by a period of ritual seclusion during which the young initiates lived apart from the tribe and were instructed in the duties of manhood. It ended with the destruction of their temporary dwellings and ceremonies to mark their admission into adult society. Only after initiation could a young man marry and take part in the councils of his community. Amongst the Nguni tribes this rite was performed at the local level and had little political significance. In Sotho tribes, however, the initiation ceremonies were performed under the authority of the chief and provided the basis for a system of military organization. The chief decided when an initiation school should be opened and whenever possible arranged for one of his sons to go through the ceremony on each occasion. All who attended the same initiation school formed an age-regiment which was associated with a particular prince. Throughout their lives the members of an age-regiment continued to recognize their affiliation though they married and settled in different parts of the tribal territory. In times of war they would fight together as a unit under the leadership of their royal age-mate and at other times they could be called together to perform such public services as building a new homestead for the chief. Amongst the Southern Sotho where tribal population was split between several villages, territorial sub-chiefs held their own initiation schools. In Tswana tribes where the people were concentrated in a single town the initiation rites and resulting age-regiments covered the whole tribe. Among some Sotho-speaking tribes there were also initiation ceremonies for women and these gave rise to female age-regiments each headed by a daughter of the chief.

The initiation-mate system could provide a horizontal link cutting across the vertical ties of the territorial chieftaincy system, but in Sotho tribes before the Mfecane it only served this purpose to a limited extent. Where sub-chiefs held their own ceremonies, centrifugal tendencies would be increased rather than diminished. Even where the system spanned the whole tribe, the association of each age group with a particular prince was likely to increase the frequency and severity of succession quarrels. The Sotho tribes were no less prone to internal struggles than the Nguni.

In all Southern Bantu tribes the fact that important sub-chieftaincies were held by close relatives of the tribal ruler tended to encourage internal disputes. Chieftaincy was regarded as inhering more in the royal lineage than in any particular individual. Though there was a definite law of succession it was not regarded as absolutely sacrosanct and where an heir was judged incapable or otherwise undesirable he might be passed over in favour of some other member of the royal family. The rule of succession itself, instead of helping to resolve problems of conflict between potential heirs, tended to exacerbate them. In addition to the normal households of commoner families a chief was expected to establish a 'great house' headed by a 'great wife'. She could only be married after the chief's accession to power and her dowry was paid by contribution from the tribe as a whole. She was thus an official state bride and in theory it was the eldest son of this household who was the rightful heir. The chief often married his 'great wife' late in his life and it frequently happened that he died leaving his official heir a minor. A regency would then be necessary, with all the temptations to usurpation which that implies. Even when the heir was not a minor he often had older half-brothers who had established their own followings before he came to the throne. Succession thus rarely passed undisputed and though the law of inheritance was universally accepted it is doubtful whether it was actually followed in a majority of cases. In these disputes one of the protagonists might overcome his opponents but more frequently the tribe divided into two or more sections. This was facilitated by the fact that the major sub-sections of the tribe possessed, in miniature, the complete structure of tribal government. The process can be exemplified from the history of the Xhosa tribe. Originally a single community, it experienced a number of minor secessions and then underwent a radical split when Rarabe, of the 'right-hand' house, broke away from Gcaleka, the official heir. The tribe was thus divided into two major sections, Gcaleka's and Rarabe's. But before long another split took place. The heir of the Rarabe chieftaincy was a minor and his uncle utilized the position of regent to build up his own following. When the young Gaika (Ngqika) at last became chief he offended against tribal custom and his uncle, Ndlambe, took the opportunity to secede and established yet another independent section. These offshoots of the original Xhosa community were politically independent and sometimes at war with one another, though the seniority of the Gcaleka branch was recognized as a matter of courtesy.[1] A similar pattern can be seen in the history of practically every Southern Bantu tribe in the pre-Mfecane period.

The process of fissiparous multiplication is not unique to the history of the Southern Bantu tribes. It is natural in a system based on a hierarchy of 'royals'. A very similar process can be seen in the history of the Soga kingdoms of Uganda and it has been suggested that Bantu state systems were inherently unstable.[2] But the tendency to constant sub-division must not be looked at in the light of political structure alone. It was the natural response of a people colonizing a new territory where the difficulties of maintaining large herds in limited areas and the abundance of unoccupied land favoured relatively small aggregations. The absence of powerful organized opposition to expansion but the ever-present threat of small-scale attacks from Bushmen or Hottentots made the development of large-scale military organization unnecessary and encouraged decentralization of authority. The history of other Bantu societies shows that this type of structure can lend itself to a process of aggregation as easily as to one of fragmentation. A conquered tribe could be simply grafted on to the territorial hierarchy, its chief becoming a regional sub-chief. Portuguese accounts of the kingdoms of Monomatapa and Congo show that both these great Bantu states grew up in this way.[3]

Conflicts between Bantu tribes were not uncommon. Succession disputes were often accompanied by fighting, and when a tribe split, the two sections sometimes continued to nourish feelings of hostility for many years. As tribes expanded, conflict over frontiers with their neighbours could often lead to minor wars.[4] Though not infrequent, warfare was not very severe. Fighting was normally limited to seizing cattle or

1 See Soga: *The South-Eastern Bantu*, pp. 128–51, and G. M. Theal: *History of South Africa*, vol. V, pp. 37–8.
2 L. A. Fallers: *Bantu Bureaucracy*, pp. 227–38.
3 See Cuvelier: *L'Ancien Royaume du Congo*, and Theal: *Records of South Eastern Africa*, vol. VII.
4 See, e.g., H. Lichtenstein: *Travels in Southern Africa*, vol. I, pp. 341–4.

grazing lands and rarely proceeded to the lengths of crushing an enemy tribe completely. Little life was lost and non-combatants were usually respected. Although the Sotho had developed their age-regiment system before the Mfecane, no Southern Bantu people possessed a permanent standing army with specialized military training or a hierarchy of military, as opposed to civil, chiefs. The purificatory rites which a warrior had to undergo after killing an enemy even in open war suggest a fundamental respect for human life and an ethos which regarded peace as the norm. After interrogating survivors of the *Stavenisse* (wrecked on the Transkei coast in February 1686), who had spent more than a year living with the southern Nguni tribes, Commander Simon van der Stell said in a report to the Council of Seventeen: 'It would be impossible to buy any slaves there, for they would not part with their children, or any of their connections for anything in the world, loving one another with a most remarkable strength of affection. . . . Revenge has little or no sway amongst them, as they are obliged to submit their disputes to the King, who after hearing the parties, gives sentence on the spot, to which all parties submit without a murmur. . . . The kings are much respected and beloved by their subjects. . . . Of their courage little can be said, as during the stay of the Netherlanders amongst them they had no wars.'[1]

Before the Mfecane the Bantu peoples of South Africa were thus organized in communities of mixed farmers which were law-abiding and relatively peaceful. Their life, however, was far from idyllic. Their material culture was very limited and though some tribes built quite substantial huts they had little in the way of furniture or utensils and nothing but skin cloaks to ward off the cold of the southern winters. The causes of disease were little understood and witchcraft was universally dreaded. Ailments which could not be immediately recognized were commonly ascribed to the malignant practices of sorcerers who were believed to act in conjunction with evil spirits. From time to time ceremonies of witch detection were held and those found guilty were put to death, often with horrible cruelty. The ill-health of a chief was generally the occasion for many such executions. Bad in itself, witch-hunting led to further abuses. The cattle of persons executed were confiscated by the chief and wealthy persons were never very secure from the imputation of witchcraft.

The Southern Bantu peoples had begun to be influenced by European contact as early as the sixteenth century, when the Portuguese established their foothold in South-east Africa. Direct Portuguese influence was largely confined to the neighbourhood of the Zambesi and Sabi

1 J. Bird: *The Annals of Natal*, vol. I, p. 46.

Rivers but fairly regular trading trips were made to Delagoa Bay where a fort was eventually built at Lourenço Marques. This contact was responsible for the introduction of maize into southern Africa where it gradually replaced millet as the basic crop. The numbers of the Portuguese were so small, however, that it is unlikely that they exercised much direct influence on the development of Bantu social systems outside the immediate locality of their forts.

The white community established at the Cape after 1652 was to have a much more profound impact. Settling at first in an area still occupied by the Bushmen and Hottentots, the Boers developed a system of cattle ranching requiring large areas of land. As population increased, the frontiers of the Colony advanced rapidly, and in the second half of the eighteenth century the settlers came in contact with the vanguard of the Bantu which was just beginning definitive occupation of the Zuurveld, between the Fish and Sundays Rivers. In 1779 the first frontier war between the races took place and relations between settler and Bantu constituted a serious problem for the temporary British administration of 1795–1803 and the government of the Batavian Republic (1803–6). In 1806 the Cape Colony came finally into the hands of Great Britain and in 1812 a determined effort was made to resolve the frontier problem by expelling twenty thousand Xhosa (belonging to Ndlambe's section) from the Zuurveld. The vanguard of the Nguni was thus driven back upon itself and this was only the beginning of a prolonged period of tension and strife. In 1818 war broke out again and still more land was taken from the Xhosa to constitute a buffer zone of uninhabited territory between the Fish and Keiskamma Rivers. This proved an impracticable device and favoured chiefs were allowed to resettle in the neutral strip on condition of good behaviour. Resentment and tension continued, however, and were to explode again in 1834. Meanwhile, under the pressure of land hunger, the colonial frontiers advanced northward to the Orange River and by the second decade of the nineteenth century white farmers were beginning to cross it and pasture their herds in Transorangia.[1]

Before the advancing colonists, a backwash of peoples was driven northward to fall upon the Sotho and Tswana tribes. The Korana, a Hottentot group originally settled near the Cape, were the first of these. Finding their lands taken over by whites they drifted northward to the Orange River and across it into Bechuanaland and the south-western Transvaal. There they encountered the southernmost Tswana tribes. With their bows and poisoned arrows the Korana proved more than a match for their Bantu enemies. The Rolong were driven from their

1 See W. Macmillan: *Bantu, Boer and Briton*, pp. 53–70.

home at Taung to Setlagole and the Korana settled in small groups in their territory. There they were joined by the notorious German outlaw, Jan Bloem. He became the leader of one of the Korana clans and with the aid of smuggled guns the Korana became a fearful scourge to their neighbours. Jan Bloem died after an unsuccessful raid on the Ngwaketsi in 1799, but he left a half-caste son of the same name who continued the tradition of cattle-raiding. After the Korana a composite group largely made up of persons of Hottentot/white descent filtered into the area round the bend of the Orange River. Under missionary influence they took the name of Griquas and established a fairly elaborate polity modelled on Boer conceptions. With their wagons, horses and guns they had a great military advantage over the Bantu and though the majority were persuaded to adopt a peaceful existence, temptation was too much for some who broke away and under the name of Bergenaars, terrorized a wide area.

In addition to this indirect influence, white society in the early years of the nineteenth century had begun to exercise direct effects on the Bantu through missionaries and traders who were starting to penetrate amongst the tribes beyond the frontiers. But though contact between the races had already produced important effects in the immediate hinterland of the Eastern Cape frontier where the reversal of Bantu expansion had produced severe overcrowding, it is doubtful if this had much influence on events far in the interior. Until the Great Trek, contact between whites and Bantu was essentially a frontier problem for both races.

2 The Zulu Kingdom

THE whole process of expansion which brought the Bantu from their original home to occupy the vast area of their present habitat can only be explained on the assumption of continuous population growth. Our uncertainties about the time-span involved and the currents and cross-currents within the overall movement, prevent an accurate assessment of the rate of this growth or of how it may have varied from time to time and place to place. When the Bantu began to settle in South Africa, however, there can be little doubt that their rate of natural increase was very high. Once they had emerged from malaria and tsetse country into the healthy South African climate the mortality rate must have declined sharply. Many of the most deadly diseases which now affect the population were unknown before contact with Europeans (smallpox, measles, tuberculosis, syphilis). So long as there was abundant land for settlement there could be little to prevent the population increasing very steeply. The process of constant sub-division which characterized the history of Southern Bantu tribes in the pre-*Mfecane* period implies rapid population growth and gives us some idea of its order of magnitude. According to Schapera[1] the Kwena tribe of Mogopa was still a single undivided group at the beginning of the eighteenth century. Yet by the end of the second decade of the nineteenth it had given rise to no less than five tribes in the area of modern Bechuanaland (in addition to other offshoots in the Rustenburg district of the Transvaal), all of them substantial in size. They included the largest and most powerful of the Tswana tribes, the Ngwaketsi. The history of the Xhosa tribe shows a similarly rapid rate of growth. In the early part of the eighteenth century it remained a single tribe though it had thrown off a number of minor offshoots. A succession dispute led to a split into two substantial sections, the Gcaleka and Rarabe. Within a generation the Rarabe divided again into followers of Gaika and Ndlambe.[2] The strength of this last section in 1812 was estimated at 20,000.[3]

1 Schapera: *The Ethnic Composition of Tswana Tribes*, pp. 8–9.
2 Soga: *The South-Eastern Bantu*, pp. 128–51.
3 This figure admittedly includes the Gunukwebe who were at that time associated with the Ndlambes.

The eastern coastal strip of South Africa was particularly favourable to Bantu settlement, with relatively high rainfall, fertile soil, good grass and excellent crops of millet, maize or pumpkins. As early as the seventeenth century we have evidence of a substantial population in Zululand and Natal. In A.D. 1622 the survivors of the wrecked Portuguese vessel, *São João Baptista*, were struggling through the area on their way to Delagoa Bay. '... in the afternoon we reached the top of a mountain from which we had the most beautiful view our eyes could desire, for many valleys lay before us intersected by rivers and smaller mountains, in which were an infinite number of kraals with herds of cattle and gardens.'[1] As this population continued to grow, grazing land became scarce.

A similar development took place throughout the whole area of Bantu settlement in South Africa but on the interior plateau southward expansion was proceeding along a wide front, from the inhabitable fringes of the Kalahari to the Drakensberg. The histories of most of the tribes now living in Basutoland speak of fairly recent southward migration in search of new land.[2] The very extent of the surface at which growth could take place in this area however, prevented very serious tension building up behind the lines.

In the coastal areas inhabited by the Nguni group the position was different, for their habitat was a narrow corridor between the escarpment and the sea. Expansion within this corridor could only take place on a very narrow front and by the eighteenth century this had advanced as far as the Fish River.[3] Further growth of population at the northern end of the corridor would inevitably produce a bottleneck. It is true that the Drakensberg was not an absolute barrier to human movement and some expansion of Nguni peoples onto the plateau did take place across it (Transvaal Ndebele onto the Transvaal highveld and Phuthi into Basutoland, for example). But the natural inertia of all human groups would predispose tribes living in the coastal area to fight for their lands before making the arduous trek across the mountains to a less hospitable environment, inhabited by tribes whose languages they did not understand.

Thus by the end of the eighteenth century Zululand and Natal were becoming overcrowded in terms of current methods of land use and warfare became more frequent and severe. The general conditions

1 Theal, *Records of South-Eastern Africa*, vol. VIII, p. 90.
2 See Ellenberger and Macgregor: *History of the Basuto, Ancient and Modern*.
3 Reports of the survivors of the wrecked Dutch ship, *Stavenisse*, show that there was a heavy Bantu population in the southern portions of the coastal corridor in the last decades of the seventeenth century. Bird: *The Annals of Natal*, vol. I, pp. 30–48.

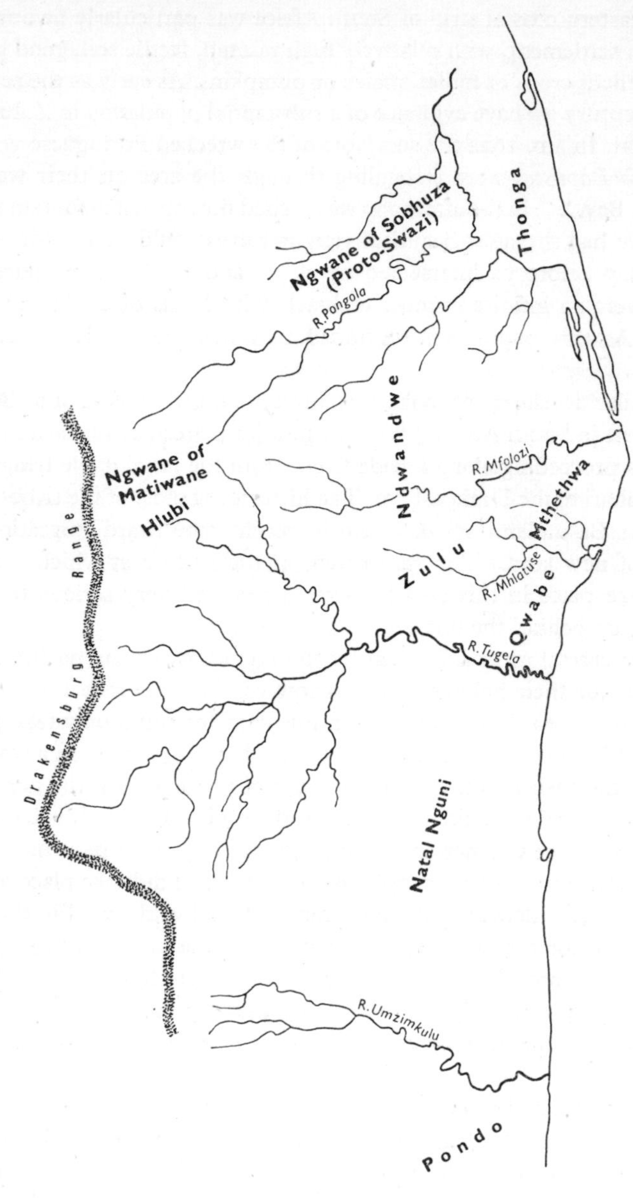

Zululand and Natal showing the approximate positions of some of the more important tribes on the eve of Shaka's rise to power

which favoured small-scale political organization and encouraged fissile multiplication had been reversed. Lack of space and the demands of more serious warfare dictated larger units and a process of aggregation began. Initially three large blocs emerged—the Ndwandwe, under Zwide; the Ngwane of Sobhuza; and the Mthethwa under Dingiswayo.

The growth of larger political units was closely bound up with a revolution in military organization. Before this time the northern tribes of the Nguni group were organized along the same lines as their cousins living further down the coastal corridor. They practised circumcision rites and they organized their fighting strength on a territorial basis. Some of them continued to do so and after the Mfecane had driven many of these tribes from their homes, the refugees still clung to the ancestral pattern. In some Northern Nguni tribes, however, a double change took place. The circumcision ceremonies with subsequent period of ritual seclusion which deprived the tribe of part of its fighting strength for considerable periods and left the initiates very vulnerable in case of war, were abandoned in response to conditions of more frequent fighting.[1] At the same time tribal armies were reorganized on an age-grade basis. It is probable that contact between Nguni and Sotho groups in northern Zululand played an important part in this change, for with the Sotho closer settlement pattern went larger initiation schools and permanent age-groupings with a military role. Though the Sotho military system was still very closely bound up with the circumcision ceremonies and provided only a very rudimentary form of military organization, it may well have suggested the idea of employing age-mate groupings as the basis of the military system. This would explain why the process of change began north of the Tugela River rather than in neighbouring Natal where population pressure was presumably just as great.

In the new system adopted by some Northern Nguni tribes young men of like age, who would normally have been initiated, were assembled together by the chief and constituted as a regiment with a name of its own. These regiments were not associated with particular princes but were assigned to one or other of the royal households (known as 'heads') which formed their rallying points. This provided a more efficient fighting force and increased tribal coherence by bringing men from different territorial segments together and uniting them in a common regimental

1 Fynn ascribes this change to an order by Dingiswayo that circumcision ceremonies be deferred till his conquests were complete. Bird, vol. I, pp. 60–71. It seems, however, to have been a development common to many tribes which can best be explained as a reaction to conditions of military insecurity. A similar development took place later amongst the Pondo, who abandoned circumcision during the Mfecane period. Hunter: *Reaction to Conquest*, p. 165.

loyalty. It also facilitated the assimilation of new groups. Under the earlier Nguni system a newly incorporated group would furnish a separate contingent in the tribal army, thus preserving its sense of identity and capacity for independent military action. Aggregations based on this system were naturally unstable. Under the age-regiment system, however, young men of newly incorporated groups were divided up according to their ages, fought alongside their age-mates from other sections of the tribe and were associated with one or other of the 'heads'. A means of welding originally different tribes into a permanent and stable unit had been created but the effects of the system were limited by the fact that the regiments only assembled occasionally.

The introduction of age-regiments is often attributed to Dingiswayo, the most famous of the three great leaders of this period. He was a son of the chief of the Mthethwa tribe but, impatient of his father's rule, he conspired with one of his brothers against the chief's life. The plot was discovered and the prince was lucky to escape only slightly wounded. In his flight he encountered a European with a horse and gun who was trying to make his way to Delagoa Bay.[1] Dingiswayo offered to serve as a guide and travelled with the stranger until they reached the territory of the Qwabe tribe. The chief, Pakatwayo, however, regarded the white man as a sea monster[2] whose presence would bring some unknown evil to his people. He had the traveller put to death. Dingiswayo took the horse and gun and about A.D. 1740[3] returned to his own people. By the time he reached home his father was dead and another brother established on the throne, but Dingiswayo was able to use the prestige of his travels and his possession of the horse and gun to rally support and successfully oust his brother from power. Once established, he commenced a deliberate policy of expansion, bringing neighbouring tribes permanently under his authority. He held the view '. . . that it was not the intention of those who first came into the world that there should be several kings equal in power, but that there should be one great king to exercise control over the little ones . . .'[4] and for this purpose he adopted the age-regiment system. It is unlikely that he was the sole inventor, however, for it was employed simultaneously by the Ndwandwe and Sobhuza's people for similar purposes. Dingiswayo's

1 The identity of the white traveller is unknown. For an account of Dingiswayo's early life see Fynn, in Bird, op. cit., pp. 60–71.

2 White people were generally believed by the Bantu to be sea monsters who floated in the ocean on gigantic shells and lived on elephants' tusks. The term 'mlungu' almost universally used for Europeans in South and Central Africa means 'sea monster'.

3 Fynn arrived at this date by calculating the number of first-fruit ceremonies said to have taken place between it and his arrival. *Diary*, p. 1.

4 Fynn: *Diary*, p. 10.

policy was generally mild. Tribes who submitted were allowed to retain their own chiefs. After a successful campaign he would return cows taken from a defeated enemy, keeping only the oxen to distribute among his warriors.[1] He had also acquired an interest in European commodities from his encounter with the traveller and took steps to open trade with the Portuguese at Delagoa Bay. A few European goods were imported and he encouraged his subjects to copy them.[2] Though he aimed at pacifying the Zululand area by bringing conflicting tribes under a single paramount ruler, his activities and those of his contemporaries were bound to result in more severe warfare and a further acceleration of the processes of change. As the three great leaders expanded their followings into multitribal blocks, collision between them could not be avoided and was naturally more serious than struggles between the smaller tribes.

The first conflict of this type took place between Zwide and Sobhuza, whose territories adjoined one another on the upper Pongola. A quarrel over the possession of farmland on the banks of the river led to a war in which the Ndwandwe were victorious. Sobhuza's following was not completely routed and retired inland to the central area of modern Swaziland. In this new home Sobhuza's people found themselves in the neighbourhood of many small Sotho and Nguni tribes. The process already begun on the Pongola was continued. The small tribes were defeated one by one and amalgamated in a composite group later known as the Swazi nation.[3] The elimination of Sobhuza left Zwide and Dingiswayo face to face. A collision was inevitable but by this time a new power had arisen under the aegis of Dingiswayo. This was Shaka, chief of what was then a small and insignificant tribe, the Zulu.

Shaka's father, Senzangakona, heir to the throne of the Zulu, had been attracted one day by the charms of Nandi, a daughter of the neighbouring Langeni tribe. He had not yet been circumcised and it was with considerable displeasure that the tribe heard the news that their prince's sweetheart was pregnant. Senzangakona wished to avoid responsibility and '. . . assured the other women that Nandi was not pregnant, but suffered from a complaint called *i-tshaka*, or looseness of the intestines, which was the cause of the swelling'.[4] This name which came to be attached to the boy is symbolic of much in his life and

1 Ibid., p. 9.
2 A wooden chair carved out of a solid block in imitation of a Portuguese prototype was seen by Fynn during his stay with the Zulu. Ibid., p. 10.
3 This can be taken to mark the true beginning of the Mfecane, but as the history of the Swazi is tangential to the main stream of development it will be discussed separately in the next chapter.
4 Fynn, op. cit., p. 12.

character. His father did finally admit responsibility and took Nandi as one of his wives, but her powerful personality and violent temper made her an unwelcome member of a chief's household.[1] She was driven away to take refuge with her own people and Shaka grew up a fatherless child subject to the teasing and bullying of his companions. His pride in his chiefly descent added to his torments for his playmates submitted him to many ordeals to test his claims to superiority and took every opportunity to mock and humiliate him.[2] He grew to manhood strong and naturally athletic. In his personality a distinct streak of sadism combined with high intelligence and a ferocious determination to prove himself by dominating over his fellows. He was personally courageous and callous of the sufferings of others. Only for his mother, and to a lesser extent his grandmother, did he show much normal human affection.

In his youth Shaka took service in Dingiswayo's regiments and soon gained a reputation for reckless bravery. The older ruler took an interest in him and tried to restrain him from the foolhardy exploits which won him the name of 'Dingiswayo's hero'.[3] The paramount also took Shaka into his confidence and gave him command over one of the regiments. But Shaka's ambition was not satisfied by the position of trusted subordinate to the great chief. About 1816 Senzangakona died and Shaka determined to seize the leadership of his father's people. His mother had never been the 'great wife' and under Nguni law he had no claim to the throne, but the support of his powerful patron gave him the opportunity to try conclusions with the rightful heir. Dingiswayo, anxious to confirm his authority over the Zulu by establishing his nominee as their chief, lent Shaka a regiment and with this assistance he was able to overcome his half-brother, Sigujana, and put him to death.

Shaka thus became a chief in his own right with a following he could train in accordance with the new military ideas which had been maturing in his mind during his service in Dingiswayo's army. The changed nature of warfare which arose when battles were no longer petty skirmishes between small tribes but large-scale encounters, called for a change in weapons and tactics. The traditional weapon of Southern Bantu tribes was a long-handled throwing spear. In addition, battle-axes were sometimes used and the warriors protected themselves with shields of cow-hide. These weapons were suited to the traditional concept of warfare which did not involve long periods of continuous fighting. As

1 Bird, op. cit., pp. 60–71. Fynn, *Diary*, pp. 12–13.
2 Bryant: *Olden Times in Zululand and Natal*, pp. 62–3. Ritter: *Shaka Zulu*, pp. 11–20, gives a more imaginative and dramatic account.
3 Fynn, op. cit., p. 13.

implements to be used in set battles between large bodies of men they had, however, serious deficiencies. Once a warrior had thrown his spear he was disarmed and the battle-line must break up. Shaka saw that if his warriors were armed with a short-handled stabbing spear, used it more as a sword than a spear and retained it throughout the battle, they would be able to maintain orderly movement in close formation. Once they came face to face with their disorganized and partially disarmed opponents they must inevitably win the day. One of his first acts on acceding to the chieftainship of the Zulu was to convince his people of the superiority of these new tactics. He took two of his regiments and armed each man with a reed. 'The two regiments thus weaponed were ordered to oppose each other, the one throwing the weapon, the other rushing on and stabbing their opponents at close quarters. The result of this collision was momentous and met with Shaka's entire satisfaction. few having escaped being wounded and several lying killed.'[1] Thereafter his followers were equipped with the new type of spear and were forbidden on pain of death to leave it on the battlefield. They could then manœuvre and fight in an ordered line protected by great cow-hide shields which covered the body from chin to feet.

The tactical formation adopted in any encounter would naturally depend on the terrain and the disposition of the enemy. There is no direct contemporary evidence of Shaka's normal battle formation but in later years the Zulu generally used a formation called 'cow's horns'. This consisted of a strong centre known as the 'chest' made up of several regiments branching out into two curving projections usually made up of one regiment each. When battle was joined the horns would attempt to surround the enemy while the chest moved forward to complete their destruction. As this formation was also employed by the Ngoni who fled to the north after defeat by Shaka, it is reasonable to assume that it was employed in his time.

Formation fighting required severe discipline and training which was impossible so long as the regiments only assembled on the eve of war. Shaka therefore made the fundamental change of keeping his regiments on permanent service for long periods. As soon as an age-regiment was formed it was accommodated in a special military settlement and remained there occupied in drilling, military displays and dances in the intervals between expeditions, until it was officially dissolved.

For the first years of his chieftaincy Shaka continued to act as a vassal of Dingiswayo and the scope of his ambitions was necessarily restricted. In 1817 or early in 1818 the decisive clash between the Mthethwa and Ndwandwe took place. Dingiswayo marched at the head

1 Ibid., p. 16.

of his forces and Shaka was summoned to bring his followers in support. According to some accounts Shaka was anxious to rid himself of his overlord and deliberately betrayed him to the enemy. Whether this is true or not, the Zulu took no part in the encounter.[1] Dingiswayo left his followers to walk up a hill from where he could survey the battlefield. He found himself in a trap surrounded by the enemy, was seized and carried captive to Zwide. The Ndwandwe chief put his great opponent to death and Dingiswayo's skull was taken to decorate the hut of Zwide's mother. With the death of their leader the Mthethwa army fled from the field and the tribal aggregation so carefully built up speedily dissolved. Shaka and the Zulu them emerged as the only nucleus of resistance to the victorious Zwide.

After the Mthethwa collapse, Shaka hastened to recruit his strength by bringing as many tribes as possible under his control. The Mthethwa themselves were conquered and their new chief, Mondisa, killed and replaced by another member of their royal family, nominated by Shaka.[2] Zwide could not afford to look on passively while the hostile bloc he had just destroyed was reconstituted under a new leader. He sent a powerful expedition against Shaka and in a fierce battle round the Gqokoli Hill[3] the new fighting methods of the Zulu were put to the test for the first time. In spite of the numerical superiority of the Ndwandwe the discipline of the Zulu enabled them to hold their ground. Time and again the Ndwandwe charged up the hill but they failed to break through the line of shields and were forced to withdraw, leaving five of their royal princes on the field. Infuriated at this repulse, Zwide determined to crush his upstart opponent for ever and towards the end of 1818 sent his whole army in overwhelming strength into the Zulu territory. Faced with this massive invasion Shaka adopted elusive tactics. He withdrew his people and their cattle before the advancing enemy, luring them ever further from their base.[4] At the same time he harried their advance with guerrilla tactics. One night a small body of Zulu crawled in amongst the Ndwandwe. They lay down alongside the sleeping bodies of their enemies and when it was almost light every man plunged his spear into the nearest foe. Before the Ndwandwe realized what was happening the Zulu had escaped, leaving many dead in the

1 Fynn, op. cit., p. 15, and Smith: *Andrew Smith and Natal*, p. 87, support the view that there was deliberate treachery. Ritter: *Shaka Zulu*, p. 117, argues that the Zulu leader arrived too late and missed the battle altogether.

2 Fynn, op. cit., p. 15.

3 A dramatic account of this battle is given by Ritter, op. cit., pp. 129–49. Bryant: *Olden Times* and *History of the Zulu*, confirms that Zwide made a first abortive expedition on which a number of his sons were killed.

4 Fynn, op. cit., p. 17.

hostile ranks.[1] Zwide's forces advanced nearly as far as the Tugela River but by then they were beginning to feel the effects of starvation. A general retreat was ordered and Shaka shadowed them until they approached the frontiers of their own country. Then on the banks of the Mhlatuze River he attacked them with all his forces. Worn out with long marches and by prolonged hunger the Ndwandwe could not stand against the Zulu. They were decisively defeated and Shaka immediately despatched some of his regiments with orders to destroy the whole Ndwandwe civil population and exorcize the threat for ever.

After the battle the Ndwandwe divided into three groups. Zwide himself had remained at home and succeeded in making his escape with some of the refugees from the battle. He moved inland and established himself on the upper Nkomati River. There he built up his following again and prepared to renew the struggle. Two other sections of the defeated army, one under Soshangane and the other under Zwangendaba, fled northward by different routes and entered Southern Mozambique.

This battle was a turning point in Shaka's career and in the whole history of the Mfecane. Though he had not succeeded in ridding himself of the Ndwandwe threat completely, Shaka had for the time being eliminated all serious rivals in Zululand and could continue to build up his power with little serious resistance. Tribe after tribe was defeated and either incorporated or driven away as homeless refugees. In a long series of campaigns the entire area between the plateau and the sea, northward from the Tugela River to within a few days' journey from Delagoa Bay, was brought under his control. South of the Tugela, Natal was devastated and the Pondo between the Umzimkulu and Umzimvubu Rivers were severely chastised. Fynn, on his arrival in Natal in May 1824, met several of Shaka's regiments returning from a prolonged campaign which had taken them right through Natal to attack Faku the Pondo chief.[2] Bryant maintains that Shaka had undertaken four previous campaigns in Natal: in 1817, 1818, 1819, 1820.[3]

As his conquests continued Shaka constructed a new type of state. Its primary purpose was to maintain and expand an efficient fighting force completely loyal to its leader.[4] The normal method of incorporating new

1 Bryant: *Olden Times*, pp. 194–5.
2 Fynn, op. cit., p. 61.
3 See Bryant: *History of the Zulu*. I have deliberately refrained from attempting a detailed analysis of the distribution of tribes in Natal before the *Mfecane* and the intricacies of the internecine strife which developed under pressure from across the Tugela. On this subject see also Bryant: *Olden Times* and *The Zulu People*. Soga: *The South-Eastern Bantu*. Bird: *Annals of Natal*.
4 A general account of the structure of the Zulu state under its third king, Mpande, is given by M. Gluckman: 'The Zulu Kingdom' in Fortes and Evans Pritchard, ed.: *African Political Systems*.

elements in an expanding tribe was employed without any important change as far as the civil administration was concerned. Conquered tribes were simply grafted onto the territorial hierarchy, their chiefs becoming territorial sub-chiefs. Shaka not infrequently removed the existing chiefs of tribes he had conquered and appointed his own nominees in their place. Even when he did not do so he made clear that they ruled at his good pleasure. In Shaka's system, however, the territorial chiefs lacked the power and importance which they had in the traditional system. Though they might continue to adjudicate over cases which arose in the territory under their control, their authority was restricted to the older men and women who still lived in traditional fashion. All young men were drafted into the army and it was in the army that all power resided. Without an effective backing the sub-chiefs could exercise no great influence on policy and were entirely at the mercy of Shaka's whims and fancies.[1]

In the central area of the Zulu kingdom a series of military settlements was established at Gibixhegu, Bulawayo, Nobamba, Isiklebhe, Mbelebele, and Dukuza. These were a development of the system of 'head's modified to meet the requirements of a permanent standing army. Each of them was circular in construction and contained a royal section opposite the entrance. On either side were the huts of soldiers around a central cattle enclosure. Gibixhegu was more than three miles in circumference and contained about one thousand four hundred huts.[2] Each settlement was under the command of a military *induna*, generally a commoner, appointed personally by Shaka. Each settlement also contained a section of the royal women under a senior woman of the royal family who exercised considerable authority in association with the commanding officer.[3] Shaka, however, never officially married and the large numbers of royal women were officially his wards. At these settlements young boys gathered from every section of the kingdom. They were employed at first to help guard the cattle and act as shield-bearers, then when they reached manhood they would be enrolled in age-regiments.[4]

The regiments were kept on permanent service until they were officially dissolved by the king. During this period they were forbidden to wear the insignia of manhood or to marry. In Shaka's time the period of active service was very prolonged as a consequence of almost con-

1 Isaacs describes the pitiable position of one of these chiefs, Zihlandlo. His tribe was '. . . once a very powerful one, until Chaka subdued it, and took away all the young warriors belonging to it to complete his own regiments'. Isaacs: *Travels and Adventures*, vol. I, p. 149.
2 Isaacs, op. cit., vol. I, p. 61.
3 Fynn: *Diary*, pp. 283–4. *Andrew Smith and Natal*, p. 42.
4 Isaacs: *Travels and Adventures*, vol. I, pp. 272–3.

Initiation ceremonies of the Cape Nguni

Shaka, King of the Zulus (from a contemporary drawing)

tinuous warfare and women of thirty and forty were without husbands.[1] Each regiment was commanded by an officer appointed by the king with junior officers under him in charge of squadrons. They were distinguished from one another by shields of different colours and other regalia such as headgear. The shields and other items of military apparel were supplied by the king. Each regiment had charge of a section of the royal herds. So far as possible the herd attached to a particular regiment would be made up of cattle of the same colour as their shields.[2] These cattle served to provide the soldiers with meat and milk and, in addition, millet beer was provided from the royal bounty.

Together with the young men, young women were also assembled in large numbers at the 'heads'. They were made wards of the king and counted as sections of his household. They too were organized into regiments for ceremonial purposes and Shaka often held great dances in which male and female regiments took part.[3] While under the authority of the king the girls were strictly forbidden to have anything to do with the soldiers but when a male regiment was dissolved its female counterpart would be dissolved also and the women given as wives to the soldiers by the king.[4] Many of the girls in Shaka's household were his concubines but he was terrified of producing an heir and any woman found pregnant by him was instantly put to death. On one occasion his mother concealed a pregnant girl until after the birth of her child but when they were brought into his presence Shaka had them both killed on the spot and beat his mother severely for allowing the child to be born without his knowledge.[5] Fear that an heir might seek to oust him from his position was no doubt an important reason for this conduct, but Shaka also may have regarded a child of his as a reminder of his own mortality. Under such a system of universal conscription there was little room for the aged and infirm. Shaka had large numbers of old and incapable men put to death on the grounds that they were a useless encumbrance and it was in commemoration of this that one of his military settlements was called Gibixhegu ('finish the old men'). He was not unnaturally in terror of growing old himself.[6]

This military system not only provided Shaka with the most efficient fighting machine in Bantu Africa but also a means of rapidly assimilating

1 *Andrew Smith and Natal*, p. 86. Fynn: *Diary*, p. 298.
2 E.g., Isaacs, op. cit., vol. I, p. 99. Fynn: *Diary*, p. 283.
3 Shaka, perhaps as a joke, named one of these female regiments 'Unkisimana' (Englishman). Fynn, op. cit., p. 30. On the subject of the organization of women in Shaka's kingdom, see also Isaacs, op. cit., p. 100.
4 Liaisons between members of the male and female regiments during their period of active service were punished by death. See Isaacs, pp. 129–33.
5 Fynn, *Diary*, p. 29.
6 Ibid., p. 30.

conquered tribes. The young men, split up amongst the regiments, soon came to feel a strong sense of *esprit de corps* and the nature of the system was such as to strengthen and emphasize the loyalty of the soldiers to their ruler in every possible way. From him they received their arms and regalia, their immediate leaders owed their position to his will. Through him lay the only hope of advancement and from him they would ultimately receive their wives. Even their food was largely provided from royal resources and as they ate the warriors would shout his praises and thank him for his generosity. The regiments had a direct interest in the wars of their ruler for they were allowed large quantities of meat which tended to outstrip the natural reproduction of the royal herds. Only by repeated victories in the king's service could their standard of living be maintained. The concentration of power in the army and its extreme dependence on the king, raised Shaka's authority far above that of the traditional Bantu chief. The sub-chiefs had lost the power to act as effective checks on the central authority. Shaka did not need to consult the traditional tribal council. He ruled to a great extent as an absolute despot, deciding cases while taking his morning bath and ordering men to death with a nod of the head.[1] Ultimately, however, his position depended on the loyalty of his troops and their commanders. The military *indunas* now held the position traditionally occupied by the territorial chiefs. Their position was weaker as they were creations of the king and had no hereditary authority of their own, but Shaka was very sensitive of the need to maintain their loyalty. The military *indunas* were thus treated as counsellors and were assembled to discuss all important questions. Shaka also took care to ensure that they did not meet behind his back and unauthorized conferences between military leaders were punished by death.[2] In addition he tried to get at least apparent public support for his policies. When he wished to embark on a course that was likely to prove unpopular he would put the proposal in the mouth of one of his *indunas* and pretend to accept it reluctantly under pressure of public opinion.

The organizational principles of the Zulu state applied only within the area under its direct control. Outside this area other chiefs like Sobhuza, Moshesh and Faku offered tribute and recognized a tenuous vassal relationship. Even within the kingdom itself the logic of the system was not perfect. The main lines had been established and the system was further perfected by later rulers, but the kingdom had been hastily created under threat of external attack. Some anomalies persisted, and at least two traditional tribal chiefs were given military authority and allowed to

1 Isaacs, op. cit., vol. I, p. 62.
2 Fynn: *Diary*, pp. 283–4. Isaacs, op. cit., vol. I, p. 284.

command forces made up largely of their own tribal following. Herein lay the basis for possible secessionist movements and about 1821 the first of these took place. Mzilikazi, chief of the Khumalo and one of Shaka's most trusted generals, defied his authority and escaped with his followers onto the highveld. Some tribes who accepted the authority of Shaka were not fully incorporated into the military system. This was especially the case with those living at the periphery of his domains. The Thonga in the northern part of his kingdom were allowed considerable autonomy partly perhaps, as Bryant suggests, because of their reputation as blacksmiths.[1] The remnant of the Natal population living around Durban accepted Shaka's authority but he did not exercise any direct control over them.

The reorganization of society on military lines was accompanied by a new ethos. The informality, hospitality and naïve curiosity which meant that the visitor to a Bantu village was immediately surrounded by a mob of men, women and children, staring, asking questions and openly begging for gifts, was replaced by a more reserved attitude. A pride almost amounting to arrogance and an indifference to human life were accompanied by a sense of discipline, order and cleanliness which at once attracted the attention of European travellers.[2] At the same time political loyalty was enhanced to a high degree, and came to be regarded as an absolute value.[3]

The peoples of Zululand had been in contact with European influences at least as early as Dingiswayo's reign when the attempt was made to encourage trade with Delagoa Bay. As a result of Shaka's conquests his kingdom extended to within about fifty miles from the the Portuguese port. Friendly relations were maintained and in 1825 a Portuguese from Delagoa Bay visited the Zulu king. The numbers of the Portuguese were so small and their military strength so negligible, however, that this contact had little influence on the Zulu. In 1823 F. G. Farewell, an adventurous English trader, organized an expedition to investigate the possibility of opening trade with Natal. An abortive attempt was made to land at St. Lucia Bay in the course of which the Xhosa interpreter, Jacob, who had accompanied the expedition, escaped. He took refuge with the Zulu and because of his knowledge of English acquired considerable influence with Shaka and later with

1 Bryant: *History of the Zulu*, p. 98.
2 E.g. Fynn: *Diary*, p. 70.
3 This is well illustrated by the attitude of a Zulu *induna* Dambuza, who was being tried by the Boers for participation in the massacre of some of their companions. When urged to repent for his sins he replied that Dingane was his only master and that if he were faithful to him, God, if there was one, would approve of his conduct. E. Walker: *The Great Trek*, p. 203.

Dingane. After the failure at St. Lucia Bay, Farewell surveyed the harbour of Port Natal (present Durban) and the following year Henry Fynn landed there in charge of an advance party of traders. From then onwards a small but permanent trading community was established in Natal. In time the overland route through Pondoland was opened and through this contact news of the situation in Natal and Zululand percolated to the Cape Colony. Shaka was quick to perceive the advantages of trade with the white strangers. He had probably heard from Jacob of the power of the British authorities and he was impressed by the potentialities of firearms. Fynn and Farewell were well received on their first visit to the Zulu king and managed to gain a strong position in Shaka's confidence. A grand military display and dance was held to impress the visitors, but during the celebrations an Ndwandwe spy succeeded in stabbing the king and inflicting a serious wound. Fynn was called upon for medical treatment and Shaka soon recovered. In gratitude he agreed to put his mark to a paper ceding much of present-day Natal to Farewell and the other members of his party.[1] Within this area the traders were allowed to live as a vassal community ruling over the small Bantu population which still remained there. They were accepted as chiefs and some of them acquired harems of Bantu wives. Shaka gave them virtually complete autonomy and in return he called upon them for military aid on several occasions.

The long-standing enmity between Shaka and Zwide had not disappeared with the passing of time. After their defeat on the Mhlatuze River the Ndwandwe had recovered their strength and prepared for a war of revenge. After the abortive assassination attempt in 1824 Zulu regiments were sent out to attack them, but failed to achieve a decisive victory. In the following year Zwide died and one of his sons, Sikhunyana, succeeded him. The succession was contested by another son, Somapunga, and early in 1826 he fled to the Zulu bringing valuable information about the Ndwandwe's intentions.[2] Shaka summoned the English traders, Fynn and Farewell, to his aid and his army advanced to encounter the enemy about twenty miles to the east of present Utrecht. The Ndwandwe had by this time adopted Zulu fighting methods and a fierce pitched battle took place. When the two armies came face to face they halted at about twenty yards from one another. The signal for battle was given by Jacob, who fired three shots into the enemy ranks. Both sides then charged with a tremendous yell and continued stabbing one another for about three minutes. They then fell back a few paces, rested and charged again. In the second encounter,

1 The text of this document is given by Bird: *Annals of Natal*, vol. I, pp. 193–5.
2 Fynn: *Diary*, p. 122.

however, the Ndwandwe were visibly weakening and the Zulu launched a third charge which routed them completely. A terrible massacre followed and about sixty thousand cattle were taken.[1] The Ndwandwe, whose numbers in this battle were estimated at forty thousand, were so completely crushed that they disappeared as an independent tribe. Numerous refugees succeeded in escaping but they were too weak to make a stand on their own and went to join Soshangane and Mzilikazi. On his way home after the battle Shaka sent some of his regiments to attack two small tribes, the Beje and the followers of Mlotsha, who were suspected of having conducted intrigues with the enemy. Mlotsha's people were defeated but the Beje, taking advantage of the natural strength of their mountain home, were able to beat off the Zulu attack. The traders were then asked to give the support of their firearms against this tribe and in February 1827 another attack was made. The Beje, terrified by the sound of gunfire, agreed to surrender and a large number of cattle were taken back to the Zulu king.[2]

In 1825 Shaka had been upset by the death of his grandmother. Not only did he feel a sense of personal loss but he was frightened at the prospect of his own death. He asked Fynn whether the white men possessed a medicine which prevented hair from turning grey, and in a weak moment Fynn had said that there was a substance called Rowland's Macassar Oil which had this effect. Thereafter the king repeatedly pestered the traders for this magic remedy which he believed was the secret of eternal youth.[3] In 1827 Shaka suffered a much more severe shock for his mother, Nandi, the only person really close to him, fell ill and died. Deeply shaken, he stood leaning against his shield while tears ran down his face. The people gathered in thousands to share the grief of their ruler and so great was the excitement that anyone found with dry eyes was instantly put to death. Fynn estimated that not less than seven thousand were killed or died of exhaustion in the first paroxysm of mourning.[4] Later the hysteria spread throughout the kingdom and thousands more were killed for not coming to mourn or on suspicion of having wished the death of the Queen Mother. After these spontaneous manifestations Shaka assembled his people to consider formal measures of mourning. Through the mouth of a favourite *induna* he proposed the most extravagant sacrifices. Cultivation was not to take place and no milk was to be used for an entire year. Throughout this period men must abstain from intercourse with their wives and any woman found pregnant would be

1 Fynn: *Diary*, pp. 123–8; *Andrew Smith and Natal*, p. 65.
2 Isaacs, op. cit., vol. I, pp. 162–8.
3 Fynn: *Diary*, pp. 141–3.
4 Ibid., pp. 132–5.

put to death together with her husband.[1] After three months the chiefs collected large numbers of cattle and brought them to the king to console him and persuade him to lighten the distress of his people. The first two prohibitions were then lifted but the third remained in force throughout the mourning period.

As this period drew to an end Shaka made plans to close it with a major campaign. He aimed to send his regiments against the Southern Nguni tribes between Natal and the frontier of the Cape Colony. Not only did this promise a rich booty in cattle but a means of establishing direct contact with the British colony and fuller access to European goods. Shaka was anxious that this campaign should be undertaken with the friendly support of the British and in March 1828 an embassy was sent under the guidance of Lieutenant King to establish diplomatic relations with the government of the Cape and bring back some of the much-desired Rowland's Macassar Oil. The embassy did not meet with a favourable reception, for rumours had reached the Colony that the Zulu were planning an attack and the embassy was regarded as a spying party. They were refused access to the Governor or any high official and after vexatious delays sailed back to Natal without even acquiring the magic oil.[2]

Before they returned the period of mourning had come to an end and Shaka called his people together to lay his plans before them. Through the mouth of an *induna* he argued that there were still people who defied the Zulu power and since they could not be forced to weep for the death of Nandi their cattle should be taken from them as a substitute for tears.[3] The warriors were to march south and open a road to the Colony, for which purpose he had already sent an embassy to the white men. Shaka himself accompanied the expedition. As the embassy had not returned he was afraid of possible complications with the British and took Fynn with him as his adviser. He also gave secret instructions that the army should not go further than Hintza's branch of the Xhosa and that some excuse for retreat should be found if they encountered any white men. The Zulu army defeated the Pondo and ravished their country. The tribes between Pondoland and the colonial border were thrown into alarm and the Xhosa and Thembu agreed to combine their

1 The accounts of Fynn and Andrew Smith agree on the nature of the restrictions imposed on the Zulu during the period of mourning for Nandi. Fynn: *Diary*, p. 136; Smith: *Andrew Smith and Natal*, p. 77. Monstrous though they may seem, the prohibitions were not entirely untraditional. Survivors of the *Stavenisse* remarked that subjects abstained from intercourse with their wives during the period of mourning for chiefs. Bird: *Annals of Natal*, pp. 30–48.

2 An account of Shaka's embassy is given by Isaacs, op. cit., vol. I, pp. 211–24.

3 Fynn: *Diary*, pp. 139–44.

forces and make a desperate stand on a plain near the Bashee River, about thirty miles from the Wesleyan mission station at Butterworth.[1] An appeal for help was also sent to the Colony and a small expeditionary force under Colonel Somerset was immediately despatched to try and persuade Shaka to retire peacefully and if not, drive him back by force. Behind this small party a larger expedition was assembled and sent northward towards Pondoland. The British forces failed to make contact with the Zulu. They encountered the marauding chief, Matiwane, and, mistaking his followers for the Zulu, attacked and defeated him at Mbholompo. Shaka, however, advanced no further than the Pondo for he still had no news of his embassy and was warned by Fynn that the British regarded the frontier tribes as being under their protection. He decided to defer his plans for the meantime. He sent a message to Hintza to keep his cattle in good condition until he returned in three months' time: he would not rest until he had reached the colonial frontier.[2]

The Zulu army then turned back on its tracks taking with it almost all the Pondo herds. Shaka was not, however, prepared to abandon his plans for a grand campaign in honour of his mother. He decided to send his army northward against Soshangane and to rouse enthusiasm he caused rumours to be spread that the northern tribes had taken advantage of the army's absence to tamper with Zulu girls. The warriors clamoured for action and Shaka was able to appear as if giving way to public pressure. Almost the entire Zulu force marched out of Zululand to the north and Shaka, who remained behind, suddenly realized that he was left without an adequate personal bodyguard. A messenger was sent to recall the young shield-bearers and they were hastily enrolled in a new regiment, the Bees.

Shortly after the expedition left, the embassy returned from the Cape to report the failure of its mission. Shaka was greatly annoyed and Fynn feared he might vent his rage on the traders. By this time, however, Shaka's tyranny and the monstrous sufferings inflicted on his people as mourning for Nandi had sapped their loyalty. Two of his brothers, Dingane and Mhlangane, deserted from the expedition and entered into a conspiracy with Mbhopa, Shaka's chief *induna*. The conspirators found their opportunity when Shaka was interviewing an embassy which had brought him a tribute of cranes' feathers from a Sotho tribe. Mbhopa broke up the meeting and distracted Shaka's attention by beating the ambassadors and driving them out of the cattle enclosure on the grounds that they had come too late. Meanwhile Mhlangane had

1 S. Shrewsbury to Secretaries, Wesleyan Missionary Society, Butterworth, 30 June 1828. M.M.S. 1828/4.
2 J. Davis to Rev. G. Morley, 16 July 1828, M.M.S. 1828/14.

crept up behind the king and stabbed him in the back. Dingane stabbed him also and as Shaka cried out 'O! children of my father, what have I done to you?' they put him to death.[1]

The assassination of the king was observed by the *induna*, Sotobe, and with a number of warriors he was about to take vengeance on the assassins. But Mbhopa addressed them and pointed out that the king had been killed by his own brothers as a means of putting an end to incessant warfare and in revenge for the deaths of those who had been killed in mourning for the Queen Mother. The appeal was successful and the immediate danger passed. The return of the army was still to be dreaded but the expedition against Soshangane had ended in disaster. The Zulu had gained an initial victory but they failed to capture the enemy's cattle and the troops were ravaged by famine and malaria. Only a fraction of the force succeeded in making its way home and they were delighted to learn that the death of the king had saved them from the punishment which would have been the reward of their failure.

In the immediate aftermath of Shaka's assassination authority was divided between Dingane and his brother. They conspired against one another and each sought to gain the support of Mbhopa. He, however, gave his support to Dingane and Mhlangane was put to death. On his accession to power, Dingane attempted to win the favour of his people by relaxing the military discipline of his predecessor. Regiments were disbanded and allowed to marry and no campaigns were undertaken for some time. The new ruler felt insecure on his throne and attempted to remove many of the more powerful men who might be a threat to his authority. The *induna*, Mbhopa, who had helped him to power was killed and Sotobe, who had shown his devotion to royalty, was restored to favour.

This proscription had an unsettling effect on the kingdom. Nqeto, chief of the Qwabe tribe, who had held a high position in Shaka's favour, feared that he might be marked out for execution and took advantage of the relaxation of military discipline to organize a rebellion. He broke away with his people and fled southward through Natal in the second major secessionist movement in the history of the Zulu kingdom. The Qwabe rebellion persuaded Dingane to change his policies. Military discipline was restored and the army was sent on numerous campaigns. Expeditions were despatched southward as far as the borders of Pondoland and onto the highveld to grapple with Mzilikazi. Sobhuza's people who had enjoyed immunity during Shaka's reign were also attacked, but they wisely retreated into the hills allow-

1 The accounts of Fynn, Isaacs and Smith agree in substance but vary slightly in detail.

ing the enemy to take their cattle without resistance. In the early years of Dingane's reign Matiwane, after his disastrous defeat by the British expedition which had been sent to make contact with Shaka, came to seek refuge in his kingdom. Dingane allowed him to settle there but feared that the famous old warrior might provide a nucleus of rebellion and had him put to death on a hill which came to be known as Matiwane's Kop.

The most serious problem facing the new Zulu king was that of relations with his white neighbours. The Portuguese did not constitute a serious danger. Friendly relations were maintained and Dingane treated them as a subject people. Members of a shipwrecked Portuguese ship were given safe conduct to Delagoa Bay[1] but in 1833 Dingane, dissatisfied with the present he had received from the governor of the fort, sent an expedition which drove most of the Portuguese on to an island and killed the Governor.[2] The fort was not destroyed, however, and the settlement was soon re-established.

Dingane was more worried by the English settlement at Natal. Increasing numbers of whites were coming to settle there and the embryonic colony had a disturbing effect on the loyalty of his own subjects. Fugitives from his justice found a ready welcome at Port Natal. Dingane was warned by Jacob that the white men would come at first in ones and twos, then more would follow and eventually an army would come to drive him from his kingdom. The interpreter told the king that when he was at the Cape with an embassy he had heard that an expedition was preparing for this very purpose.[3] Dingane began to be persuaded and Fynn was so alarmed that he withdrew with his Bantu followers to Pondoland for a time, but the mood passed and Fynn persuaded the king that Jacob was guilty of treachery and he was put to death. In January 1831 Captain Alan Gardiner, an ex-naval captain, arrived at Natal to commence missionary work. He managed to establish a measure of authority over the English settlers for a time and entered into an agreement with Dingane to return refugees who escaped to the infant settlement. The king's mind was set at rest and permission was given for mission work to begin among the Zulu. In 1836 three American missionaries and the English missionary, Owen, began work in the new field.

1 Governor Lourenço Marques to Dingane, 29 April 1830. A.H.U., Codice 1425, p. 6.

2 This is attributed by Bryant and others to the followers of Soshangane but documents in the Lisbon archives show that it was the Zulu who were involved. See document entitled *A Guerra dos Reis Vatuas vizinhos do Prezidio de Lourenço Marques em 1833*. A.H.U. Mozambique, Maca IA 1827–41.

3 Isaacs, op. cit., vol. II, pp. 219–20; Gardiner: *Journal of a Journey to the Zooloo Country*; *Andrew Smith and Natal*, pp. 70–2.

Jacob's warning was true enough, however, for ever since Farewell had obtained his charter from Shaka the English settlers had been trying to persuade the Cape Government to make Natal into a colony.[1] In 1832 Dr. Andrew Smith had been sent on a visit to Dingane with secret instructions to examine the potentialities of the area with a view to colonization. On his return, a society of Cape Town businessmen was formed to lobby for the implementation of this policy. The British Government was not prepared to undertake a move which it believed would increase expenditure.

News of the rich lands of Natal had, however, reached the ears of many settlers in the Cape Colony and in 1834 the Boers, who were thinking of seceding from the Colony, sent a small party under Uys to spy out the prospects there.[2] When the Great Trek took place Natal was selected as the main destination. Quarrels between the leaders delayed the arrival of the Boers but on 5 November 1837 Piet Retief rode into Natal to see Dingane and asked for the cession of this fertile territory to form the homeland of the Boer Republic. Dingane realized that the Boers were different from his British allies but he was in a quandary as to how to deal with them. He tried to temporize at first and told Retief that some of his cattle had been stolen by Sikonyela, the Tlokwa leader. If the Boers brought them back they would be given the grant they asked for. Dingane hoped that Sikonyela would destroy the Boer party but he was greatly disappointed. Retief rode to Sikonyela's capital and engaged the chief in friendly conversation. A pair of sparkling handcuffs were dangled before his eyes and he was tempted to try them on. They were snapped shut and Sikonyela was a prisoner. He was forced to surrender the cattle required by Dingane as the price of his release.

Two Zulu *indunas* had accompanied the Boer party. They marvelled at the powerful sorcery of the whites, their unscrupulous treachery and their lack of respect for chiefs. Dingane became more alarmed than ever at the thought of such dangerous neighbours. Further news was even more disquieting, for Retief wrote in overbearing tones telling Dingane of a Boer victory over Mzilikazi, urging him to keep faith and telling him to consult the missionaries who would explain to him the fate of evil kings. Finally on 3 February 1838 Retief came down to hold Dingane to his promise and even before he had seen the Zulu king the Boers began pouring down the passes of the Drakensberg to settle in the rich lands of Natal. Dingane decided to risk everything on a single decisive blow. If the Boers were allowed to consolidate their position they

1 Bird, op. cit., vol. I, pp. 191–3.
2 E. Walker: *The Great Trek*, pp. 94 and 139.

would be too strong for him, but if he could catch them unprepared the danger might still be averted. Retief was apparently well received and Dingane signed a charter granting Natal to the Boers. Suspicions were lulled and the party was enticed unarmed into the midst of the assembled warriors. Then the king cried 'Kill the sorcerers' and they were dragged away to be put to death on Matiwane's Hill. Immediately afterwards the regiments were despatched to fall on the Boer wagons unexpectedly and obliterate the threat for ever. At the same time Dingane did his best to keep the two white groups from combining. The missionaries were untouched and Dingane made it clear that his quarrel was with the Boers alone, not with the English.[1]

The Zulu king's plans miscarried. The attack on the wagons was only partially successful. The first to be attacked raised an alarm by firing their guns; the others were able to form a defensive *laager* and the regiments were driven off with heavy losses. The English too could not be prevented from sympathizing with their fellow whites. The missionaries insisted on leaving Zululand and the Natal traders launched an abortive expedition against Dingane. It resulted in a fiasco and the English were evacuated by a warship which happened to enter the port.

In spite of his initial failure it looked for some time as if the Zulu king might succeed in his plans, for the regiments had swept away many of the Boer cattle and while they were forced to remain in *laager* the others could not be pastured. The first Boer counter-attack ended in lamentable failure and many began to think of recrossing the Drakensberg to the highveld which offered opportunities for settlement free from Bantu opponents. The majority, however, chose to cling on. More reinforcements came in from the Cape and Pretorius rode down from the highveld to lead a new campaign. Then a strong force took the field and advanced directly into Zululand. On 16 December 1838 the sanguinary battle of Blood River demonstrated the futility of Zulu fighting methods in face of firearms. The victorious expedition pressed on to Dingane's capital itself. On Matiwane's Kop the bones of Retief and his companions were found together with the precious piece of paper ceding Natal.

Dingane had no wish to risk his regiments again against Boer guns, and the Boers, in spite of their victory, had not destroyed the Zulu kingdom and were not free to break up their *laagers* and pasture their cattle in the rich grass of Natal. Both sides were thus ready for peace. By this time a small British contingent had arrived at Port Natal to watch developments and its commander, Captain Jarvis, took the

1 See Owen's *Dairy*, p. 107, and *Letters of the American Missionaries*, nos. 59 and 60, pp. 223–42.

initiative in bringing both sides together. Peace was made but the Boers imposed hard terms and in a secret clause unknown to Jarvis they made Dingane undertake to withdraw his people further up the coast leaving, in addition to the whole of Natal, a strip of territory beyond the Tugela River for Boer occupation. Dingane attempted to carry out this arrangement. His regiments were sent to devastate Sobhuza's people and to open a road for his own withdrawal. The Zulu were told to abandon their settlements and accompany their king on his northward migration, but the humiliation of military defeat and bitterness at the thought of abandoning their homeland placed intolerable strains on the Zulu state system.

One of Shaka's brothers, Mpande, still survived. He was believed to be politically incompetent and harmless and had been spared when Dingane was destroying potential rivals. He now saw his opportunity, refused to follow Dingane and fled across the Tugela into Natal where he begged for Boer protection. The number of his followers increased steadily while those of Dingane dwindled until Mpande felt strong enough for an attempt to seize the Zulu throne. His army recrossed the Tugela supported by a Boer commando which marched separately. The forces of the Zulu rivals fought the severe battle of Magongo (February 1840). Dingane was defeated and fled to the country of his old enemy, Sobhuza, where he was put to death by a minor chief in revenge for the havoc he had created. The Zulu war machine had thus temporarily destroyed its own fighting potential. The Boers did not fire a shot, but received the reward in the shape of immense herds which the humble Mpande gladly paid for their support.

The reign of Mpande, so inauspiciously begun, really marked the beginning of a second phase in the history of the Zulu kingdom. During his lifetime he maintained good relations with the Boers and the British Government which succeeded them in Natal. The Zulu were thus left alone and were able to recoup their forces. In the immediate aftermath of Dingane's defeat the kingdom was weakened by the mass desertion of peoples who fled into Natal, but in the long peace that followed these losses were restored by natural increase. Regimental discipline was relaxed in the absence of war but it was not abandoned and only awaited an energetic leader to bring it once again to the high pitch of Shaka's day. Prolonged peace did, however, produce severe internal strains and these were increased by the longevity of the old chief who survived long after he was capable of effectively controlling affairs. His sons fell to squabbling over the succession and two powerful factions, the Usutu and the Usibebu, emerged which continued to divide the Zulu for many years thereafter. While Mpande was still alive a bitter battle was fought between the factions. The Usutu were victorious and their leader, Cetewayo, assumed the regency and was assured of the succession. In 1873 he was officially crowned by Sir Theophilus Shepstone, Natal's Secretary for Native Affairs. Under Cetewayo the Zulu military system was restored to its full vigour and the Zulu fighting force reached what was probably the highest point of its perfection. Shepstone's influence, however, prevented the army from being used on any major campaigns.

It was Cetewayo's tragedy to be caught up in the politics of white South Africa. Like Shaka, Dingane and Mpande before him, he was anxious to avoid conflict with white forces but the mere existence of his army was a cause of offence. When Carnarvon, anxious to precipitate the federation of white states in South Africa, cast his eyes on the Transvaal the threat of a Zulu invasion of the Republic after its defeat by the Pedi chief, Sekukuni, was used as a pretext for British annexation (April 1877). When the federation still failed to materialize, the Zulu kingdom came to be seen as the key to the problem. If the Zulu were crushed the Cape's fears of the financial burdens of defending Natal would evaporate, while good grazing lands could be given to the Transvaal Boers to soothe the bitterness of annexation. Britain would also rid herself of the association with Exeter Hall philanthropy and show the Boers that she could deal firmly with the Bantu. Thus Sir Bartle Frere decided that the Zulu must be humbled. A pretext was found for war and Cetewayo was faced with an ultimatum which demanded the demolition of the entire Zulu state system. British forces advanced into Zululand in January 1879 but mistakes and miscalculations led to the disaster of Isandhlwana where a whole British regiment was destroyed by the Zulu forces. Fortuitous accident though it was, the battle shook the British Government's resolve with regard to its South African policies and prepared the way for the Transvaal rebellion, the Pretoria Convention and the abandonment of Carnarvon's policy. It did not, however, save the Zulu. The heroic defence of Rorke's Drift and the restraint of Cetewayo who ordered his regiments to restrict themselves to repelling the British invasion, prevented an attack on Natal. Overwhelming British forces were assembled and the march into Zululand resumed. On this advance the Prince Imperial of France was killed. The troops reached Cetewayo's capital, Ulundi, where the Zulu made their last stand. The regiments advanced with perfect discipline in their 'cows-horns' formation but in face of modern weapons their courage and training were of no avail. They were decisively crushed and Cetewayo was taken captive to Cape Town.[1]

The defeat of Ulundi (July 1879) may be said to mark the end of

1 For a recent account see R. Furneaux: *The Zulu War*.

the great period of the Zulu kingdom but not of the Zulu as a people. The unity which Shaka had forged in ten brief years survived even this disaster. In the aftermath of their victory the British declined to annex the country but tried to break the power of the Zulu by dividing them into thirteen different states, some under chiefs who traced their lineage to the pre-Shaka period and one under John Dunn, an English friend of Cetewayo, who had betrayed him at the last minute. The experiment was doomed to failure. Zululand became the prey of anarchy and such a danger to its neighbours that in 1883 it was decided to bring Cetewayo back again. In his absence, however, the old faction dispute had grown up again. The Usutu had been seriously weakened in the preceding war and shortly after Cetewayo's restoration the Usibebu gained a victory. The king was forced to leave and died shortly afterwards in exile (1884). Zululand was then torn by a succession dispute and one of the contenders, Dinizulu, appealed for the aid of Boer volunteers who placed him on the throne but took half of his kingdom in return and established a republic there which was shortly afterwards amalgamated with the Transvaal. In 1894 the remnant of the Zulu kingdom was annexed to Natal but Zulu pride found the new yoke hard to bear. In the Bambata rebellion of 1906 the old fighting spirit flared up again in one of the most serious revolts faced by any colonial power in Bantu Africa, and even after this had been crushed the sense of Zulu identity was not destroyed. Under white rule, traditions of the exploits of earlier days have been kept alive in songs and stories and to this day the old men become enthusiastic when they talk about the kings and they love to recite their praises.[1] The fame of the Zulu name and the fact that Europeans tend to use it indiscriminately for all the Nguni-speaking Bantu of Natal has led to a situation where many, who were never part of Shaka's state, now believe and feel themselves to belong to the Zulu people. The work of Shaka in creating a sense of unity wider than the traditional tribe is still continuing.

1 Gluckman, 'The Zulu Kingdom' in Fortes and Evans Pritchard, ed.: *African Political Systems.*

3 The Birth of the Swazi Nation

THE Ngwane of Sobhuza were a Northern Nguni tribe living on the Pongola River near the Ndwandwe. In this area tribes of the two great language groups lived in close proximity to one another. The Ngwane, under a series of chiefs of the Dlamini clan, had conquered a number of small Sotho groups and incorporated them in an expanded tribe. In the early years of Sobhuza's reign relations between the Ngwane and Ndwandwe were friendly, but the course of expansion followed by both groups and the economic pressure of land shortage finally brought them to blows. A quarrel over farming lands[1] on the banks of the Pongola River led to war and the Ngwane were defeated. The Ngwane retreated to the central area of modern Swaziland and there continued the process of expansion by conquering numerous small Sotho and Nguni-speaking tribes to build up a large composite state.

When the Ngwane entered their new homeland they were organized on the same lines as the Mthethwa of Dingiswayo. The age-regiment system was employed as the basis of their army but only operated in times of war.[2] This system proved quite adequate in warfare with the small tribes of modern Swaziland who were outnumbered by the invaders and defeated one by one. Sobhuza's policy towards the conquered peoples was similar to Dingiswayo's.[3] Their identity was not destroyed and great pains were taken to preserve their royal dynasties. They retained a considerable measure of autonomy under their own chiefs but their young men were expected to serve in the age-regiments when need arose. A certain prestige naturally attached to the members of the original nucleus who were known as 'Bomdzabu' in contrast to the 'Emakhandzambili' ('those found ahead'), but as the latter proved their loyalty there was a tendency to accord them the same status as members of the original group. The slight element of class distinction

1 Bryant: *History of the Zulu*, and Kuper: *An African Aristocracy*, p. 13, agree that this was the cause of conflict.

2 On Swazi military organization, see H. Beemer: 'The Development of the Military Organisation in Swaziland', *Africa*, vol. X, no. 1, 1937.

3 For the structure of the Swazi political system I have relied largely on Kuper: *An African Aristocracy*.

thus encouraged devotion to the new state and hastened adoption of the Nguni language and culture. This was facilitated also by the fact that the Nguni were considerably more numerous than the Sotho.

Sobhuza's policy was to consolidate his position and avoid conflict with his more powerful neighbours. After the first struggle with the Ndwandwe, friendly relations were maintained even when their defeat by the Zulu in 1818 left them temporarily disorganized and Sobhuza married one of Zwide's daughters as his 'great wife'. To Shaka, Sobhuza sent a tribute of young girls including princesses of the royal clan. Some of these were put to death when they became pregnant to the Zulu king but Sobhuza was not to be moved from his policy of conciliation. During Shaka's reign Sobhuza secured immunity from Zulu attack but on the succession of Dingane he was in a less favourable position. The Zulu king needed a raiding ground in which to employ his regiments where cattle might be found to maintain the heavy consumption of the army. Sobhuza's people lay conveniently near and in the years of peace their herds had greatly increased. Zulu regiments ravaged the country but Sobhuza warned his people to avoid a struggle and take refuge on hills and in caves until the enemy withdrew. Early in 1839 the Zulu attacked again when Dingane, anxious to fulfil the secret clause in his treaty with the Boers, sent his regiments to clear a path for the Zulu to move into Swaziland. But his army was tired and dispirited by their defeat at the hands of the Boers. Sobhuza's forces, sensing the demoralization of their foes, stood firm and the Zulu were driven back to seek for reinforcements.[1] This was the signal for Mpande's rebellion and soon afterwards Dingane fled into Swaziland with a small following. He fell into the hands of one of Sobhuza's chiefs and was put to death. Sobhuza did not long survive him. He died before the end of 1840 and after a short succession dispute was succeeded by Mswati, the son of Zwide's daughter.

Mswati was to be the greatest of the Ngwane kings and from him they took the name Swazi by which they are now generally known. Contact with the Zulu regiments led to a modification of the Swazi military system along Zulu lines. This was not taken to the full extent of Shaka's system, however, and Swazi political organization also showed many traces of Sotho influence.

As in the Zulu state, the territorial hierarchy of traditional chiefs was preserved. Most of these belonged to the royal clan but some to dynasties prior to Sobhuza's conquest. These chieftaincies were associated with the various royal homesteads which constituted the administrative

1 Bryant: *History of the Zulu*. Kuper mentions that this campaign is known to the Swazi as *impi yobuya*.

Great dance at Mbelebele in 1836

headquarters of different parts of the tribal territory. In the Swazi state, however, the system of royal households was slightly different from that of other Bantu tribes because of the great importance attached to the Queen Mother. She occupied a position of higher prestige than even the king himself and her homestead was the official capital of the state. Her political authority, however, was less than that of the king and her functions were largely of a ritual nature, but she was expected to exercise a restraining influence on her son and automatically acted as regent in case of an interregnum. The king's households were separate from the Queen Mother's; one of them was always fairly close to the capital and the others distributed in different parts of the tribal territory.

Under the system of military organization which developed as a result of contact with the Zulu, the king's towns became military settlements. Age-regiments were formed on a nation-wide basis but the majority of the young men remained at home under the authority of their local chiefs. Some of the young lads from each district, however, would go to the royal headquarters to 'drink the king's milk'. After a period when they acted as cattle herds and weapon-bearers they were enrolled in regiments and remained at the royal homesteads until their regiment was dissolved. There they were fed from the king's bounty and constituted a standing force available at short notice. They used the Zulu stabbing spear and fought in typical Zulu fashion. These sections of the national age-regiments enjoyed considerable prestige and there was never a lack of adventurous and ambitious recruits.

On occasions when a major expedition was planned or a serious danger threatened, the whole national force would be mobilized. Youths who had stayed at home would march to the capital and join up with their age-mates, already in barracks, to form the full age-regiments. Each of these was under the command of an officer personally appointed by the king from a commoner family and each regiment was also associated with a royal prince in a manner reminiscent of the Sotho system. In addition there was a supreme military commander, always a commoner, with responsibility for the entire military system.

The system of partial mobilization gave the Swazi an army which was more than a match for the Sotho tribes with which it was in contact, though it could not expect to hold its own against equal numbers of Zulu. The system also encouraged the rapid assimilation of conquered peoples and made for centralization, but it did not give rise to the absolutism of the Zulu state. In spite of the development of the military system the Swazi state remained a 'constitutional monarchy' and even evolved away from the more authoritarian and oligarchic Nguni pattern towards the greater democracy of the Sotho tribes. Though the existence of a standing army strengthened the position of the king and the senior military officers, the territorial chiefs had not lost all their powers. Except in times of national emergency they had young men belonging to all the age-regiments under their authority and could use this force on their own initiative in local struggles. Their consent in matters of policy was therefore important, and together with the chief commoner officials, they formed a council which met to discuss matters of major importance. In addition, a wider assembly of all leading men which was open to all adult males was summoned from time to time. This assembly had great freedom to criticize the king and could sometimes secure the rejection of decisions already agreed by the smaller council. It could even impose a fine on the king himself if, for example, he failed to attend the assembly after summoning it. As lineage ties were weakened by the incorporation of many originally separate groups within a large state system, the Swazi developed a form of personal affiliation reminiscent of the process of 'commendation' in feudal Europe. A man would seek out an important political figure and offer to become his personal follower. In return he would be treated as a member of his superior's family and receive the support and protection normally extended to close relatives.

A man was thus a member of a number of different sub-communities and recognized multiple overlapping loyalties. He was a member of his own clan group (which might in some cases be the nucleus of a pre-conquest tribe). He was a member of an age-regiment and might spend part of his early life on active service at one or other of the royal homesteads. He was also a member of the nation as a whole and entitled to participate in the public councils of the kingdom. In administrative and judicial matters he recognized the authority of his district chief (who might in some cases be the hereditary successor of the chief of a pre-conquest tribe). In military affairs he was under the command of his regimental officers and the chief military commander. In his personal capacity he looked up to his 'lord', often a member of the central hierarchy and a different person from his immediate district chief. At the head of all these societies and chains of loyalty were the Queen Mother and the King, the embodiment of the principle of authority in the kingdom as a whole. As none of the subordinate units of loyalty had overriding importance in relation to the others, centrifugal forces were reduced. The complex network of loyalties held the kingdom together and facilitated the transition from small clan-based tribe to multitribal nation.

The death of Dingane and the succession of Mpande opened the way for the rapid expansion of the Swazi. The new Zulu king's mild disposition and the influence of Sir Theophilus Shepstone prevented further attacks by the Zulu regiments. The Swazi continued extending their authority over neighbouring tribes until they became one of the most powerful Bantu peoples in Southern Africa. In 1860 Mswati saw an opportunity to extend his influence to the Shangana kingdom of Southern Mozambique. Soshangane died about 1856 and his heir, Mawewe, succeeded him. But the new king proved unpopular and his brother, Mzila, who had taken refuge in the territory of the Transvaal Republic, came back with popular support and drove Mawewe from the throne. Mawewe then appealed to Mswati for aid and a Swazi army advanced into Southern Mozambique. Mzila turned to the Portuguese at Delagoa Bay and with their support defeated his rival in two bitter battles. The Swazi, who do not seem to have taken an active part in the fighting, withdrew taking Mawewe with them. Thereafter Mswati considered himself the protector of Mawewe's claims. Swazi forces drove Mzila's people north of the Limpopo River and devastated Sotho settlements in the Transvaal lowveld and the foothills of the Drakensberg. Fighting between Mzila and the Swazi continued until 1862 but without decisive results. The Limpopo came to form the boundary between the two kingdoms and the Swazi remained in possession of the lowveld. Special officers were placed in charge of this area, but Mswati's rule mainly took the form of annual raids which turned the area into a virtual desert.[1]

By this time the Swazi were in increasingly close contact with Europeans. In 1845 Mswati had ceded a large territory inhabited by vassal Sotho to the Transvaal Boers and in 1864 the Swazi army assisted Boer forces in crushing the Poko tribe. Boer farmers were also beginning to enter the Swazi kingdom itself. They were well received and allowed to graze their herds alongside those of the Swazi people.

When Mswati died in 1875 he left his heir, Ludonga, a minor, and the Queen Mother together with another prince acted as regent. Ludonga fell ill and died before he could be crowned and suspicion fell on the prince regent, who was put to death. Dispute about the succession then followed but finally Mbandzeni was chosen. The confused situation gave the Transvaal government an opportunity to confirm its influence with the tribe and a Boer commando of four hundred men assisted at the coronation of the new king. In Mbandzeni's reign the problem created by European infiltration into the kingdom assumed new proportions. At first the new king ruled much as his father had done. The military system was in full operation and raids were made on tribes as far afield as the Zoutpansberg and Lydenburg districts of the Transvaal. In 1880 the British asked the Swazi for military assistance against the Pedi

1 Stevenson-Hamilton: *The Lowveld: Its Wild Life and Its People*, pp. 169–79.

chief, Sekukuni, whose successful defiance of the Transvaal had precipitated the British annexation of the Republic in 1877. The Swazi forces went out to battle under a great war leader, Mbovane Mkudze, and with their aid the Pedi were completely defeated.

When the Transvaal regained its independence the British were anxious to prevent it extending its territory towards the sea and in two conventions, 1881 and 1884, both governments guaranteed the independence of the Swazi kingdom. The Transvaal, however, remained anxious to gain control of a territory which promised much rich grazing land and the position was complicated by the activities of British and other concession hunters.

At first the Swazi attempted to deal with European immigrants as if they were small Bantu families coming to join the tribe. They were given land to graze their herds and were expected to respect the king's authority, but whites could not be easily assimilated. They did not accept the customary law and jurisdiction of the king's courts. They claimed freedoms and privileges which even chiefs did not enjoy and they retained links with their own communities outside the frontiers. Some were lawless vagabonds who raided the Swazi for cattle and labourers. The white governments could take no cognizance of offences committed by their subjects within the territory, which they recognized as an independent kingdom, but Mbandzeni feared the consequences of punishing white law-breakers himself. In 1887 he informed the British High Commissioner that Transvaal Boers were threatening to attack him. He was given no promise of British aid but merely told that if his country were invaded he should not remain idle but collect his forces and expel the aggressors.

In the same year the king decided to create special administrative machinery to deal with the problem of white residents. He naturally thought of treating them as an incorporated tribe and proposed to provide them with a chief of their own who would be responsible, under the authority of the king, for dealing with their affairs and for settling any disputes between them and his subjects. The man chosen for this task was Theophilus 'Offy' Shepstone, son of Sir Theophilus (senior) whose influence with the Zulu had been valuable to the Swazi in earlier years. 'Offy' was appointed Resident Adviser and Agent of the Swazi nation. He was given powers to act in all matters where white persons were concerned, but the sovereignty of the king was carefully guarded. The Agent was paid a salary and was liable to dismissal. His task was not an easy one, for apart from the fact that he could only act effectively with the support of the king, his authority was not readily acceptable to all the white residents who were themselves divided into hostile factions of British concessionaires and Boer farmers. Shepstone formed a white committee to help him in his work, consisting of elected members and nominees of the king. It was given a charter empowering it to regulate affairs concerning whites, but subject to the ultimate veto of the Swazi ruler. This system arrested total chaos but it cannot be said that it gave the Swazi much protection from the designs of the concession hunters.

Tempted by lavish gifts Mbandzeni continued to fix his mark to documents he did not understand, often without the knowledge of his official Adviser. Before the end of his reign he had signed his entire kingdom away more than once. Concessions were of the most varied and complex types: the right to import tobacco or extract oil, to undertake auctioning or photography. Most comprehensive of all were two great concessions: the Unallotted Lands concession and the Unallotted Minerals concession.[1] As the process of concession hunting continued, Boer and British differences crystallized around their respective interests. The Boers were interested in farming and the British in industrial and mining activities, but Boer farmers objected to British concessionaires undertaking operations on their grazing lands. Only conflict between the two groups prevented the country from falling to one or other party. The Transvaal was anxious to annex the kingdom and had acquired concessions which virtually gave it governmental powers, but their implementation was resisted by the British concessionaires supported by powerful pressure groups in Britain, including the Chambers of Commerce of London, Birmingham and Liverpool.

In 1890 Mbandzeni died and the situation deteriorated further. After much dispute a young prince, Bunu, not yet of age, was chosen as the new king but the decision was not universally popular and there were outbreaks of violence among a people frustrated at the contrast between nominal independence and actual white control of much of their territory. The white committee was dissolved and a joint commission of the Transvaal and British Governments was sent to the kingdom to investigate the problem of white residents. Swazi independence was confirmed and a Provisional Government was established by means of an 'Organic Proclamation' issued by the Swazi authorities. The government was designed to represent Swazi, Boer and British interests, with 'Offy' as the representative of the Swazi. This system survived for three years but failed to provide a stable administration. It was at the mercy of the white concessionaires and confirmed the great majority of existing

1 Documentary evidence on the bizarre 'concession hunting' phase of Swazi history can be found in the Swaziland Blue Books, Cmd. 5,089, 1887; Cmd. 6,200, 1890; Cmd. 6,217, 1890; Cmd. 7,212, 1893; Cmd. 7,611, 1895.

concessions. Riddled by internal corruption and inefficiency it provided one of the most expensive governments in the world.

As the whites grew increasingly resentful at the lack of orderly government the Transvaal continued to press its claim for annexation. President Kruger offered to abandon his Republic's claims to territory north of the Limpopo River if Britain would make a concession in Swaziland. The British government, anxious to ensure the success of Rhodes' venture in Southern Rhodesia, agreed to allow the Transvaal to take over the kingdom if the Swazi authorities could be persuaded to agree. But when the document was placed before the queen regent and her council they refused to accept it. They sent a deputation to ask for British protection and also repudiated the Organic Proclamation. The Transvaal, however, continued to press its case and in 1894 Britain agreed that the Swazi kingdom should become a protected dependency of the Transvaal even if this were not acceptable to the Swazi.

Realizing the impossibility of resisting the Transvaal's forces the Swazi made no open resistance. The short period of Boer Republican rule was far from happy. The Swazi resented the imposition of taxation which forced them to take service with the whites. The Boer government, in order to ensure its control over the country, was anxious to destroy the authority of the Swazi ruler. Bunu had recently come of age and when one of his counsellors was put to death for witchcraft the Boer authorities tried to arrest him. He fled to Natal and asked for British protection. His people mobilized and a dangerous situation arose, but under British pressure the Transvaal agreed to restore him though with much curtailed authority.

The outbreak of the Great Boer War brought this phase to an end. Swaziland came under British administration and in 1910, together with Basutoland and Bechuanaland, it was excluded from the South African Union. The Swazi hoped that their land would be restored to them but the new government could not repudiate concessions which had been accepted as valid for so long. About two-thirds of the agricultural land remained in the hands of Europeans and the Swazi, like other South African peoples, have been forced to supplement the agricultural returns of their depleted territory by service on the farms and in the mines of white South Africa. In spite of the loss of so much of their homeland, however, the Swazi have retained their identity as a nation. Even the age-regiment system has not entirely disappeared and the Swazi, though still encumbered by the legacy of the period of concession hunting, now stand on the verge of independent nationhood.

4 Soshangane and the Empire of Gaza

SHAKA'S victory on the Mhlatuze River started a general northward movement of several Nguni tribes. Two leaders of Zwide's army, Soshangane and Zwangendaba, led their followers by different routes into Southern Mozambique. A similar direction was taken by two other peoples, the Maseko and the Msene, who combined under the leadership of the Msene chief, Nxaba. Early in 1821 some of these peoples were in the vicinity of Lourenço Marques. They had driven the chief, Capella, to take refuge on an island and by mid-July they had crossed the Temby River and were devastating the lands of chief Matola. The Portuguese fortress was in no position to defend itself and the governor was fortunate to persuade the invaders to retreat in return for presents.[1] In 1822 Captain Owen called at Delagoa Bay in the course of his expedition to survey the East African coast. His party met Soshangane with some of his followers on the Temby River and during the night the British camp was attacked. The attackers were beaten off by gunfire and Soshangane was believed to have been killed.[2] Shortly afterwards Owen's people took part in a joint attack with the Portuguese on another group of Soshangane's warriors. By this time Zwangendaba and his followers had moved further ahead and Owen's party encountered them on the River Manice. The southern invaders had devastated the country and subjugated the peoples as far as Inhambane and Owen was surprised that the officer in charge of the fort at Delagoa Bay continued to trade with them.[3]

When the main Ndwandwe body under Zwide's son, Sikhunyane, were finally defeated by Shaka in 1826 Soshangane gained a great many recruits to his following.[4] He remained near Delagoa Bay until 1828

1 Letters, Governor Lourenço Marques to Governor Mocambique, 11 July 1821 and 28 July 1821. A.H.U. Mocambique, caixa 68.

2 Captain Owen: *Narrative of Voyages to Explore the Shores of Africa, Arabia and Madagascar*, vol. I, pp. 93–100.

3 Ibid., p. 80.

4 C. Montez in 'As invasoes dos Mangunis e dos Machanganas', *Mocambique*, 9–10, 1937, pp. 25–55, argues that Soshangane did not break away from the

when he was attacked by the Zulu regiments engaged on Shaka's last campaign. Though the Zulu gained no more than a pyrrhic victory, Soshangane decided to withdraw out of their reach and moved northward to the region of the middle Sabi. There he found himself in the proximity of the other two invading groups.

The three hordes were loosely associated for a time but rivalry between the leaders led to conflict. About 1831 a bitter struggle between Soshangane and Zwangendaba left the former victorious. Zwangendaba led his followers away to the west through modern Southern Rhodesia. Soon afterwards another war took place between Soshangane and Nxaba and again Soshangane emerged the victor. The composite Msene and Maseko army broke up. Nxaba led his followers westward in the wake of Zwangendaba while the Maseko under Ngwane took a northward path, crossed the Zambesi and passed through much of modern Mozambique to enter the Songea district of modern Tanganyika.

With the defeat of his major rivals, Soshangane was able to build up and consolidate an empire which was known after his grandfather as the empire of Gaza. His headquarters were at Chaimite in the highlands of the middle Sabi and from that centre his regiments undertook expeditions in all directions. On 10 October 1834 the Portuguese captain at Inhambane rallied the local tribes for an attack on the invaders but in the ensuing battle the captain and all but ten of his men were killed.[1] The following year the regiments reached the outskirts of the territory of Sofala. They retreated before a Portuguese counter-attack[2] but on 10 October 1836[3] they attacked again and virtually the entire garrison was wiped out. Thereafter the post existed at the good pleasure of Soshangane and was subject to repeated alarms.[4] The old kingdom of Manica was devastated and the Portuguese abandoned their trading posts there for about fifty years. The Portuguese settlements of Sena and Tete also suffered from repeated attacks and were reduced to buying peace with an annual tribute.

Nothing of the nature of a major war between the Portuguese and Soshangane took place, however. The Portuguese settlements were in

---

main Ndwandwe body until after their final defeat by Shaka in 1826. While the evidence is not conclusive I have preferred the view that when Soshangane encountered Owen and his party in 1822 he had already established himself as an independent chief.

1 Montez, op. cit.

2 Letter, Governor Mocambique to Governor Sofala, 20 May 1835, congratulates him on this success. A.H.U. codice 1424, p. 38.

3 On the precise dating of this see S. Alberto: 'Os Angones os ultimos povos invasores da Angonia Portuguesa', *Mocambique*, September 1941, pp. 79–103.

4 Letters, Governor Mocambique to Governor Sofala, 22 Nov. 1841 and 11 May 1842. A.H.U. codice 1424, pp. 80–6.

the last stages of decay. Lacking arms and men they could only act on the defensive. No attempt was made to prevent Soshangane extending his control over the whole hinterland south of the Zambesi and the Portuguese only came in conflict with his warriors when they happened to approach one or other of the forts. Soshangane on the other hand had no grand scheme to drive the white men into the sea. He sought to reduce them to a position of vassalage and to secure tribute, but not to destroy the forts which could supply him with valuable commodities. Apart from the trading posts in Manica most of the Portuguese settlements survived, though in very distressed circumstances. When Livingstone visited Sena and Tete (1856 and 1858) he found them in a lamentable condition. The Portuguese were treated as a conquered tribe and forced to pay a tribute which was collected every year by a party of armed warriors. The *prazo* lands which had been occupied along the river were deserted and the settlers were deterred from making any improvement in their situation by the knowledge that this would lead to the tribute being increased.[1]

It was with the Bantu peoples of Southern Mozambique that Soshangane fought his main campaigns. One by one they were conquered and incorporated in a Zulu-type kingdom which extended its authority from the Zambesi to a little south of the Limpopo. In building up his kingdom Soshangane employed the age-regiment system and Zulu fighting methods. The chiefs of conquered tribes were treated as vassal sub-chiefs and the young men were taken and trained by military *indunas* in the fighting methods of their conquerors. Members of the Nguni nucleus, however, constituted a distinct class called 'ba-Ngoni' in contrast to the newly incorporated peoples who were known as 'ba-Tshangane'. The new recruits were segregated in regiments of their own under 'ba-Ngoni' officers. They were subject to discrimination and on the battlefield these more expendable subjects were put in the front line.[2]

In course of time the incorporated peoples came to identify themselves with their conquerors and take pride in their loyalty to the king, but the process of assimilation only operated to the full at the heart of Soshangane's empire. Away from the vicinity of the royal households many tribes remained virtually independent, simply paying tribute on demand. Even within the ranks of those who were members of the state in the full sense, tensions based on cultural differences persisted. As Sosha-

1 D. and C. Livingstone: *Narrative of an Expedition to the Zambesi*, p. 30.

2 Stevenson-Hamilton: *The Low Veld: Its Wild Life and Its People*, p. 169. On the subject of the incorporation of conquered peoples in the military system, see W. Mhlanga: 'The story of Ngwaqazi' and 'The History of the Amatshangane', *Nada*, 25, 1948, pp. 70–1, 71–3.

ngane grew old he began to believe himself bewitched. Suspicion fell on the newly incorporated peoples and many of the 'ba-Tshangane' were killed. A party of Thonga broke away and succeeded in escaping to the Transvaal where they settled in small parties.[1]

Between 1856 and 1859[2] the old chief died and the succession passed first to his son, Mawewe, who shifted the capital from the highlands of the middle Sabi to Biyeni near Delagoa Bay. His rule was unpopular, however, and his brother, Mzila, who had taken refuge in the Transvaal was able to oust him from power. Mzila then sought Portuguese aid while Mawewe turned to the Swazi. Mawewe failed to recapture his throne and died in exile in Swaziland. He had been accompanied by a few followers, and their descendants are still to be found near the Crocodile and Nkomati Rivers.[3] The Portuguese subsequently claimed that in return for their aid Mzila had agreed to become a tributary chief and accept orders from the governor of Lourenço Marques, but the document in proof of this was signed by four Portuguese officers only.[4]

In spite of his victory Mzila was moved by the Swazi invasion to withdraw his people north of the Limpopo and to shift his capital away from the Swazi frontier back to the highlands of the middle Sabi near Soshangane's original centre. The process of conquering and incorporating new peoples was continued and raids were made on those of the Shona of Southern Rhodesia who fell outside the limits of territory raided by Mzilikazi's regiments. Good relations were maintained with the Ndebele and Mzila's son, Gungunyana, married a daughter of Mzilikazi's heir, Lobengula.

In 1870 messengers sent by Mzila visited Natal and called on Sir Theophilus Shepstone.[5] They asked him to help them settle the quarrel with the Swazi, open trade and send an official to visit their king. They denied that the Portuguese had any control over them and expressed a wish for British protection. Shepstone gave a non-committal reply, but the following year Mr. St. Vincent Erskine was sent by the Natal government to visit Mzila and report on the situation. He found most of the fighting force concentrated near the capital where he calculated there were about thirty thousand men. Outposts were maintained at other strategic points, one near the Limpopo to guard against a renewed Swazi attack. The traveller was annoyed by the treatment he received at

1 Stevenson-Hamilton, op. cit., p. 170.
2 The precise date is a matter of dispute; see, e.g., Montez, 'As invasoes dos Mangunis e dos Machanganas'.
3 Stevenson-Hamilton, op. cit., p. 176.
4 Warhurst: *Anglo-Portuguese Relations in South-Central Africa*, p. 79.
5 Ibid., pp. 79–80.

Mzila's hands and gave a generally bad report of his people.[1] Another embassy from Mzila visited Natal in 1872 but it was dismissed with a few presents.

In spite of Mzila's apparent contempt for the Portuguese the balance of power began to shift in their favour during his reign. The metropolis was starting to take a new interest in its East African dependencies. Trade with the Transvaal was bringing new life to the settlement of Lourenço Marques and on the Zambesi an energetic Portuguese subject of Indian descent, Gouveia de Andrada, built up an armed following from the tribes around Sena and drove Mzila's people back. The Zambesi settlements were relieved of the burden of tribute and much of the *prazo* land was recovered.[2]

Mzila died in 1885 and was succeeded by Gungunyana. In the same year two of his subjects put their marks to a treaty with Portugal, and shortly afterwards the Secretary-General of the province of Mozambique led an expedition to his capital, Manhlagazi, on the middle Sabi with the object of establishing a Resident there. Gungunyana responded by sending another embassy to Natal which stated that he wished to be guided by the British Government like his father before him.[3] The proposal was rebuffed on the grounds that the Gaza kingdom was under Portuguese authority. In 1889 Gungunyana decided to shift his capital southward again to a site near the Limpopo and although many died *en route* the march was successfully accomplished. In his new home the monarch allowed a missionary of the Swiss Evangelical Society to begin teaching his people and continued his policy of attempting to play one white power off against the other while at the same time building up his own strength.[4] For this purpose he encouraged trade with the Europeans and strove to build up his supplies of firearms. His control over his own people, however, was weakened by contact with Europeans. Young men were drifting away to work for the whites instead of taking their place in the regiments and rum imported by traders on a large scale was demoralizing his subjects. In 1890 the internal weakness of the state was made apparent when the Chopi broke into open revolt. But decay had not gone so far that the fighting machine could not operate. The regiments assembled and the revolt was ruthlessly suppressed.

In the same year Gungunyana was approached by an agent of the

1 Ibid., p. 81. Also St. Vincent Erskine: 'Journey of Exploration to the mouth of the River Limpopo', *Journal Royal Geographical Society*, 39, 1869, pp. 233–76.
2 Theal: *The Portuguese in South Africa*, pp. 290–1.
3 Warhurst, op. cit., p. 81.
4 Liengme: 'Un Potentat Africain: Goungounyane et son Règne', *Bull. Neuchatel Geog. Soc.*, 13, 1901, pp. 99–135.

British South Africa Company. Rhodes was already planning to gain an outlet to the sea for his future empire in Southern Rhodesia and Dr. Schultz persuaded Gungunyana to give verbal consent to a treaty similar to the Rudd Concession made by Lobengula. Mining rights and rights to everything necessary for the operation of a mining industry throughout his kingdom were conceded to the Company in return for the promise of one thousand rifles, twenty thousand rounds of ammunition and an annual subsidy of £500. This was the first step in a complicated diplomatic struggle between the British South Africa Company and the Portuguese authorities to establish legal claims to the Gaza empire.[1] Rhodes' attempts to seize Gazaland were finally frustrated by the disinclination of the British Government to act contrary to its existing treaties with Portugal and Gungunyana was faced with the failure of his attempts to maintain independence by pitting one European power against another. A last embassy was sent to Natal offering allegiance to Britain and asking that if this were refused Gunganyana's people might be allowed to settle in the British sphere. It was sent back empty-handed and Gungunyana faced the Portuguese alone. Though his warriors possessed about two thousand rifles they could not hope to defeat a serious Portuguese attack and the Portuguese were determined to destroy the kingdom which stood between them and effective occupation of the country they claimed. A pretext for war was found in 1895 and Gungunyana's followers, weakened by internal dissensions, were overcome. The king himself was captured and died in exile in the Canary Islands. The last of the great independent Bantu monarchies in Southern Africa had been brought to an end.

After their victory the Portuguese systematically hunted down Gungunyana's remaining followers. Some of them fled to the Transvaal and settled between the Sabi and Oliphants Rivers by the foothills of the Drakensberg. They were ruled at first by one of the junior sons of Gungunyana but in 1922 the rightful heir who had been deported to Portugal and later transferred to Angola, escaped and succeeded in rejoining his people.[2] They are all that remain of Soshangane's following. The numbers of the 'ba-Ngoni' aristocrats had always been small and their assimilation of conquered peoples was incomplete. The thoroughness of the Portuguese suppression broke up the empire for ever. Subject peoples reverted to their original tribal system though they retained some of the conquerors' words in their vocabulary, particularly words relating to warfare and cattle.[3] The empire disappeared

1 On the diplomatic struggle for control of the Gaza kingdom, see Warhurst, op. cit., chapter III, pp. 78–108. 2 Stevenson-Hamilton, op. cit., p. 181.
3 Ibid.; Junod: *The Life of a South African Tribe*, pp. 26–34.

as a political and cultural unit, but the memory of its existence persists and the Bantu of Southern Mozambique are proud to associate themselves with it. To this day mine-workers from this area who go to work in South Africa call themselves Shangaans.

5 The Ngoni Invasions of East-Central Africa

ZWANGENDABA, chief of the small Nguni-speaking Jere tribe, was one of the most remarkable leaders in African history. Contemporary accounts and traditional histories give little insight into his character as a man but he led his people on a successful migration over thousands of miles, preserved them in innumerable encounters and presided over the development of a system of socio-political organization of great ingenuity. The Jere tribe were one of the many small tribes inhabiting northern Zululand which were caught up in the process of empire-building by rival powers. The Ndwandwe were their closest neighbours and the Jere accepted Zwide as their overlord, but the desire for tribal autonomy persisted and the opportunity came when Zwide's forces were defeated on the Mhlatuze River. Zwangendaba and his people broke away in the confusion of the retreat, and in company with other fleeing Nguni groups, penetrated into Southern Mozambique. The Jere formed the vanguard of this movement and in 1822 they were found by Captain Owen on the River Manice (Lower Nkomati).[1]

The lessons of the Zulu war were not lost on the defeated and Zwangendaba together with other Nguni leaders drilled his followers in Zulu fighting tactics. With these they were more than a match for the Thonga and other peoples of Southern Mozambique and though their numbers were small they met with no effective opposition. As they advanced, Thonga captives were incorporated in the regiments and the host grew more formidable with every victory. After 1826 it was further strengthened by new recruits from the defeated Ndwandwe.

About 1831 Zwangendaba encountered Soshangane and Nxaba. The three leaders fell to blows and after bitter fighting the defeated Zwangendaba led his followers westward. They pursued a course near the Zambesi at first, alarming the inhabitants of the Portuguese settlements of Sena and Tete,[2] and passed into modern Southern Rhodesia. The

1 Captain Owen: *Narrative of Voyages*, vol. I, pp. 142–3.

2 Letter, Governor Mocambique to Governor Quilimane and Rivers of Senna

Jere, or Ngoni as they came to be known, were then within the territory of the age-old Monomatapa empire. This empire was then dominated by the Rozwi tribe, ruled by chiefs of the Shangamire dynasty which had conquered the earlier Kalanga rulers in the seventeenth century. In spite of centuries of Portuguese penetration the Monomatapa empire was still a living force and the stone-building culture which created the striking ruins at Zimbabwe, Inyanga, Dhlo Dhlo and other sites was at its height on the eve of the invasions from the south. The Rozwi and Kalanga, however, lacked a system of military organization comparable to that of the invaders. Zwangendaba's forces secured a series of easy victories and the empire was irremediably broken. The stone buildings were captured and the huts they enclosed set on fire. As he continued his march westward Zwangendaba adopted captives of the two Shona[1] peoples into his tribe until they became a significant element in the composite group.

Shortly after Zwangendaba's defeat by Soshangane, Nxaba suffered the same fate and also led his following into Southern Rhodesia, completing the devastation of the Monomatapa empire. Somewhere between Mozambique and modern Matabeleland the two leaders encountered one another. Zwangendaba was defeated and hastened on his westward flight.[2] When he reached the vicinity of modern Bulawayo he halted for a while and his regiments tracked down the last Rozwi emperor who fled to a hilltop fortress. Even the cleverly constructed stone defences could not keep the Ngoni regiments at bay. The hiding place was stormed and the Rozwi dynasty expired.[3]

Whether the long migration had generated a restless love of movement or whether fear of another conflict with Nxaba kept the Ngoni on the move, they did not delay long in the healthy upland cattle country of modern Matabeleland but turned their steps northward to the Zambesi. They reached the river near the Kebrabrassa Rapids and on 19 November 1835, a day marked by a solar eclipse, the greater part of the

---

29 Oct. 1831, refers to arms and ammunition sent to Senna and Tete to make it possible to resist the caffres who had invaded the immediate neighbourhood of those towns. A.H.U. codice 1422, p. 29.

1 The name Shona is in general use as a collective name for the various peoples who formed part of the Monomatapa empire. Together with the Ndebele they constitute the present-day population of Southern Rhodesia. Many of the Ndebele moreover are of Shona origin. The derivation of the name is unknown.

2 Chibambo: *My Ngoni of Nyasaland*, p. 15.

3 Posselt: 'Mzilikazi and the Rise of the Amandebele', *Proceedings of the Rhodesian Scientific Association*, vol. XVIII, part I, July 1919. Woods: 'Extracts from the Customs and History of the Amandebele', *Nada*, 1931, pp. 16–23.

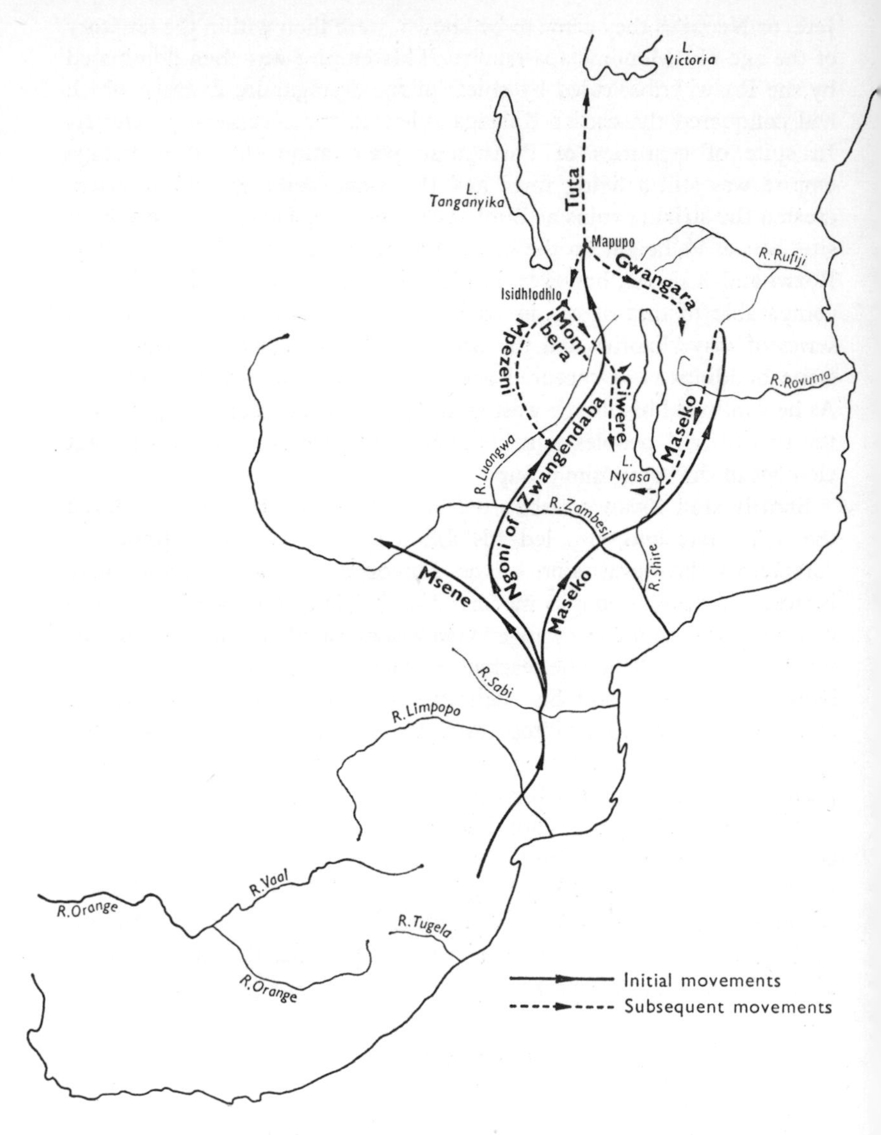

Northward migration routes of Zwangendaba's Ngoni, the Maseko Ngoni and the Msene

host crossed the flood.[1] One section under a woman leader, Nyamazana, refused to follow and remained in Southern Rhodesia continuing the devastation of the Shona peoples until the arrival of the Ndebele with whom they were finally incorporated.[2]

After crossing the river the Ngoni established a settlement in the lands of the Senga people.[3] For about four years their regiments ravaged the neighbourhood bringing large numbers of captive Senga to swell their ranks. Then, like a swarm of locusts forced to continue advancing as it destroys its own livelihood, the Ngoni moved off again to the north. Keeping the Lwangwa valley on his left Zwangendaba passed up the west side of Lake Nyasa until he reached the small lakes of Mawiri. There the Ngoni halted again for another period of about four years. In this new home they were in the territory of the Cewa tribe, a branch of the Maravi peoples of modern Malawi. Like other members of this group the Cewa had not developed a large-scale political system and their small clan villages were at the mercy of the invaders.

At no great distance, however, were three more powerful groups. The Bemba, with an elaborate state system centring on their king, the Citimukulu, had their base near Lake Bangweolu and were expanding eastward at the expense of the less highly organized and militant Bisa and Lala.[4] Their stockaded villages could be defended even against Ngoni attack. To the north of them in the valley of the Luapula River, Cazembe, a general of the Lunda king, Mwata Yamvo,[5] had built up a kingdom in the early eighteenth century which still remained strong. On the highlands near the northern end of Lake Nyasa another such kingdom had been created in the eighteenth century by an adventurous elephant-hunter named Mlowoka. He had brought together a number

1 The coincidence of the occurrence of a solar eclipse while the Ngoni were crossing the river makes this one of the few firm dates in the history of the *Mfecane*. It has nevertheless been a subject of some controversy. See Barnes: *Politics in a Changing Society*, pp. 16–17.

2 See Jones (Mhlangazanhlansi): *My Friend Kumalo*; Woods: 'Extracts from the Customs and History of the Amandebele', *Nada*, 1931, pp. 16–23.

3 On the route taken by the Ngoni under Zwangendaba I have followed Chibambo and Barnes.

4 On the structure of the Bemba kingdom, see Whiteley, 'The Bemba and Related Peoples of Northern Rhodesia', *Ethnographic Survey of Africa, East Central Africa*, Part II. A. Richards: *Tribal Government in Transition*. Livingstone gives a good impression of the military strength of the Bemba stockaded towns: *The Last Journals of David Livingstone*, vol. I, p. 199.

5 For a general account of the Lunda of Cazembe, see S. Laski: *Peoples of the lower Luapula Valley*. The kingdom was visited by a Portuguese expedition under Lacerda in 1798 and again by Gamitto in 1831–32. See Burton: *The Lands of Cazembe*; Cunnison: *Pedroso Gamitto*.

of Tumbuka clans to form the Kamanga kingdom which continued after his death under a dynasty known as Chikurayamembe.[1]

The Ngoni avoided a major conflict with any of these powerful states but raided the defenceless Cewa and those Tumbuka clans which fell outside the Kamanga kingdom. Many captives taken from these tribes swelled the Ngoni ranks and the original Nguni-speaking nucleus, though politically and culturally dominant, had by then become a minority in a composite group of great diversity. Internal tensions based on cultural differences could not be avoided altogether and the Ngoni passed through a serious crisis. Their chief was growing old and he fell ill. Suspicions of witchcraft were aroused and the newly recruited Senga, Cewa and Tumbuka diverted the danger from themselves by laying the blame on the Thonga who had been incorporated in Mozambique. An orgy of killing followed and a large proportion of the Thonga were massacred.[2]

By this time constant raids had largely destroyed the resources of the area within easy reach of the Ngoni camp. A war party led by an energetic *induna*, Pinceya, had passed beyond Lake Nyasa into the Fipa country near the south-eastern shores of Lake Tanganyika. They brought back fine red cattle like those the Jere tribe had known in northern Zululand and the old Zwangendaba decided to lead his people in pursuit of them.[3] The Ngoni passed out of the Cewa territory to the north, moving up the Luwewe River to the source of the Luangwa. There they halted and Zwangendaba sent out a large expedition to reconnoitre the western shores of Lake Tanganyika. The regiments returned with an adverse report of the area but on their march they had attacked the Holoholo and driven some of them across the lake to settle on its eastern shores.[4] The Holoholo profited by their defeat by mastering Ngoni tactics and when they encountered the invaders again they were in a position to give a good account of themselves. Disappointed in the prospects on the west bank of Lake Tanganyika, Zwangendaba proceeded with his original plan and led his people round the head of Lake Nyasa through the Sukuma territory on to the Fipa plateau. A settlement called Mapupo ('dreams') was built near present Ufipa and there Zwangendaba died about 1848.[5]

1 See T. C. Young: *Notes on the History of the Tumbuka-Kamanga Peoples.*

2 Chibambo, op. cit., pp. 22–3.

3 Ibid., p. 23.

4 This expedition and its consequences for the Holoholo are discussed by Hatchell: 'The Angoni of Tanganyika Territory', *Man*, 35, 1935, pp. 69–73. Because of this expedition some writers accepted the view that one section of the Ngoni marched up the west side of the lake. The evidence for this is discussed by Barnes, op. cit., pp. 22–3.

5 The date is a rough estimate given by Chibambo, op. cit., p. 25, on the basis of a calculation of the number of years taken on the migration from the Zam-

On the long march from their original homeland the Ngoni developed a system which enabled them to absorb heterogeneous alien groups very rapidly, while still preserving their identity as a community with a recognizable way of life and set of values. It allowed for strong leadership and maintained the military efficiency essential to survival in alien territory. It achieved this through the development of the traditional clan system to allow for the incorporation of captives in a quasi-kinship relationship and through the age-regiment military organization.[1]

In the turbulent times in which the Ngoni system was born, members of the original nucleus attached themselves to one or other of the leading members of the Jere royal clan. As these leaders acquired more wives and followers they established several households, each of which constituted a separate village. The position of the households in relation to one another was fixed by the customary order of seniority. The territorial distribution of the households of all clan heads in relation to the king was also regulated by a fixed rule. Even within individual villages, huts were arranged in an order determined by the status of their occupants. Though the Ngoni were so often on the move this scheme was always remembered and when a halt was made villages and huts were reconstructed in the same territorial pattern. When captives were taken they were distributed between the king, his major chiefs and the ordinary warriors. Once handed over to a master the prisoner was treated as a junior member of the master's family. He built his hut near that of his lord in a position appropriate to his humble status and in return for services of cattle herding he was entitled to protection like any member of the family. When the overlord's family increased and was divided into households the ex-captives were distributed amongst these.

A captive's position was low at first but if he distinguished himself in war he could acquire captives of his own though he was still subject to his original master. As his followers increased, the ex-captive's hut became the centre of a subsidiary cluster of dwellings within his master's village. Ultimately he removed to establish a satellite village which in turn continued growing until it too was divided into households. Early captives thus rose to positions of importance, but their subordination to their original masters was not forgotten and as the system proliferated the Nguni aristocracy remained at the top. The prestige of the original Nguni-speaking nucleus (known as the 'Zansi') was maintained and

---

besi to Mapupo. Rangeley suggests 1842 as an approximate date: 'Mtwalo', *Nyasaland Journal*, vol. 15, no. 1, pp. 33–7. Barnes gives about 1845: *Politics in a Changing Society*, p. 16.

1 The following account has been largely based on Barnes: *Politics in a Changing Society*.

served to support the cultural values they had brought with them from the south. Conscious of the danger of losing their identity in the flood of strangers the 'Zansi' always tried to marry aristocratic women as their 'great wives' though junior spouses might be taken from other groups. The 'Zansi' daughters always married within the aristocratic class and the older women enjoyed great respect. They were the repositories of Nguni tradition and the children of ex-captives were often sent to them to help with the chores, wait on the 'Zansi' children and learn something of Nguni culture.

As the Ngoni community expanded, long and complex chains of quasi-lineage affiliation stretched through society from top to bottom. The original followings of the royal clan heads grew into great territorial chieftaincies and the community as a whole could be described as a loose bundle of enlarged clans. Holding this together was the age-regiment system. As in the Zulu kingdom, boys first took part in cattle herding and when they reached maturity were enrolled in age-regiments. These were nation-wide, included captives and their children as well as aristocrats, and could only be constituted by the king. When a new regiment was formed it was immediately sent on its first expedition. This marked the decisive break with childhood and thereafter its members could no longer take part in cattle herding or drink milk. Instead of each regiment having a name of its own the Ngoni had a fixed number of age-grade names. When a new regiment was formed the older ones changed their appellations and the oldest was dissolved.[1]

The age-regiments did not live in separate military towns but were only summoned as need arose. Each major territorial division of the tribe constituted a military district and contained companies of all the national age-regiments. Their headquarters were the households of the king or of his relatives established in their area, and they sometimes undertook local expeditions under the command of a territorial chief. Major campaigns, however, could only be undertaken on the king's command. A messenger from the king's settlement would arrive at each important village at dawn and deliver the royal instructions to prepare food and arms.[2] A few days later local contingents converged on the royal settlement where ceremonial dances and magic rites prepared the army for war. At the assembly point, companies of age-mates from different districts united to form the full age-regiments, each of which thereafter acted under the command of a single regimental *induna*. On each occasion the king nominated a commander-in-chief for the

1 C. Wiese: 'Expedicão Portuguesa a M'Pesene', *Bulletin Lisbon Geographical Society*, no. 10, 1891, pp. 235–73, 331–430, 465–97; no. 11, 1892, pp. 372–599.

2 See the description by Chibambo in M. Read: *The Ngoni of Nyasaland*, pp. 29–37.

expedition. Sometimes he was an important individual but sometimes a relatively recent captive chosen for his military abilities. Throughout their wanderings the Ngoni preserved the Zulu battle tactics: 'The arms are two short spears, one in the right hand, the other in the left, concealed by a large shield, . . . disdaining bows and arrows, and they never use the spear as an assegai. . . . Their thousands march in four or five extended lines and attack by attempting to envelop the enemy.'[1]

In Central and East Africa the Ngoni only rarely fought set battles with powerful enemies. Military activity generally consisted of storming the stockaded villages in which the inhabitants tried to defend themselves. When the army drew near to one of these settlements it halted while a council of war decided the order in which the regiments were to attack. Every attempt was made to take the enemy by surprise and attacks were usually launched at dawn or nightfall. When the signal was given the first regiment rushed down on the stockade yelling and beating spears against shields to create panic. If it wavered, a second regiment was sent in support and once a breach was made in the palisade the whole army made a simultaneous charge which normally carried all before it. When the stockade fell, all who offered resistance were speared to death. Foodstocks were looted, captives and cattle rounded up to be taken back in triumph to the king. Often, captured villages were set on fire and the progress of an Ngoni army could be followed by the trail of smoke. In the course of a battle the commanders took note of those who first entered the stockade or performed other feats of valour, and when the army returned home the heroes were rewarded by the right to dance a solo portraying their exploits before the monarch. They were sometimes allowed to wear distinctive regalia and received a greater amount of the spoils than their companions.[2] Major expeditions involved large numbers of men and might be very protracted. The missionary Elmslie once saw an army of ten thousand set out in June and return in September. When they were not encumbered by captives and stock the Ngoni marched with great rapidity and generally caught their victims unprepared.

The age-regiment system maintained the position of the king above that of all other clan heads. He remained the supreme political authority of the community. He was the symbol of the unity of the state and only

1 R. F. Burton: *The Lake Regions of Central Africa*, vol. II, p. 77, describing the tactics of the Tuta branch of the Ngoni. The military success which attended these methods led to such military conservatism that Wiese noted that Mpezeni's Ngoni in 1889 still preferred to rely on their traditional weapons though they possessed considerable quantities of firearms. See 'Expedicão Portuguesa a M'Pesene'.

2 M. Read: *The Ngoni of Nyasaland*, pp. 29–37, and Wiese, op. cit.

he was entitled to the royal salute. The Ngoni prided themselves on possessing true kings, in contrast to the Central African peoples who only had clan heads. Unity was strengthened by the hostility of the outside world. The Ngoni attacked their neighbours almost indiscriminately and their settlements were often surrounded by tracts of devastated country, outside which other peoples looked on them with universal fear and hatred.[1] Thus within their own ranks they developed a strong sense of coherence, a devotion to law and peaceful order—the exact opposite of their relationships with external groups. Violence or insulting behaviour of any kind, even towards the most lowly member of the community, was deplored and the ideal of personal behaviour was one of peaceableness and orderly living reminiscent of the Roman 'gravitas'.[2] Captives were often ill-treated on the march home from a successful raid but once assigned to a particular lineage they were entitled to be treated with consideration and respect. Even if they deserted their original masters they could not be put to death.[3]

In spite of the forces making for coherence, the natural tendency for the artificial lineage groups to split into separate kingdoms could not be prevented altogether. The very success of the Ngoni meant that the community grew too large to live together conveniently and to be governed as a unit. It divided into a number of sections, each of which continued growing independently. The death of Zwangendaba precipitated this development. The question of the succession was very complicated. Normally the heir of the 'great house' should have succeeded, but during the long northward march the 'great house' had fallen into disgrace. One of its wives had brought Zwangendaba some beer but when he was about to drink it he noticed some hairs floating in it. Witchcraft was suspected and the king ordered the 'great house' to be destroyed. Many of its members were killed and its dependants were distributed among the other houses, but one wife and her son, Mpezeni, were secretly preserved. Later they were presented to the king and the prince was received into his favour. On the destruction of the 'great house', however, Zwangendaba had nominated another to provide the heir and in this house there was a son named Mombera. When Zwangendaba died both boys were still minors and it was very difficult to know which of them had legal seniority.[4]

1 Barnes: *Politics in a Changing Society*, pp. 26–7.
2 M. Read: 'The Moral Code of the Ngoni and their former Military State', *Africa*, vol. XI, no. 1, January 1938, pp. 1–41.
3 Elmslie: *Among the Wild Angoni*, pp. 117–18. Wiese, 'Expedicão', gives a similar impression of the treatment of captives.
4 On this question, see Chibambo: *My Ngoni of Nyasaland*; Barnes: *Politics in a Changing Society*; M. Read: *The Ngoni of Nyasaland*.

The course of events was determined by two other senior members of the royal clan who were bitter rivals. Zwangendaba's junior brother, Ntabeni, first assumed the regency and he supported the candidature of Mpezeni but this was opposed by a cousin of the late king named Mgayi. Ntabeni's regency was cut short by his death and power passed to his rival. The first secession then took place. Ntabeni's followers feared reprisals and broke away. They were hotly pursued for a time but succeeded in making their escape in a northward direction. They came to be known later as the Tuta. A second secession followed soon after. Zulu-Gama, another member of the royal clan, led his people away to the east where they became known as the Gwangara.

Mgayi then led the main body of the Ngoni southward from the Fipa country to a point between the northern tip of Lake Nyasa and the southern end of Lake Tanganyika. There his candidate, Mombera, came of age and was installed as king. The supporters of Mpezeni had not abandoned their pretensions and it only needed a small incident to precipitate a further split. One of Mombera's first expeditions ended in failure and Mpezeni's supporters took this as an omen that the wrong man was on the throne.

The main Ngoni body then divided into two. Mpezeni and his followers travelled westward towards Lake Bangweolu while Mombera and his section turned back along the route of their original march and entered the territory of the Kamanga kingdom. There, yet another break-away occurred. Mombera sent a large expedition southward down the west side of Lake Nyasa under the command of a Senga ex-captive, Ciwere Ndhlovu. The army reached the area of the modern Dowa district and finding good grazing land decided to remain there. They became an independent kingdom under a dynasty founded by the Senga war *induna*.

The original following of Zwangendaba had thus broken into five separate Ngoni groups but in the meantime another Nguni-speaking horde had migrated into Tanganyika from the south and founded what can be regarded as the sixth Ngoni kingdom. When Nxaba was defeated by Soshangane, the confederation of two tribes he had led disintegrated. While he and the Msene travelled westward into Southern Rhodesia the Maseko were led northward by Ngwane. They crossed the Zambesi further downstream than Zwangendaba and continued northward across the Rovuma River until they entered the Songea district of modern Tanganyika. On their way they incorporated captives from many different tribes and became a powerful group which terrorized a wide area around their new home.[1]

1 The Maseko Ngoni were once thought to be a branch of Zwangendaba's

The Tuta

After the death of Ntabeni, his following escaped northward under the leadership of two of his sons, Mtambulika and Mtambara.[1] Shaking off pursuit they established their first camp at the northern end of the Rukwa valley and from this base sent raiding parties as far as the shores of Lake Tanganyika. There, however, they encountered the Holoholo, who not only successfully resisted the Tuta attack but counter-attacked their camp. The assault was beaten off and the Holoholo chief was killed, but the Tuta decided to abandon the area in search of easier prey. They passed up the eastern side of Lake Tanganyika till they approached its head. There they found themselves amongst the Nyamwezi tribes and in the vicinity of the great Arab trade route which passed through Tabora to Ujiji, the port on the north-eastern shore of the lake. Ujiji was attacked at least twice. On one occasion the Arabs and the local population were driven to take refuge on Bangwe Island.[2] Another attack in 1858 was foiled when the Arab merchants returned from an expedition just in time to drive off the attackers with their guns.[3] Finally the Tuta settled on hilly country in the Runzewe district to the north-west of Tabora. From this centre their raiding parties reached as far as the southern shores of Lake Victoria.[4] As their conquests continued they captured many Nyamwezi and their activities encouraged others to seek stronger political organization in self-defence.

One of the Tuta captives was a young chief, Mirambo.[5] He was trained in Ngoni fighting methods and learnt their language, but he made his escape and began building up a following of his own. The raids of the Tuta and the activities of Arab slavers had broken many tribes, and Mirambo gathered the floating population together to form a motley force known as the Ruga-Ruga. Partly armed with guns from the proceeds of trade with the Arabs, the Ruga-Ruga became a powerful force. Mirambo remained on good terms with the Tuta and could rely on the support of their regiments on major campaigns. He extended his

---

people. Barnes suggested that they might be a breakaway from the Ndebele. M. Read has shown their separate origin and succeeded in tracing their route through the study of surviving clan names. M. Read: *The Ngoni of Nyasaland*, pp. 3–10. See also map, p. 207.

1 This account of the route taken by the Tuta is based on G. W. Hatchell: 'The Angoni of Tanganyika Territory', *Man*, 35, 1935, pp. 69–73.

2 Stanley: *Through the Dark Continent*, vol. I, p. 392.

3 R. F. Burton: *The Lake Regions of Central Africa*, vol. II, pp. 75–6.

4 Kollman: *The Victoria Nyanza*, p. 106, describes the effects of these raids on the population near the southern shores of the lake.

5 R. J. Harvey: 'Mirambo, the Napoleon of Central Africa', *Tanganyika Notes and Records*, no. 28, January 1950.

authority over a large, though ill-defined, territory which intersected the main trade route to Ujiji and he attempted to enrich himself by levying transit tolls on the Arab caravans. This involved him in a long struggle with the Arab traders in which he was generally successful. In 1870 Stanley, who was staying at Tabora, was persuaded to accompany an Arab party to fight the combined Ruga-Ruga and Tuta forces. He was lucky to escape unharmed, for his companions were defeated. Tabora was sacked and five of the leading Arabs killed.[1] The numbers of the Tuta were never very great and as they continued to recruit Nyamwezi captives into their ranks the Nguni culture was diluted almost to vanishing point. When the Germans occupied Tanganyika the Tuta were conquered by Captain Langheld. They suffered very severely and their numbers were greatly reduced. The survivors remained in the Runzewe area in north-west Tabora district. They were enumerated as a separate group in the Kahama district in the census of 1931, but the conflict with the Germans had reduced them to a very small group. They were not counted as a separate group in the census of 1948 and no longer appear in the tribal map of Tanganyika.

The Gwangara

When Zulu-Gama broke away from the main body he was pursued by a powerful expedition but succeeded in beating it off and making his escape.[2] He and his people travelled south-east, traversing much of present-day Tanganyika to Mlangala. About 1858 Zulu-Gama died and the leadership of the community passed to Mbonani, another clan head with a large following who had exercised considerable power even in Zulu-Gama's lifetime. The change in dynasty was never fully accepted by Zulu-Gama's lineage and the foundations were laid for a future split.

At Mlangala the Gwangara came in contact with the Maseko Ngoni who had been settled for some time in the Songea district. Ngwane, their original leader, had died and his place had been taken by his heir, Maputo Maseko. Under his authority the Maseko raided as far as Lake Nyasa to the west and the sea to the east.[3] They were far stronger than the Gwangara and Maputo was accepted as ruler of both groups. The arrangement was not a stable one and Maputo tried to strengthen his

1 Stanley: *How I found Livingstone*, pp. 275–99.
2 This account is largely based on Gulliver: 'A History of the Songea Ngoni', *Tanganyika Notes and Records*, VI, December 1955, pp. 16–30, and Fr. E. Ebner: *History of the Wangoni*.
3 They had even attacked the Arab town of Kilwa. Johnston: 'Native Routes in East Africa', *Proceedings of the Royal Geographical Society*, vol. I, 1879, pp. 417–22.

position by destroying the Gwangara leaders. A number of their *indunas* were put to death and Mbonani himself was killed. The Gwangara, however, prepared to take their revenge. They found an opportunity during an expedition against a tribe living on the lower Ruhaha River. Maputo had accompanied his forces, but the regiment with which he marched suffered a defeat and he was forced to take refuge with a Gwangara regiment. Instead of saving him they put him to death and succeeded in convincing the Maseko that he had been killed by the enemy. Suspicions were lulled while preparations were made for revolt and then the Gwangara attacked the Maseko unawares. Caught off their guard the Maseko fled and the Gwangara pursued them till they crossed the Rovuma River.

In the confusion of the Maseko defeat many newly recruited members of that community were left behind. Most of them belonged to the Ndendeuli tribe but had acquired a knowledge of Ngoni tactics and political organization. With their masters gone, they began building up an Ngoni state of their own and were steadily increasing their strength when they were attacked by the Gwangara about 1862.[1] The incipient kingdom was smashed and most of its members fled to settle on the far side of the Kilombero valley where they are known today as Mbunga. Three chieftaincies were eventually created which still show traces of Ngoni influence. Other refugees from this defeat fled eastward into present Tunduri, Masasi and Newala districts, and some penetrated into what is now Portuguese territory.

Having destroyed this upstart kingdom the Gwangara had secured their position in the Songea district. The old quarrel between Mbonani's and Zulu-Gama's people then came to a head and the two sections separated to found independent kingdoms. Mbonani's people were led by his senior son Chipeta. Their kingdom was known as Mshope, after Mbonani's father. Chipeta established his capital first at Seluka just south of the confluence of the Hanga and Putukiva Rivers. Later he shifted his headquarters to Mtakano, to the north of the Hanga. The regiments of this group raided northward and north-east of their headquarters to the vicinity of Bagamoyo. In 1882 they made a lightning raid on Masasi. The mission station there was completely destroyed and the district reduced to a tributary status.[2]

Zulu-Gama's section took the name Njelu and their headquarters were established further south at Nyalanga and later at Mbinga (Matamondo). They were ruled at first by Hawagi and later by Mhalule, their most famous war chief (died 1889). Under his leadership they terrorized

1 Gulliver, op. cit.
2 G. H. Wilson: *History of the Universities' Mission to Central Africa*, pp. 56–9.

a wide area to the south, south-east and south-west of their kingdom from Lake Nyasa to the Indian Ocean. The two kingdoms remained in contact and were prepared to co-operate in face of common danger, but their leaders were always jealous and suspicious of one another.[1]

The Ngoni invasion of south-eastern Tanganyika threw the peoples of the area into confusion. Most were easily overcome but the Hehe offered stiff resistance. Before the coming of the Ngoni the Hehe had been a group of loosely organized clans living in hilly country. They had no centralized political system and no particular martial reputation, but under the impact of Ngoni raids they rapidly adopted the age-regiment system and struck back at their attackers. In 1878 they attacked the Mshope kingdom, stormed the capital and killed the chief. The Mshope had asked for aid from their brother kingdom but the Njelu forces were also defeated. The Hehe then withdrew without making a further assault on the Njelu kingdom. In 1881 the Hehe attacked again but the Gwangara had sufficient time to prepare resistance. The two kingdoms united their forces and met the enemy in a pitched battle. The two sides were so equally matched that the struggle ended in a stalemate. Neither side wished to continue fighting and an agreement was made to preserve peace until the next generation should have grown old enough to resume the war.[2]

The coming of the Germans marked the end of the great period of Gwangara history. Impressed by the overwhelming power of the whites, they submitted without resistance, but bitterly disillusioned by the realities of German rule they played an active part in the Maji-Maji uprising of 1905–6. In return they were visited by severe reprisals. The Germans arrested their chiefs and made a systematic attempt to break up their society. The 1914–18 war, however, put an end to the German period and under British trusteeship the principle of indirect rule was adopted. The successors of Zulu-Gama and Mbonani were recognized as paramount chiefs and the sense of Ngoni identity survived.

The Maseko Ngoni

After their defeat by the Gwangara the Maseko crossed the Rovuma River and continued southward till they reached the southern end of Lake Nyasa. They then turned westward, crossed the Shire River and settled in the highland country of the Kirk Range in the late 1860s. Under their new leader, Cikuse, they continued to send out raiding

1 *Journals and Papers of Chauncy Maples*, pp. 133–53.
2 Gulliver, op. cit.

expeditions and rapidly recovered from the losses they had suffered on their flight. At first their expeditions were confined to the west of the Shire but in 1875 one of their armies crossed the river and attacked the Yao living to the east.[1] Active slave raiders though they were, the Yao were no match for the Ngoni. Their wretched trade muskets proved little protection against a mass charge of well-drilled regiments and they began to take refuge on the mountain-tops. About a year later another Ngoni army crossed the Shire and most of the accessible Yao villages were destroyed. By this time, however, the Kololo who had been left behind during Livingstone's Zambesi expedition, had succeeded in establishing their hegemony over the mixed population of the Shire valley. They attempted to prevent the Ngoni crossing the river and established a series of fortified villages at the fords. In 1884, however, a strong Ngoni army arrived on the river-bank when the water was exceptionally low. They shouted to the chief of the village guarding the ford that they would leave him unmolested if they were allowed free passage but otherwise would certainly put him to death.[2] The Kololo sub-chief let them pass and they devastated the population of the Shire Highlands until the mission station at Blantyre was like an island in a sea of flames.[3] The missionaries bravely went out to interview the leaders of the expedition and the Ngoni agreed to retire.

The coming of Sir Harry Johnston brought the fighting days of the Maseko Ngoni to an end. The missionaries pleaded to be allowed to try and win them over to peaceful ways by moral suasion but Johnston determined on a show of force. Their regiments were defeated by a British military expedition in 1896 and Cikuse's successor, Gomani, was shot when he refused to submit to the indignity of walking alongside the horses of his captors. The chieftaincy was not extinguished, however, and although the Maseko today speak Chi-Nyanja and remember only a few Nguni words they are very conscious of their history and heritage. The greater mobility provided by modern means of transport enables them to keep in contact with other Ngoni groups and in this way the memory of old customs and institutions is preserved.[4]

Mpezeni's Ngoni

When the main division took place between the two heirs of Zwangendaba, Mpezeni and his followers travelled south-west into the Bemba country. Many bitter fights took place around the stockaded villages,

1 Rangeley: 'The Makololo of Dr. Livingstone', *Nyasaland Journal*, vol. 12, no. 1, January 1959, pp. 59–98.
2 Ibid.
3 W. P. Livingstone: *A Prince of Missionaries.*
4 See M. Read: *The Ngoni of Nyasaland.*

but the Bemba offered such fierce resistance that Mpezeni's people abandoned the struggle and turned south-east to re-enter the country where Zwangendaba had first halted on his long march north of the Zambesi. The Senga peoples were devastated a second time and so many captives were taken that, together with those absorbed on the first occasion, they constituted the majority of Mpezeni's following.[1] Their settlement was established in the neighbourhood of present Fort Jameson. Mpezeni's people did not forget the claims of their king to be the rightful ruler of the entire Ngoni people but distance and the presence of the upstart Cewa leader, Mwase Kasungu, between the two kingdoms prevented any major clash with Mombera's people.

In the last years of the nineteenth century Mpezeni's people were caught up in the process of European competition in Africa. The German adventurer, Carl Wiese, was asked by the Portuguese to visit Mpezeni and acquire concessions which would establish Portuguese claims. He visited the kingdom in 1889 and was well received. Other concessionaires soon followed in his wake and a complicated diplomatic battle took place between the Portuguese and the British South Africa Company. In this situation the continued independence of Mpezeni's kingdom was seen as an obstacle to the establishment of effective occupation. His people were prodded into war and the regiments were mowed down with Maxim guns.[2] Mpezeni's power was decisively broken and much of the tribal land was taken for white settlers.

Some newly incorporated peoples abandoned their Ngoni status and rejoined their original tribes. Shortage of agricultural land forced Mpezeni's Ngoni to go out to work with white employers on a large scale and the instability produced by the migrant labour system added its effects to the consequences of military defeat. In spite of this the sense of Ngoni identity survives and paradoxically the migrant labour system has helped old traditions to be maintained. At the mines of Zambia, Rhodesia and South Africa, Ngoni meet their fellows from other kingdoms and also other Nguni-speaking peoples like the Ndebele. The prestige of the past urges them to re-learn at least a few phrases of the forgotten language and they return home with their sense of history strengthened.

1 By 1889 Senga had become the language in general daily use. The Nguni tongue was still, however, employed in court ceremonial. See Wiese, 'Expedicão'.

2 Baxter: 'The Angoni Rebellion and Mpeseni', *Northern Rhodesia Journal*, no. II, December 1950, pp. 14–24, gives an account of the campaign. Mpezeni was imprisoned for a time but later reinstated and died as chief of his people in 1900.

The Ngoni of Mombera

After the break with Mpezeni's people, Mombera, with what remained of the main Ngoni nucleus, doubled back along the line of Zwangendaba's march and re-entered the Tumbuka country. This time a direct attack was made on the Kamanga kingdom and about 1855 the seventh Chikurayamembe was defeated and killed. The Ngoni settled on the healthy uplands and from there their expeditions reached the lake to the east, while to the west they penetrated as far as the fringes of the kingdom of Cazembe and the Bemba country. Numerous captives, particularly Tonga, Henga and Tumbuka, were assimilated. Campaigns were not uniformly victorious. The Bemba often succeeded in repelling attacks on their villages and in the Cewa country a powerful leader arose in the person of Mwase Kasungu. He made use of guns acquired from Arab traders to build up a powerful following. The Ngoni made an attack on his stockade but were beaten back by gunfire. Mwase Kasungu realized that a subsequent attack might be more successful and offered his allegiance to the Ngoni king. He proved a valuable ally and supported them with his firearms at a critical moment in their history. He was also useful as a buffer state between Mombera and Mpezeni's people.[1]

Because Mombera's kingdom was the largest of the Ngoni states it contained several powerful territorial sections which were strong enough to insist on a measure of autonomy. The supreme position of the king was still recognized and national campaigns were organized from time to time, but the major territorial chiefs often used the local sections of the national army on expeditions of their own.[2] On such occasions captives taken were naturally retained within the district which had organized the raid and, as a result, captives from neighbouring tribes were not evenly distributed throughout the kingdom but concentrated in the districts closest to their tribal territory. Mombera's people were not completely ruthless in their treatment of conquered peoples and they allowed villages of subjugated tribes to survive, living their own lives as tribute-paying vassals.

About 1875 tensions within the composite community came to a head. The Ngoni territory was crowded and rumours spread that the chiefs were planning to massacre all the old people belonging to conquered tribes and to keep only the warriors.[3] A movement of secession

1 Barnes: *Politics in a Changing Society*, map, p. 67.

2 This is clear from the accounts of the missionaries. See for example Elmslie: *Among the Wild Angoni*.

3 T. C. Young: *Notes on the History of the Tumbuka and Kamanga Peoples*, p. 118.

was begun by the Tonga, who fled *en masse* to the lake shore. They sent back a defiant message saying, 'If you want to follow us with war, do it; we no longer intend to be your people.'[1] The Ngoni regiments were summoned to deal with the revolt but the Tonga had learnt Ngoni fighting methods and found good defensive terrain in the marshy land around the lake. Stockades were hastily erected and a maze of pitfalls was dug to trap the enemy and break up their charge. A mass Ngoni attack met with a heavy defeat and Mombera's people were forced to abandon the attempt to crush the revolt by a direct onslaught. Thereafter they confined themselves to frequent small raids, hoping to wear down the Tonga resistance by keeping them pinned against the lake shore. This policy was nearly successful, for the Tonga began quarrelling among themselves. Some drifted back to the Ngoni of their own accord and when in 1878 they were first encountered by the Livingstonia missionaries they were in a pitiable condition.

The revolt of the Tonga was the signal for other secessionist movements. Shortly after their revolt, the Kamanga and Henga also broke away. They combined their forces and organized them along Ngoni lines. In a mood of premature enthusiasm the Kamanga restored their vanquished dynasty and chose a new Chikurayamembe. Their success was short-lived. In 1879 the Ngoni launched a full-scale attack on the rebels and administered a severe defeat. The renascent Kamanga kingdom was broken up, the new Chikurayamembe killed and the majority of the Kamanga brought back within the Ngoni ranks. The victory was not complete, however, for some of the Kamanga and the Henga managed to defend themselves on strong hilltop positions and repel the Ngoni attack. A nucleus of rebellion persisted and Mombera's kingdom remained in danger. At this point the alliance with Mwase Kasungu proved decisive. The Cewa gunmen came to the aid of the Ngoni regiments and in a second campaign (1879–80) the remaining rebels were dispersed.[2] Scattered groups of refugees fled to the northern end of Lake Nyasa huddling on islets which were little more than heaps of stones. 'Driven off the face of the earth, as might literally be affirmed, they had to rear their families, crabling them in the cracks of the rocks or crannies between the boulders to prevent them rolling off into the water.'[3]

In the midst of the struggle to crush this second rebellion a third broke out. The Tumbuka took advantage of Ngoni preoccupation with the Henga and Kamanga to make their own bid for freedom. In 1880

1 Ibid., p. 119.
2 This account is based on T. C. Young, op. cit.
3 Elmslie, op. cit., pp. 83–91.

they fled up the Hora Mountain and prepared to defend themselves. A first assault was repulsed but the Ngoni then began a systematic siege and the mountain position proved a deathtrap. Its defenders were weakened by starvation and then the Ngoni attacked again. The leader of the revolt with a few faithful followers made his escape but all the other Tumbuka were captured and put to death.[1]

While Mombera's kingdom was in the throes of this internal upheaval it began to be affected by new influences. The Livingstonia mission, founded to commemorate the work of the great missionary explorer, commenced its work in Africa at Cape Maclear on the southern tip of Lake Nyasa. The prevalence of malaria, however, led to the search for a new location and in 1878 an exploring expedition was undertaken around the shores of the lake. The Tonga were visited and it was decided to establish the new headquarters of the mission amongst them. For this purpose it was essential to secure peaceful relations with Mombera's Ngoni and the Livingstonia Mission was logically led to extend its work onto the Ngoni highlands.

The commencement of mission work with the Ngoni was helped by the internal difficulties of the kingdom which had shaken confidence in the old ways, and still more by the fact that the Livingstonia Mission was accompanied by a dedicated Xhosa missionary, William Koyi. He was left behind at the headquarters of one of the major Ngoni section heads, Chipatula, to prepare the way for the opening of mission work. The fact that he spoke an Nguni language gave him respect and he was able to win the confidence of the people. Though he died of malaria within two years, he had laid the basis for future success. The mission had many difficult moments, but it survived and gradually expanded its operations throughout the kingdom. As it spread, Ngoni raids became less and less frequent, competition for education came to take the place of service in the regiments, and in 1896 there were already twenty-one schools taught by local teachers in Mombera's kingdom.[2] As European authority was steadily spread over the surrounding areas Mombera's Ngoni realized the futility of struggling against a much greater power. Faced with the difficulties caused by European infiltration into their territory they decided to place themselves under British rule and this was brought about by peaceful agreement in September 1904.[3]

Because they had never been involved in armed conflict with the British authorities Mombera's Ngoni were allowed to retain their tribal lands. Some of the conquered peoples severed their allegiance with

1 T. C. Young, op. cit. Elmslie saw the bones of the victims still lying around the foot of the mountain. Op. cit., p. 93.

2 D. Fraser: *Winning a Primitive People*, p. 40. 3 Ibid., pp. 239–44.

Mombera's community. The Kamanga eventually succeeded in restoring the Chikurayamembe dynasty. But the coherence of Mombera's Ngoni state survived. Though, like other Ngoni communities, they have abandoned their original language, Mombera's people have been able to keep old traditions alive to a greater extent than any other Ngoni people.

Ciwere's Ngoni

When the Senga war leader, Ciwere Ndhlovu, decided not to lead his victorious army back to Mombera's capital but settle on the highlands of the present Dowa district in territory of the Cewa people, he founded another Ngoni kingdom. Though he was not of royal blood or even a member of the 'Zansi' aristocracy he was accepted as king and founded a dynasty which still survives. The army which he commanded contained some 'Zansi' but was mainly made up of fairly recent captives and in its new home captive Cewa soon came to constitute the majority. The traditional Nguni culture was therefore less strongly entrenched than amongst other groups and Ciwere's Ngoni were strongly influenced by Cewa culture. Nevertheless, the main features of the Ngoni political system survived and to this day those who regard themselves as Ngoni keep the patrilineal descent pattern and the bride-price customs which distinguish them from their neighbours.[1] Mission work among Ciwere's people was begun by the Dutch Reformed Church Mission Society in 1889.[2] Ciwere's Ngoni were not powerful enough to offer resistance to the establishment of European rule and they were allowed to remain in peaceful possession of their lands. Though a small community they are still proud of the traditions of their conquering days.

Consequences of the Ngoni Invasions

The Ngoni invasions were a terrible disaster for the peoples of East-Central Africa. They combined with the effects of the expanding Arab Slave Trade to bring a long era of peaceful peasant existence to a violent end. Almost every people in the whole vast area between Lake Bangweolu and the Indian Ocean was affected.[3] Villages were destroyed

1 Hodgson: 'Notes on the Achewa and Angoni of the Dowa district of the Nyasaland Protectorate', *Journal Royal Anthropological Institute*, vol. LXIII, 1933, pp. 123–64.
2 See A. C. Murray: *Nyasaland en Mijne Ondervindingen Aldaar*.
3 Livingstone's accounts of his Zambesi expedition and the Journals of his last journey contain numerous references to Ngoni depredations and give a clear impression of the chaos they produced throughout East-Central Africa.

and burned. Thousands were massacred and others dragged away to join the Ngoni ranks. The terror of Ngoni raids prevented normal cultivation and famine was widespread. Great displacement of population was another result. Crowds of refugees huddled round both shores of Lake Nyasa, while elsewhere fertile country was virtually untilled. Thick forest and mountains provided natural places of refuge and at the north-western end of Lake Nyasa terror-stricken peoples lived in holes scooped out of steep mountain-sides where the only protection from the elements was a few sticks pushed into the earth above and covered with grass.[1]

The relationship between the Ngoni invasions and the growth of the Slave Trade is difficult to analyse. The two developments overlapped in time but were largely independent of one another. The nature of the Ngoni socio-political system encouraged the retention of captives as subjects and mitigated against the Ngoni becoming slave traders. They did sometimes engage in the Trade but not on a large scale.[2] Their raiding parties are known to have attacked Arab caravans,[3] and by making routes unsafe they may have acted as a check on the expanding business. On the other hand, the disruption of normal life, the famine and desolation which they left in their wake, created ideal conditions for the growth of slave-trading. Where life was so unsafe, famine so prevalent and the need for firearms a matter of life and death, it was easier for the Arabs and their agents to find customers than it would have been in more normal times.

Though the destructive effects of the Ngoni invasions are so obvious, they were a part of the process of constructive political change which had begun in Zululand. More than any other group in this period they perfected a system for uniting peoples of different cultures in enduring units. The Zulu only brought together peoples who shared a basically similar culture and language, but the Ngoni united patrilineal and matrilineal peoples speaking a host of different languages and gave them a permanent sense of common identity. Starting as two small bands of plunderers they created six substantial kingdoms which, in spite of geographical separation and their different languages, still take pride in their common origin.

In building up these powerful states the Ngoni stimulated others to

1 Elmslie, op. cit., pp. 83–91.

2 Livingstone was exaggerating when he remarked that the Ngoni never sell their captives. D. and C. Livingstone: *Narrative of an Expedition to the Zambesi and its Tributaries*, p. 386. Kerr, who spent some time with the Maseko Ngoni, remarked that Chikuse's court was one of the greatest slave markets in Africa. M. Kerr: *The Far Interior*, vol. I, p. 125.

3 Wiese, op. cit.

follow them. The rise of such strong leaders as Mirambo and Mwase Kasungu owes much to the Ngoni as well as to Arab influence. The adoption of new military methods by the Holoholo, Hehe and other peoples was a direct result of contact with Ngoni regiments. The rotting corpses and smoking villages were not just the results of an epidemic of senseless butchery. To some extent they were the inevitable sufferings of a period of rapid political change.

6 The Invasion of the Highveld by Mpangazita and Matiwane

Two of the largest Nguni tribes living in the area of modern Natal at the beginning of the nineteenth century were the Ngwane[1] who herded their cattle in the vicinity of the present town of Wakkerstroom and their close neighbours, the Hlubi, who were then led by Mtimkulu. As the two rival empires of Dingiswayo and Zwide enlarged their spheres of action these two tribes inevitably became involved. The Ngwane were attacked by Dingiswayo and shortly afterwards by Zwide also. Hoping to save their herds from total destruction they entrusted the greater part of them to the safe-keeping of their neighbours, but when the Hlubi saw the owners defeated in battle they refused to return the cattle. This was the origin of a bitter feud between the two tribes and about 1821 the Ngwane launched a surprise attack and killed Mtimkulu. The Hlubi lost not only the cattle they had stolen but most of their own herds as well, and under the impact of the disaster most of the tribe abandoned their homeland and followed the energetic Mpangazita who led them across the Drakensberg on the first stage of a long course of wandering among the Sotho peoples of Transorangia. (A smaller section remained near its ancestral home. It was incorporated in the Zulu state for a time, but in the reign of Mpanda its leader fled to Natal and was settled by the British Government near the borders of Basutoland. Langalibalele, the chief of this section, was treated as a rebel in an incident which alarmed the whole of white South Africa in 1892.) The Ngwane did not long enjoy the fruits of their victory for about a year later they were attacked by Shaka's regiments and under the leadership of Matiwane they also fled across the Drakensberg following the path taken by their enemies the Hlubi.

The sudden intrusion of Mpangazita into the country inhabited by the Sotho peoples began the process whereby the military and political

1 Bryant: *Olden Times*, p. 136, gives their name as Ngwaneni. They should be distinguished from the Ngwane of Sobhuza who came to form the Swazi nation.

ferment among the Nguni tribes of the coastal strip was spread to the interior plateau. Tribe after tribe was driven from its lands and forced to a life of pillage. Numerous marauding groups moved hither and thither, their trails crossing one another in a pattern of great complexity.[1] The first tribe encountered by the Hlubi were the Tlokwa. The chief of this tribe had recently died leaving an heir, Sikonyela, who was still a minor. His mother, Mma Ntatisi, a woman of outstanding strength of personality, was acting as regent. Caught unawares by the Hlubi invasion, the Tlokwa were driven from their homes and began their own career of wandering and conquest. They fled westward to the vicinity of Kurutlele Mountain near the Sand River where they attacked one section of the Fokeng and put them to flight. Before they could enjoy the fruits of their victory the Tlokwa were attacked again by the Hlubi who had followed in their footsteps and after a struggle which failed to give a decisive victory the two hordes moved away from Kurutlele in separate directions. Mpangazita led the Hlubi to Mabolela where he set up his headquarters and the Tlokwa travelled south-east to establish a base close to the mountain of Butha-Buthe in the north-west corner of modern Basutoland.

The mountain was occupied by Moshesh (the future Basuto chief), who was then the leader of a fairly small following. The Tlokwa attacked but failed to storm the mountain stronghold and in a daring counter-attack Moshesh's men forced their way into the heart of the Tlokwa camp. Mma Ntatisi's followers were almost routed when a woman named Maseile caught hold of one of the warriors who was running away and berated the Tlokwa for allowing themselves to be put to flight by an inferior force. This turned the tide and the Tlokwa drove Moshesh's men back up the mountain and seized most of his cattle, though they did not dislodge him from his hill-top position. Many of the Tlokwa cooking-pots were broken during the struggle in their camp and the battle is known in Sotho tradition as the 'Battle of the Pots'.[2]

After this encounter the Tlokwa moved westward to the Caledon River at Peka and from there they undertook a series of raids. Sikonyela was now old enough to lead the army and was tempted to make a surprise attack on the Hlubi at Mabolela. The attempt failed and Mpangazita sent out a retaliatory expedition. It came upon the Tlokwa unexpectedly at Tlapeneng when their camp was virtually undefended.

1 In attempting to trace the routes taken by the various groups in this area I have been guided to a great extent by Ellenberger and Macgregor's *History of the Basuto*. As the evidence is largely that of oral tradition which cannot be expected to be precise, particularly in such a chaotic situation, complete accuracy is probably unattainable.

2 Ellenberger and Macgregor, op. cit., p. 126.

Sikonyela had led nearly all the fighting men on a raid in the vicinity. Only the quick wit of Mma Ntatisi saved the day. Forming all the available men into a single rank she made the women line up behind them waving the handles of hoes instead of spears and holding up sleeping-mats to look like shields. Faced with what looked like a compact body of warriors drawn up in a combat formation the Hlubi hesitated and as they did so Sikonyela, returning with the fighting men, came upon them and inflicted a severe defeat.[1]

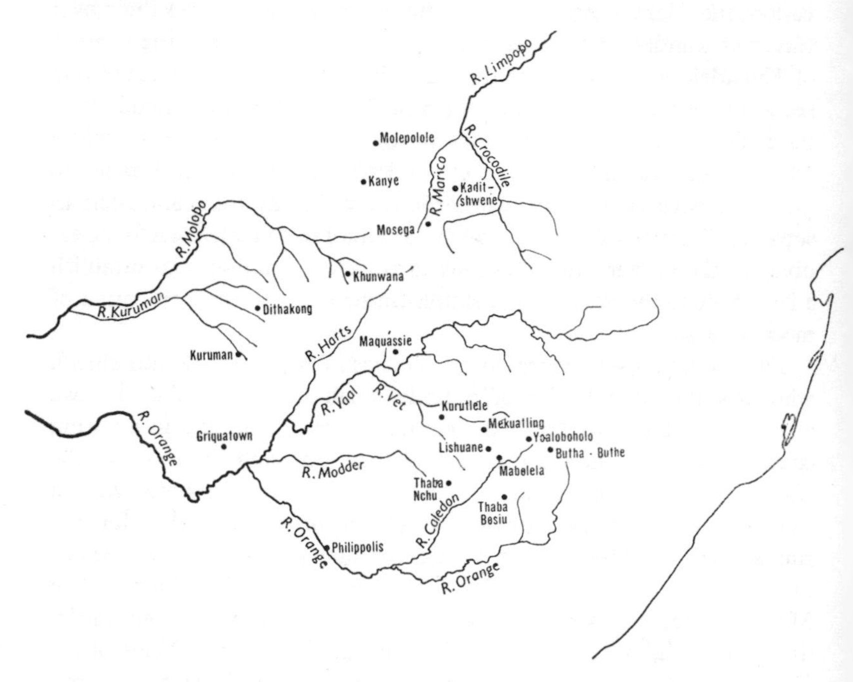

Area affected by the invasions of Mpangazita and Matiwane

The Tlokwa then travelled northward, back to the area of Kurutlele where they defeated the Taung, and then turned south, crossed the Caledon River and traversed the plain which lies in the angle between it and the Orange. They intended to cross the Orange but found it in flood and moved back to the north again.[2]

1 Ellenberger and Macgregor, op. cit., p. 127.

2 Ellenberger and Macgregor, op. cit., pp. 134–42, maintained that the Tlokwa travelled north to the Vaal, crossed it and went on to attack Dithakong (Lattakoo). This was based on a misunderstanding of Moffat's account of the battle of Dithakong (see below). The route of the Tlokwa between their return from the banks of the Orange and their arrival at Butha-Buthe is unknown.

About 1824–25 they returned to the neighbourhood of Butha-Buthe and began a determined attack on Moshesh's stronghold. The future ruler of the Basuto attempted to persuade them to limit the struggle to a contest for the cattle, but Sikonyela was not to be deterred and settled down for a prolonged siege. Shut up on their mountain-top Moshesh's followers ran short of food and after two months were reduced to the verge of starvation.[1] Unable to defeat his more numerous enemies on his own, Moshesh made an alliance with an Nguni-speaking tribe who came down on the Tlokwa unexpectedly and so weakened their forces that they called off the siege.[2]

Abandoning the scene of Butha-Buthe, the Tlokwa moved on in search of a permanent home. Their experience in the struggle with Moshesh had taught them the value of defensible mountain strongholds and they seized possession of the mountains of Kooaneng and Yoalo-boholo. The former was a naturally strong position and they further fortified it by building walls to protect the narrow entrances to the summit.[3] Thereafter the Tlokwa continued to play an important part in the history of Basutoland until their final defeat by Moshesh in 1852. In 1837 their numbers were estimated as twenty to thirty thousand.[4] By this time Sikonyela was the effective ruler of the tribe though his mother continued to enjoy great respect.[5]

The Ngwane of Matiwane had crossed the Drakensberg in the wake of the Hlubi. Their army, organized in age-regiments distinguished by the colours of their shields, was the most powerful military force in Transorangia.[6] Passing through the land of the Tlokwa they pursued a path to the westward on the track of the Hlubi. The Sotho tribes,

1 Arbousset and Daumas: *Narrative of an Exploratory Tour to the North East of the Colony of the Cape of Good Hope*, p. 290.
2 Arbousset and Daumas, op. cit., pp. 291–2, describe this group as the Matabele of Sepeka. Msebenzi in his account of the history of the Ngwane (Van Warmelo, ed.: *History of Matiwane and the Amangwane Tribe*, p. 24), remarks that when the Ngwane visited Basutoland they found two chiefs quarrelling over a mountain and intervened on the side of Moshesh. If it were the Ngwane who took part in this incident it would explain how Moshesh came to be a tributary of Matiwane.
3 The fortifications of Sikonyela's mountain are described in a letter of the Missionary Archbell to the Secretaries of the Wesleyan Missionary Society from Thaba Nchu, 11 May 1834, M.M.S. Albany 1834.
4 Estimates by Wesleyan Missionary Edwards. Edwards to Rev. John Beecham, Umpukani. 4 Oct. 1837, M.M.S. S.A. 1837.
5 When the Missionary Archbell visited the Tlokwa he was introduced first to the aged Queen Mother before meeting her son who was the effective chief. Archbell to Secretaries, Wesleyan Missionary Society, M.M.S. Albany 1834.
6 That the Ngwane were organized on a regimental pattern somewhat similar to that of the Zulu is clear from Ellenberger and Macgregor's accounts of their final battle with the Hlubi (op. cit., pp. 154–5), also from Msebenzi's *History*.

already weakened by the impact of the Hlubi and Tlokwa, were in no position to offer effective resistance. Some groups fled across the Vaal before the new invaders and Moshesh offered his allegiance to Matiwane. The Ngwane leader established his camp at Senyiotong and from this base resumed his old quarrel with the Hlubi at Mabolela. For two years the Nguni tribes struggled for mastery of the territory they had invaded, while at the same time devastating the remnants of Sotho tribes over the whole area between the Caledon and the Vaal. Matiwane shifted his camp to Mekuatling in the northern corner of Basutoland and from this position attacked the Hlubi again but still without any decisive result. In 1825 Mpangazita risked his whole force in a mass assault on Matiwane's camp. His army descended on the enemy settlement one afternoon when the bulk of the Ngwane regiments were away on a foraging expedition. Only one regiment which formed the bodyguard of the chief had stayed behind. With their greatly superior numbers the Hlubi drove the Ngwane from their camp, but the bodyguard held firm around their leader until the other Ngwane regiments arrived and the tables were turned. The Hlubi were driven back and made a stand around a great rock in the valley between Mekuatling and Lishuane. As the fight continued the Ngwane discovered the whereabouts of the enemy leader. A concerted attack was made in his direction. Mpangazita was killed and the defeat of the Hlubi was turned into a rout.[1]

This decisive battle brought the career of the Hlubi as a powerful marauding group to an end. A section of the tribe escaped under Mehlomakhulu. Crossing the Vaal they were encountered by one of Mzilikazi's regiments and taken to the chief. They joined the Ndebele for a time but Mehlomakhulu sensed that the Ndebele king was jealous of him and feared for his safety. He escaped with his followers and fled back into Transorangia pursued by Ndebele regiments. The majority of the Hlubi had remained in Transorangia and been incorporated in the ranks of the Ngwane. When they saw their kinsmen's plight they drew the Ndebele attack upon themselves and Mehlomakhulu escaped over the Drakensberg. He entered the area known as Nomansland where he allied with the Bhele in an attack on the Bhaca leader, Ncapayi. It ended in a disastrous defeat and Mehlomakhulu fled back into Basutoland. He was given shelter by Moshesh and remained there until 1854 when he and a few followers were established by the British Government in the Herschel district of the Cape.[2]

1 Ellenberger and Macgregor, op. cit., pp. 154–5. This account was taken from Moloya, a member of the Ngwane who had been present at the battle.
2 Bryant: *Olden Times*, p. 154, and Theal: *Baustoland Records*, vol. 2, pp. 86–7. See also Ayliff and Whiteside: *History of the Abambo*, pp. 12–13.

With the defeat of the Hlubi, Matiwane became the paramount power in Transorangia. His forces, strengthened by numerous adherents from the conquered foe, were more than a match for any army the Sotho-speaking peoples could put into the field. But his position was an unstable one. His large host could only be supported by continuous plunder and Transorangia had been so devastated in the long chain of disturbances that it no longer provided a valuable raiding ground. Only Moshesh still possessed substantial herds of cattle and a conflict between the two chiefs was inevitable.

At first Moshesh attempted to rid himself of the importunities of his overlord by bringing a greater power against him. Though he paid tribute to Matiwane, the Basuto ruler had also offered his allegiance to Shaka and sent him an annual tribute of cranes' feathers and other regalia used by the Zulu warriors. One year he failed to deliver the tribute and declared that the depredations of the Ngwane made it impossible for him to fulfil his obligation as a vassal to the Zulu king. A Zulu expedition then crossed the Drakensberg and the Ngwane were attacked.[1] The fight ended indecisively and the Zulu withdrew, but Matiwane began to feel that his position was becoming impossible and to seek for a new venue for his activities. An expedition was sent across the Orange River to reconnoitre the situation in the Thembu country. It lost most of the cattle it captured in a Thembu counter-attack and contracted smallpox which led to its members being placed in quarantine on return, but it brought information about large herds and rich grazing lands in the Thembu country.[2]

When the Ndebele were pursuing Mehlomakhulu across Transorangia some of Matiwane's followers had come into conflict with them, and he was involved in a quarrel with Mzilikazi. His determination to remove to safer country was increased, but before they left his followers could not be restrained from making an attack on Moshesh's position at Thaba Bosiu. The attack was made in July 1827 but though the Ngwane were more than a match for the Basuto in the open field they did not succeed in storming the mountain. Decimated by large boulders and showers of spears hurled down from above, their ranks began to waver and they were routed by a Basuto charge.[3] Matiwane was furious with his subordinates who had risked battle on such unfavourable terms and

1 Bryant: *Olden Times*, p. 142, states that there is no Zulu tradition of this expedition and suggests that it may have been the Ndebele who were involved. Not only, however, do Ellenberger and Macgregor state that it was the Zulu but Msebenzi repeats this view and discusses at some length the intrigues of Moshesh with Shaka.

2 Ellenberger and Macgregor, op. cit., pp. 178–9.

3 See the account by Arbousset and Daumas, op. cit., pp. 294–8.

exposed the insecurity of his position. Only the strength of public opinion prevented him from putting the leaders of the expedition to death. The Ngwane position in Transorangia had become untenable and a second encounter with the Ndebele caused them to abandon the area and follow the route mapped out by their scouting expedition. In January or February 1828 they crossed the Orange and entered the Thembu country.

The move was undertaken at a most inauspicious time, for Shaka's regiments were advancing through Pondoland and the colonial authorities, alarmed at the prospect of hosts of refugees being driven into the Colony, were preparing to go to the assistance of the border tribes. The advance party of the colonial forces encountered Matiwane and engaged his forces in a skirmish. A month later the larger colonial force, together with numerous Xhosa and Thembu auxiliaries, met Matiwane and his people at Mbholompo. Still mistaking the Ngwane for the Zulu the British attacked them and routed them completely.[1]

The battle at Mbholompo put an end to the career of the Ngwane as a powerful invading group. Most of the survivors, both Hlubi and Ngwane, settled down among the Thembu and Xhosa in a subordinate capacity where they came to be part of the composite group known as the Fingo (Mfengu). Matiwane himself with a small group of followers escaped from the field and fled to his one-time vassal Moshesh. He was well received but he was homesick for the land of his birth and against the advice of his host he decided to go and seek pardon from the Zulu king and permission to settle with the remnants of his followers in their ancient home. Shaka was dead by this time and Dingane received the Ngwane well. He allowed them to settle in his kingdom but he felt that the presence of such a famous warrior as Matiwane within his kingdom was a danger to his authority. The Ngwane leader was summoned to court and put to death on Matiwane's Kop.

His people continued to live in Zulu territory under Matiwane's son, Zikhali, but the young prince felt that his life was also in danger from the jealousy of his overlord and he fled with his people to seek the protection of the Swazi. This was the first stage of a second prolonged and complex odyssey[2] which only ended when the remnant of the Ngwane tribe finally settled in Northern Natal under British rule not far from Langalibalele and his section of their old enemies, the Hlubi. From this

1 The documentary evidence on this affair is published by Van Warmelo as Chapter 26 to Msebenzi's *History*. The commanders were much criticized for their conduct in the matter but letters from Wesleyan missionaries with the coast tribes make it clear that the confusion of Ngwane with Zulu was general at the time.

2 A detailed account of this period is given by Msebenzi.

centre, messengers went out to tell the scattered members of the erstwhile tribe that a chief of the royal house survived and a new home had been found. Many came to rejoin the community from as far afield as Grahamstown and the Ngwane became once more a substantial people though many more remained as part of the Fingo group.[1]

Immigration from Transorangia to the Cape Colony

Under the impact of the devastation caused in Transorangia by the spread of the Mfecane, hundreds of Sotho refugees flocked into the Cape Colony hoping to find protection and support among the white colonists. They came at a favourable time, for the 1820 experiment in settling British settlers on small farms in the Zuurveld area where they were to till the land without the aid of Bantu labour, had failed disastrously. Those of the settlers who remained on the land were demanding large farms of the traditional Boer type and labour to work them. This created a difficult problem for relations with the Xhosa tribe across the border were strained and the government was anxious to restrict contact to a minimum. Sotho tribesmen, having no traditional links with the Xhosa and speaking a different language, constituted no menace to security.[2] The settlers were allowed to employ them and the economy of the Eastern Cape revived. The Sotho recovered from their harrowing experiences and in return for their services acquired cattle and other commodities. Eventually most of them returned across the Orange and settled in Moshesh's kingdom, their place in the Colony being taken by Fingos and some Xhosa.

The Disturbance spreads to the Southern Tswana Tribes

Before 1823 the area inhabited by the southern Tswana tribes (now divided between the British Bechuanaland District of the Cape Province and the Bechuanaland Protectorate) had enjoyed relative peace and prosperity. The cattle-raiding of the Korana and the banditry of the lawless Griqua Bergenaars had brought much suffering to some tribes but it had not fundamentally affected tribal distribution and way of life. The Tswana devoted much of their attention to agriculture and though their military methods were little developed they possessed a rather higher material culture than other South African people. The dominant tribe of the area were the Ngwaketsi with their headquarters

1 This is clear from the fact that a considerable proportion of the Fingo (Mfengu) trace themselves to the Ngwane and Hlubi. See Ayliff and Whiteside: *History of the Abambo*, pp. 17, 55, 90–1, and Msebenzi's *History*, ch. 27.
2 Theal: *History of South Africa*, vol. 5, p. 391.

at Kanye. In 1798–99 they had defeated an attack by Jan Bloem the elder,[1] and though they made no attempt to build up a tribal empire they were looked up to and feared by other tribes. The second most powerful tribe of the area was the Hurutshe whose capital, Kaditshwene, was estimated by the missionary traveller, Campbell, in 1820 to have a population of 16,000.[2] Close neighbours of the Hurutshe were the Kgatla, another powerful people, and further to the north there was a tribe of Kwena and a Tlokwa tribe (this was not related, however, to the Tlokwa of Mma Ntatisi). On the Molopo River one section of the Rolong had its headquarters at Khunwana while another was established further south at Maquassie.

Mission work had been started among the southernmost of the Tswana tribes. Robert Moffat was settled with the Tlapin, whose capital was known as Dithakong (Lattakoo). His mission station was at Kuruman and by the use of water drawn from the spring the missionary created a veritable oasis in the generally arid environment. The presence of Moffat at Kuruman and his close connections with the missionaries working among the Griquas gave the Tlapin considerable security. Their herds grew large and their reputation for prosperity was widespread. Moffat was anxious to spread mission work to other tribes and the Wesleyan Missionary Society was preparing to open a station with Rolong at Maquassie when the disturbances in Transorangia reached that neighbourhood.

The invasions of the Hlubi and Ngwane and the devastations caused by the Tlokwa drove four large tribes from Transorangia to take refuge across the Vaal. As they had lost their cattle they were forced to live by plunder and traverse the land as devastating hordes. The Phuting crossed the river and travelled northward to the Hurutshe country. The Hurutshe capital, Kaditshwene, was sacked and the Phuting then turned southward again. The Hlakoane also crossed the Vaal and began a career of destruction. The Fokeng, driven from their home near Kurutlele by the Tlokwa, joined another tribe of the same name on the northern bank of the Vaal. They found an able leader in the young chief, Sebetwane, and set off westward in search of a more peaceful home. Finally the Taung and a section of the Leghoya tribe abandoned their home near the site of the future Boer settlement of Winburg and fled from the disturbed conditions in Transorangia. Under the leadership of Moletsane they advanced up to the Molopo River. They attacked the Hurutshe before they could recover from the Phuting attack and also devastated the northern Rolong.

1 Stow: *The Native Races of South Africa*, pp. 289–91.
2 Campbell: *Travels in South Africa . . . Second Journey*, vol. I, ch. XX–XXI.

The rich herds of the Tlapin at Dithakong were a powerful attraction and in 1823 three of these wandering hordes converged by different routes on the capital of the tribe. The first to arrive were the Fokeng and soon afterwards came the Phuting. The two robber bands resented one another's presence and a battle took place in which the Fokeng were victorious. A woman of the Kololo tribe who had been one of the wives of the Phuting chief was captured by Sebetwane and thereafter his people were known as the Kololo. In spite of their defeat the Phuting did not abandon the area and shortly afterwards the Hlakoane also arrived on the scene. The whole mass of peoples impelled by starvation then moved down on the Tlapin capital.

For some time terrifying rumours had been spreading among the Tlapin that the Mantatees[1] were coming in an irresistible horde. Moffat dismissed them at first but soon the close approach of the composite mass removed all doubts. The Tlapin were incapable of offering effective resistance to the invasion. They appealed to Moffat for protection and the missionary determined to do his best to save his flock. The only hope lay in the Griquas and Moffat hastened to Griquatown to seek their aid. At this time the Griquas were far from united, for mission policy had led to the deposition of Adam Kok (son of Cornelius Kok the first Griqua leader) and the establishment of Waterboer, an ex-catechist, as chief. Adam Kok had seceded with a section of the people and the half-caste leader, Barend-Barends, also maintained his independence at his settlement, Boetsap. In face of the common peril the Griqua leaders were persuaded by Moffat, Melville, the resident missionary at Griquatown, and the traveller Thompson to sink their differences and mount a combined expedition.[2]

A force of about 100 Griquas equipped with guns and horses rode out with Moffat to face the invaders and on 25 June 1823 the enemy was sighted near Dithakong. Moffat attempted to enter into negotiations but the enemy refused and made a sally at the horsemen. The Griquas then retired and prepared for a full-scale encounter the following day. On 26 June the Griqua force drew itself up for battle. Another attempt was made to parley but the enemy began the attack at once, throwing out

1 Because Moffat described the composite group who attacked Dithakong (Lattakoo) as Mantatees it was long thought that Mma Ntatisi and the Tlokwa were responsible for the spread of anarchy to the Tswana country. M. How in 'An Alibi for Mma Ntatisi', *African Studies*, vol. 13, no. 2, 1954, pp. 65–76, however, showed that this was not so and a close study of Moffat's writing confirms that it was not the Tlokwa who were involved. Moffat: *Apprenticeship at Kuruman*, p. 103. The account given here is based upon E. Smith: 'Sebetwane and the Makololo', *African Studies*, vol. 15, no. 2, 1956, pp. 49–74.

2 Moffat: *Apprenticeship at Kuruman*, pp. 87–8.

wings to surround the horsemen. The Griquas were at an immense advantage for the mobility of their horses enabled them to keep out of range of their opponents' spears while they shot them down from a distance. The tribesmen kept up the struggle bravely for seven hours but they could never get within reach of the horsemen and at every volley more of their number fell. At last, when four to five hundred had been killed, they broke and fled towards Dithakong where another body almost as numerous had remained throughout the battle.[1] As they entered the town the fugitives set fire to the huts and after a brief last stand the whole mass streamed out of the settlement towards the north. Moffat turned his attention to saving the wounded and women and children from the Tlapin, who had taken little active part in the battle but were anxious to take revenge on their enemies now that they were helpless. He was struck by the starving condition of the invaders. Even in the course of the battle itself '. . . the poorer class seized pieces of meat with the utmost avidity, tearing and eating it raw'.[2]

After the defeat at Dithakong the composite group broke up again. Sebetwane and the Makololo took a northward route while the Phuting and Hlakoane drifted to the east.[3] These two groups came into conflict with one another and the Phuting allied with a Korana clan to attack their companions in misfortune. The Hlakoane were driven into the Vaal and only a handful escaped. They found refuge at last with Adam Kok who had set up his capital at Philippolis.[4]

The Taung did not participate in the attack on Dithakong. They remained in the vicinity of the Hurutshe country and were joined there by Sebetwane and the Kololo. The two chiefs ravaged the northern Rolong until their activities attracted the attention of the Ndebele.[5] The alliance then broke up and Moletsane turned southward while Sebetwane continued on his way to the north. In the course of his conquests Moletsane absorbed members of many different tribes and towards the end of 1823 his horde began to approach Maquassie, where the Wesleyan missionary Samuel Broadbent had just commenced his labours with the Rolong of Sifunelo. Sifunelo unwisely made an attempt to avenge the losses of a neighbouring tribe by a raid on Moletsane's

1 Moffat, op. cit., pp. 91–7, gives a description of the battle. 2 Ibid., p. 95.

3 The stragglers after the battle at Dithakong were reduced to a pitiable condition. The Missionary Hodgson on his way to join Broadbent with the Rolong at Maquassie found some of them devouring the body of one of their companions. S. Broadbent: *Narrative of the First Introduction of Christianity amongst the Barolong Tribe*, p. 71.

4 Information collected by Ellenberger from Nkharahanye, one of the survivors. Ellenberger and Macgregor, op. cit., p. 139.

5 See 'Statement drawn up at the request of Chief Molitsane', Theal: *Basutoland Records*, vol. I, pp. 517–32.

people[1] and on 24 April 1824 the Taung swooped on his capital. Broadbent was away in Griquatown to recuperate his health. The Rolong were completely defeated and the mission station was sacked. The plunderers suffered an unpleasant surprise, for Broadbent had left a bag of gunpowder in the mission house. It was seized by the Taung who assumed that it must be something edible and placed it carefully in the middle of a fire to cook. It exploded, wounding several of the warriors severely.[2]

When news of the attack on Maquassie reached Griquatown a commando was hastily assembled and despatched to help the Rolong. It found the town in ruins and the enemy departed. Seeing no prospect of valuable loot the Griquas turned on the unfortunate Sifunelo and accused him of robbing mission property himself. They levied a fine of four hundred cattle on his already depleted herds. In spite of this harsh experience the Rolong chief still hoped for Griqua support against his enemies.

In August 1824 Moffat made an exploring journey to visit the Ngwaketsi tribe. He was accompanied by a number of Griquas and on his return he met Sifunelo on the Molopo River. The Rolong chief had come to ask for help against the Taung and Moffat went to his support.[3] On his way the missionary's party was attacked by Moletsane's men and on 20 August a major battle took place. Griqua and Rolong faced the Taung together but at the first charge the Rolong gave way and fled. Tshabadira, brother of Sifunelo and the most energetic leader of the tribe, was killed. Fleeing Rolong brought news to Maquassie of a complete disaster but the battle was not over.[4] The small number of Griquas kept up the struggle with the triumphant Taung. They were too small a body to rout the enemy completely but they recovered much of the cattle which their allies had lost and also killed one of Moletsane's chief lieutenants. Because of the death of leaders on both sides the battle came to be known as the 'Battle of the Chiefs'.[5] The Griquas showed themselves more generous than on the previous occasion and the recaptured stock was returned to the Rolong, but Sifunelo had little hope of maintaining his position at Maquassie once the horsemen withdrew, and the missionaries were forced to abandon the station they had just reconstructed. A new Rolong capital was established at

1 E. Edwards, Journal sent to Secretaries, Wesleyan Missionary Society, Griquatown, 10 Jan. 1824, M.M.S. 1824/6.

2 There are numerous accounts of the attack on Maquassie in the published and unpublished sources. See for example S. Broadbent: *Narrative of the First Introduction of Christianity amongst the Barolong Tribe*, pp. 128–33.

3 Moffat: *Apprenticeship*, pp. 144–8.

4 Ibid., pp. 151–3.

5 Ellenberger and Macgregor, op. cit.

Platberg and the Taung remained in the vicinity of Maquassie. No further major hostilities between the two tribes took place, though Sifunelo made an abortive attempt to attack the Taung in alliance with a Griqua, Piet Witvoet.[1] In 1827 Moletsane, alarmed at the proximity of the Ndebele regiments in the Transvaal, decided to move further out of their range and set up a new capital a little to the south of the Vaal. Hodgson, missionary with the Rolong, visited him there and friendly relations were established between the Rolong and Taung.[2]

In the following year Moletsane invited the Rolong to take part in a large-scale expedition to attack the Ndebele in company with a number of Korana under the leadership of Jan Bloem (junior). After initial success the Korana commando was ambushed as it was making its way home, but Moletsane succeeded in making his escape. In 1830 he tried the same device again. He joined Barend-Barends who was planning a great war of revenge against the Ndebele. Once again victory was followed by an ambush but this time the Taung were not so fortunate. The fighting power of the tribe was almost destroyed and Moletsane moved eastward with a mere handful of followers.[3] For some time he lived under the protection of Adam Kok at Philippolis, but in 1836 he sought shelter with the French missionaries at Beersheba.[4] He then had only about 150 followers, but some of his tribe, together with some Leghoyas, had remained behind in their old home at the time of the Tlokwa attack. They had migrated subsequently to the vicinity of Mekuatling in the north-west corner of Basutoland and Moletsane decided to join them. Later in 1836[5] he moved to Mekuatling where he soon succeeded in asserting his authority over the other chiefs and became a powerful leader once again. He was to play an important part in the subsequent history of Basutoland.

1 Hodgson and Archbell to Secretaries, Wesleyan Missionary Society, Vaal River, 4 Oct. 1825, M.M.S. 1825/49.
2 Hodgson to Secretaries, Wesleyan Missionary Society, Platberg, 23 June 1827, M.M.S. 1827/21.
3 A further account of these campaigns is given below, Chapter 9, pp. 138–40.
4 Letter of M. Rolland, Beersheba, 28 June 1836, *Journal des Missions Évangéliques*, vol. 12 (1837), p. 23.
5 Letter of M. Rolland, Beersheba, 15 Sept. 1838, *Journal des Missions Évangéliques*, vol. 14 (1839), pp. 42–53.

Chief Sikonyela of the Tlokwa (from a contemporary drawing)

Thaba Bosiu—the mountain stronghold of Moshesh (from a contemporary drawing)

7 Moshesh and the Basuto Nation

BEFORE the invasion of Mpanganzita and Matiwane the mountainous areas of modern Basutoland had a sparse Bantu population. Some Nguni speakers (now known collectively as Phuthi) had entered the area from across the Drakensberg, but apart from these the hilly country was still largely inhabited by Bushmen who found caves in the mountain-sides ideal shelters. On the surrounding plains to the north and west were many different tribes of Sotho-speaking peoples mainly belonging to branches of the Kwena and Fokeng. These tribes had not as yet begun to amalgamate into powerful states but the beginning of a process not altogether dissimilar from that started by Dingiswayo, Zwide and Sobhuza, in Zululand, could perhaps be seen in the career of Motlomi. He was chief of a small Kwena tribe and possessed a keen imagination and lively curiosity for the culture of other peoples. He travelled widely and built up connections with many tribes by marrying daughters of their chiefs. He was said to have seen visions and was widely loved for his tolerance, wisdom and preference for peace. He was also much in demand as a rain-maker. As a result he was able to exert moral influence over a wide area and was often called upon to adjudicate disputes between tribes. His influence rested on personal qualities rather than an institutional framework and after his death about 1815 the experiment in philosopher kingship came to an end.[1]

While Motlomi was still at the height of his influence his attention was attracted to the son of a sub-chief of the Mokoteli, another sept of the Kwena. The Mokoteli were an insignificant tribelet and Mokachane by no means distinguished but Motlomi saw in his son, Moshesh, qualities of intelligence and leadership which marked him off from the ordinary. He summoned the young lad and gave him sage advice on how to conduct himself if he should be called to be a ruler. He urged on his pupil the need for impartial justice, the advantages of peace over war and the foolishness of reliance on the devices of witchdoctors.[2] His

1 For accounts of Motlomi, see Arbousset and Daumas, op. cit., pp. 262–77; Ellenberger and Macgregor, op. cit., pp. 90–8.
2 Arbousset and Daumas, op. cit., pp. 262–77.

advice found a receptive ear and Moshesh grew up to be one of the greatest of Bantu statesmen, a master of diplomacy and a strong believer in the superiority of rational argument to force. Ambitious though he was, Moshesh was a kindly man with none of the delight in the sufferings of others which characterized Shaka. He had the strength of character to learn readily from white missionaries without falling completely under their influence, and the singleness of purpose to build up a nation from many different tribes and preserve it from destruction through the most complex vicissitudes.

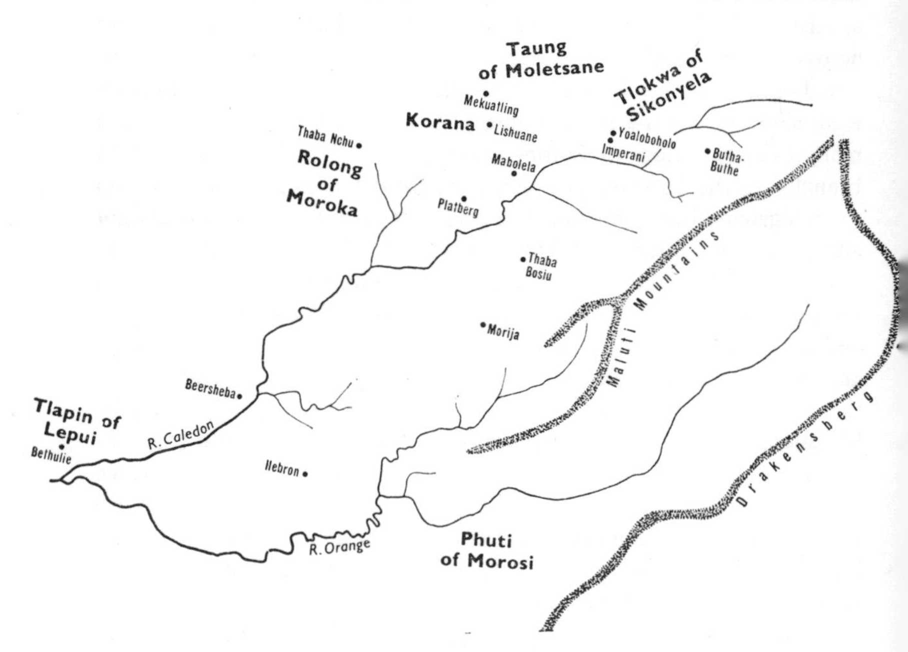

Basutoland and neighbourhood in the Mfecane period

Early in his life Moshesh realized the advantages of the strong defensive positions provided by the Basutoland mountains. With a small body of young men, some of whom had been attracted from tribes other than his own, he set up his position on the mountain of Butha-Buthe in north-eastern Basutoland. The passes up the hillside were blocked by boulder walls allowing access to no more than one beast at a time. Look-out huts were built at vantage points near these entrances and caves were fortified with stone walls to serve as provision stores in case of need.[1] The precautions were well advised, for when Mpangazita's invasion drove the Tlokwa from their home they made a fierce attack on Butha-Buthe but were beaten off at the 'Battle of the Pots'.[2] The second Tlokwa attack was a more serious affair. The Mantatees invested the mountain and Moshesh's followers were reduced to dire straits. The intervention of an Nguni force persuaded the Tlokwa to retire but Moshesh had drawn the conclusion that Butha-Buthe was inadequate as a permanent home for his people and began to search for a more satisfactory site. His spies brought news of a great flat-topped hill standing isolated in a fertile plain in western Basutoland. Its summit with an area of about half a square mile could provide for the accommodation of a large number of people with livestock and other provisions in time of siege. Its steep cliffs with narrow passes would be easy to defend and the surrounding country could support a substantial population in times of peace.[3] A small Phuthi tribe, under None, was living in the vicinity but they had made no attempt to utilize the potentialities of the mountain-top as a defensive stronghold.

The march from Butha-Buthe promised to be a dangerous one. A tribe on the move is easily vulnerable and the intervening country was occupied by a turbulent population, the remnants of many tribes broken in the epidemic of wars and migrations. Loss of their food supplies had forced them to live by robbery and many were reduced to such extremities that they had resorted to cannibalism and hid in caves to fall upon passers-by. Nevertheless Moshesh decided to make the attempt. Butha-Buthe was abandoned and the Mokoteli set off by forced marches to their new home. On the way some of the old people could not keep up and as they dropped behind they fell into the hands of cannibals. Moshesh's grandfather, Peete, was one of these.[4] Only blood and some garments were found by his relatives who went back to look for him. Finally, the mountain was reached by night and in commemoration they called it Thaba Bosiu ('the hill of night'). The courageous decision to undertake this march was a turning point in Moshesh's life and in the history of the Basuto nation. Moshesh had established himself in a position so strong that it could stand against Boer commandos as well as the most formidable Bantu enemies. The southern Sotho peoples had a stable focus around which they could cluster.

1 Walton, 'Villages of the Paramount Chiefs of Basutoland I—Butha-Buthe', *Lesotho*, vol. 1, 1959. 2 See above, Chapter 6, p. 87.

3 For a description of the site, Walton, 'Villages of the Paramount Chiefs of Basutoland II—Thaba Bosiu the Mountain Fortress of Chief Moshesh', *Lesotho*, vol. 2, 1960.

4 Ellenberger and Macgregor, op. cit., p. 146.

From his new home Moshesh began the long process of extending his influence over neighbouring peoples. He tried to win them over peacefully whenever possible and unite them with his own people in a composite following. The first attempt in this direction was unsuccessful, for the grazing land in the near vicinity of Thaba Bosiu was inadequate for the greatly increased population. Moshesh failed to restrain his sons from attacking None and driving his people away.[1] Nevertheless the policy generally succeeded and even Morosi, the most powerful Phuthi leader, was persuaded to become a loyal vassal of Moshesh.

One of the first difficulties which had to be faced was the lawless state of much of the country filled with desperate groups of bandits and cannibals. Moshesh realized that their behaviour was the result of circumstances and believed that they could be won back to normal life by generosity, but he was faced by the repugnance of his own people who wished to massacre the cannibals in revenge for their losses on the march from Butha-Buthe. The chief succeeded in winning support for his mild policy by the ingenious argument that cannibals were living tombs sacred to the spirits of their victims.[2] He provided them with cattle from the royal herds which they were to look after in return for the milk and a guarantee that his own people would not be attacked.[3] In a short time the majority of the cannibals had settled down to normal peaceful life and thereafter became some of Moshesh's most faithful followers.

The expansion of his influence took place under difficult circumstances for he was surrounded by powerful neighbours who might be attracted, by the presence of substantial herds, to launch an attack on the infant state. In Zululand, Shaka's regiments were a peril to be feared, and nearer home the Ngwane of Matiwane were a force which Moshesh's followers could not face in the open field. The Tlokwa also, though no longer at the height of their power, were firmly established on their own mountain fortress and were to remain a danger for many years. Moshesh offered tribute to Shaka and also to Matiwane but the presence of the Ngwane in Transorangia was a serious threat to his kingdom. He persuaded the Zulu to attack them but they did not immediately withdraw and in 1827 Matiwane's men attacked Thaba Bosiu. The mountain fortress proved too strong for them and shortly afterwards they withdrew to the Thembu country to meet their fate at Mbholompo.

In 1831 an Ndebele army sent out to attack the Taung entered Basutoland and launched an attack on Moshesh's mountain. The first wave of attackers was repulsed by showers of stones and spears. The

1 Ellenberger and Macgregor, op. cit., p. 147. 2 Casalis, *The Basutos*, p. 19.
3 Arbousset and Daumas, op. cit., p. 58.

regimental *indunas* were furious and could be seen urging their men to a new attack, tearing the plumes from their heads and trampling them under foot in shame and in indignation. A second more desperate charge was made but it met with the same fate and the attempt to storm the mountain was abandoned. Moshesh then seized the opportunity to achieve a diplomatic triumph. He sent a messenger after the defeated Ndebele with a gift of cattle to say, 'Our master assumes that you must have been hungry to have attacked his people. He sends you these cattle so that you may eat and go in peace.' The Ndebele were so impressed that they resolved never to attack Moshesh again.[1]

By this time Moshesh had consolidated his authority over most of modern Basutoland and refugees from many different tribes came to seek his protection. Matiwane, defeated by the British, passed through his kingdom but could not be dissuaded from journeying on to meet his death in Zululand. Mehlomakhulu and the Hlubi, driven back from Pondoland, found a home for some time amongst the Basuto and several small groups from Natal settled near Mekuatling. As news of the return of peaceful conditions reached the Cape Colony, many Sotho, who had been working on the white farms, flocked homewards.[2] They came with the cattle they had earned as wages and put themselves under the authority of Moshesh, who settled them on fertile lands between the Caledon and Orange Rivers. This area had previously held a very sparse population but soon began to bourgeon with villages and gardens. The only major remaining rival to Moshesh was Sikonyela. Every attempt was made to maintain friendly relations and negotiations were undertaken with a view to a marriage between Sikonyela and one of Moshesh's daughters, but the Tlokwa were too numerous and their chief too strong a personality for them to be peacefully incorporated in Moshesh's kingdom.

The defeat of the Ndebele expedition did not bring complete peace and security to Basutoland. The devastation of Transorangia had left the area virtually denuded of cattle and as the strength of Mzilikazi's regiments deterred raiding parties from venturing into the Transvaal, the predatory Korana and Griqua bands turned their attention to Moshesh's people. The number of these robbers was small but the mobility of their horses and their possession of guns made them formidable. They would swoop on Basuto villages at dawn, throwing the inhabitants into a panic by firing their guns and sweep off the cattle before effective resistance could be organized. Constantly repeated attacks forced the villagers to take refuge on the mountain-tops and

1 Casalis, op. cit., pp. 22–4.
2 Arbousset and Daumas, op. cit., p. 304.

interfered with normal economic life.[1] In response to these raids the Basuto organized counter-ambushes, waiting till the Griquas fell asleep round their camp-fires and charging down on them before they could seize their arms. In this way the Basuto began to acquire considerable quantities of horses and guns and Moshesh did everything he could to increase the supply. In a remarkably short time the Basuto had bred their own 'Basuto pony'[2] and begun to convert themselves into a nation of mounted gunmen, so expert in handling their steeds that they were compared by a British officer to the Cossacks in the Crimean War.[3]

Conflict with the Griquas and occasional contact with Boers who had been grazing their cattle for short periods in the lands between the Caledon and the Orange from about 1818, led Moshesh to seek more information about the white people. A wandering Christian Griqua, Adam Krotz, visited Thaba Bosiu in 1832 and told the chief about the work of missionaries with the tribes. He determined to secure their services for himself and sent two embassies to Philippolis with gifts of cattle and a request for missionaries to come to him. The cattle were stolen by Griquas but the second embassy reached Philippolis in 1833, just as a party of French missionaries belonging to the Paris Evangelical Missionary Society was staying there on their way to commence mission work among the Hurutshe. Disheartened by news of Mzilikazi's activities Casalis, Arbousset and Gosselin took Moshesh's message as a divine call and travelled to Thaba Bosiu where they were received with open arms. A central mission station was established at Morija and shortly afterwards others at Beersheba and Mekuatling. The work rapidly expanded and the missionaries undertook to regard themselves as Basuto and make the welfare of the nation their highest aim. Their support was to prove invaluable to Moshesh in the difficult times which lay ahead.

The arrival of the missionaries took place just as the Griqua menace was beginning to recede, but it was followed by a new development which further increased the difficulties of Moshesh's position. The long period of insecurity among the southern Tswana tribes had reduced the missionaries in that area to the verge of despair. The relative peace of Moshesh's kingdom offered greater hope for the pursuance of their work and a general drift of population towards Basutoland took place.

1 A good impression of the conditions produced by the Griqua and Korana raids can be gained from the Letters and Journals of the French missionaries.
2 See Thornton: *The Origin and History of the Basuto Pony.*
3 Governor Cathcart, Despatch to Colonial Secretary, 13 Jan. 1853. Theal: *Basutoland Records*, vol. II, pp. 2–5.

Many Tlapin had fled to Philippolis to take refuge with Adam Kok. In April 1833 the French missionaries acquired the Caledon Mission Station from the London Missionary Society (it was subsequently renamed Bethulie) and by the end of the year Pellissier had persuaded the Tlapin chief, Lepui, to take up residence there with five to six thousand followers.[1] In 1836 Moletsane came to the station at Beersheba and in 1838 moved to Mekuatling where he became an important vassal of Moshesh.

Another migration took place under the auspices of the Wesleyan Missionary Society. After their station at Maquassie had been twice abandoned they had set up a new post at Platberg, but conditions remained unsettled. The vicinity of the new station had been devastated and offered little prospect for expansion, and it was widely separated from the chain of Wesleyan stations that was being built up between the Eastern Cape frontier and Natal. In 1833 Archbell travelled across the depopulated wastes of Transorangia to Basutoland and decided to find a new station for his congregation there.[2] Under his leadership the Rolong of Moroka, together with a small group of half-caste Hottentot/whites and another of Koranas, abandoned their old home and journeyed towards Moshesh. They chose a position for their new settlement near Thaba Nchu, a Basuto outpost where a sub-chief, Seme, was living with a considerable following.[3] Moshesh welcomed the new immigration which would strengthen him against the Griquas and agreed to allow the Rolong to settle alongside his own people. He regarded the arrangement in the light of traditional practice and the gift of cattle he received as recognition of his sovereignty. Moroka was invited to councils at Thaba Bosiu and Moshesh considered him a chief within the Basuto kingdom.[4] The Wesleyan missionaries, however, were not anxious to place their congregation under the sovereignty of a chief whose people were the mission field of another society. They persuaded the Basuto ruler to put his mark to a document which gave their society and the Rolong people absolute rights of ownership to the lands of Thaba Nchu.[5] In addition to these immigrants a group of Thembu,

1 Letters of Casalis and Pellissier: *Journal des Missions Évangéliques*, vol. 9, 1834, pp. 26, 129–34.
2 See Letter Archbell to Secretaries, Wesleyan Missionary Society, Platberg, 2 Sept. 1833, M.M.S. 1833/28.
3 Arbousset earlier in the year had estimated the population of Thaba Nchu together with that of neighbouring Thaba Patsoa at about 1,000. *Journal des Missions Évangéliques*, vol. 9, 1834, pp. 43–4.
4 See statement by Moshesh, Theal: *Basutoland Records*, vol. I, pp. 1–4.
5 Theal: *Basutoland Records*, vol. I, pp. 4–6. It is significant that the document was not witnessed by any of the Paris Evangelical Missionary Society missionaries who could have explained its meaning to Moshesh.

disturbed by the frontier war of 1834–5, fled into Moshesh's kingdom and placed themselves under his authority.

In the task of uniting these heterogeneous elements Moshesh lacked the advantages provided by the Zulu age-regiment system. His own immediate followers were organized in accordance with age, but on the lines of the old Sotho system under which young initiates were associated with a prince of the royal house.[1] In Moshesh's kingdom, chiefs of large incorporated tribes held their own initiation ceremonies and the system did not play a very large part in the process of nation-building. Instead, Moshesh relied on traditional principles slightly modified to apply to a greatly expanded following. Small groups that had lost their tribal identity were governed through headmen of their own, but placed under the authority of members of Moshesh's family whose headquarters were established in different parts of the kingdom. Larger groups who could not be handled in this way were left under their own chiefs so long as these recognized the supremacy of the paramount. Unity was encouraged by the process of consultation on all major matters which Moshesh employed to the full and by external pressures. The Basuto kingdom was thus a patchwork of tribal groups, the largest being Moshesh's own following divided up among members of his family. The longer it survived the greater internal cohesion became, as cultural differences between tribes were modified by contact with one another, but throughout Moshesh's lifetime and for some years after that it was problematic whether it would hold together. Because of the structure of the kingdom every major political decision involved a complex diplomatic exercise. Interested parties had to be consulted even if it meant long delays, and sometimes Moshesh was forced into actions which he would have wished to avoid to gratify the impatience of one or other section and preserve the fragile bonds which held the community together.

Hardly had Moshesh consolidated his position in Basutoland and gained a measure of security from Bantu and Griqua enemies than his life's work began to be threatened from a new source. Ever since the second decade of the nineteenth century farmers from the Colony had been crossing the Orange and grazing their herds in Transorangia. At first this was a seasonal movement but later a permanent white population began to grow up north of the Orange River.[2] Some penetrated into land which Moshesh claimed between the Orange and the Caledon, but their numbers were small and they lived peacefully enough alongside the Basuto. The majority of these pre-Trek immigrants kept outside

1 See Ashton: *The Basuto.*

2 See, for example, Macmillan: *Bantu, Boer and Briton*, pp. 53–70.

Moshesh's kingdom and settled on lands claimed by the Griqua of Philippolis.

The Great Trek brought a great increase in the white population of Transorangia. The farmers asked Moshesh to allow them to graze their cattle on his lands until they were ready to move on. Permission was given, but the chief pointed out that he was not granting any permanent rights of ownership. He told the farmers that they should not erect substantial buildings or sell their grazing rights to one another.[1] Many of the travellers, however, did not move on and, in spite of protests from the chief, began to treat the land they occupied as their personal property.[2]

Hoping that the British Government would protect him against such encroachment Moshesh agreed to enter into a treaty with it. But the question of a treaty immediately raised the problem of the true boundaries of Moshesh's state and precipitated latent trouble between him and the Rolong. Moshesh regarded Thaba Nchu as falling within his domains, but Moroka, strongly supported by the Wesleyan missionaries, protested that he was an independent chief and supported his arguments by reference to the deed of sale. The differences could not be resolved and in the Napier Treaty of 1843 it was agreed that the northern border of Moshesh's domain should be left undefined pending a clarification of the problem.[3] The treaty did not give Moshesh the protection he had hoped. The Boers remained where they were and consolidated their position. They refused to submit to Bantu jurisdiction and tension between them and the Basuto grew.

It was not, however, Basutoland but relations between the Boers and the Griquas which precipitated new developments. A Boer was arrested by Adam Kok for a crime committed on territory over which the Griqua chief claimed sovereignty. A Boer commando assembled at once and released the prisoner, and the Boers remained under arms threatening to solve the Griqua problem once and for all. The Colonial Governor, Maitland, responded promptly and a force of British troops together with Griquas dispersed the Boer commando at Swartkopjes, but it was evident that some stable and permanent system governing relations between the races in the area was needed.[4] Moshesh asked for full British protection, and a British Resident at Thaba Bosiu but the British Government was anxious to limit its responsibilities and decided to try the experiment of placing the separate races under separate authorities. Moshesh and Adam Kok were asked to mark out parts of their land

1 Theal: *Basutoland Records*, vol. I, pp. 36–7, 81.
2 Ibid., pp. 80–1. 3 Ibid., pp. 54–79.
4 For an analysis of the development of British policy towards Transorangia, see de Kiewiet, *British Colonial Policy and the South African Republics, 1848–1872.*

as alienable territory. The ultimate sovereignty of the chiefs over these areas was to be preserved but white farmers could acquire rights there in return for payment. Jurisdiction over such Europeans was to be delegated by the chiefs to a British Resident who would have his seat at Bloemfontein. Tribal land outside the demarcated area was to be regarded an inalienable and no whites could acquire land rights there. A treaty drawn up along these lines was signed by Moshesh in 1846.[1] The arrangement was better on paper than in practice, for the Resident at Bloemfontein had no effective force to support him and no means of exercising control over the activities of the white farmers which were the root cause of the trouble. Moshesh agreed to set aside some land between the Caledon and the Orange for Boer settlement, but they regarded the area as much too small and refused to abandon farms they had established much further into Basuto territory. The position remained confused and unstable until Sir Harry Smith, newly appointed as Governor of the Cape and High Commissioner for South Africa, rode into Transorangia in 1848 on his way to visit Natal.

He had come from dealing with yet another war on the Eastern Frontier and had decided that the annexation of frontier areas was the only answer to repeated outbreaks of violence. The lands between the Fish and the Kei were annexed as British Kaffraria and Sir Harry appreciated that the problems of the Eastern Frontier could not be separated from those of Basutoland and Transorangia. A situation in which Boers lacking stable government or means of education were living in the close proximity of Basuto and Griquas was bound to lead to trouble. Moshesh and the Boer leaders were summoned to Bloemfontein for a brief discussion and Sir Harry declared the whole area between the Orange and Vaal rivers annexed as the Orange River Sovereignty.

The general principles on which the Governor acted were undoubtedly right and were welcomed by Moshesh, but the measure was taken far too hastily and with inadequate appreciation of the difficulties. The home government was reluctant to ratify the annexation and only did so on condition that it should not become another charge on the revenue.[2] The Boers summoned Pretorius to their aid from the Transvaal and broke into open rebellion. The revolt was suppressed after the Boer forces had been scattered at Boomplaats but the situation in the Sovereignty remained highly unstable. Warden, the Resident in charge of the new dependency, lacked political experience and still did not possess a force adequate to assert his authority. He could only hope to

1 Text of the agreement given by Theal: *Basutoland Records*, vol. I, pp. 88–92, 118–19.

2 See, for example, de Kiewiet, op. cit., p. 32.

govern with the co-operation of the Boers who were already disaffected, and was bound to make concessions to them in order to win support.

The most perplexing problem facing Warden was the definition of frontiers between different groups. The original line proposed by Moshesh was quite unacceptable to the Boers. On the other hand Boer farms and Basuto villages were interspersed amongst one another and no line could be drawn which would neatly separate them. The problem of the Boer/Basuto frontier was not the only one. The population of all the tribes in Transorangia was rising and as westward expansion was rendered impossible by Boer settlement, tension between the major tribes came to a head. An attack by Sikonyela on some Basuto villages which were established on land claimed by his own people started a whole chain of raids and counter-raids in which Moshesh and his vassal, Moletsane, were ranged against the Tlokwa and the Rolong.[1]

Warden's method of determining boundaries was highly unfavourable to the Basuto. A commission which contained no Basuto representatives marked off a frontier between tribesmen and farmers which included nearly all white farms on the white side of the line but cut many Basuto villages off from their fellows. Then, as he became increasingly impatient with the Basuto chief, Warden demarcated boundaries between the Basuto, the Rolong and the Tlokwa in a way which further reduced Moshesh's territory.

The Basuto ruler long insisted that the definition of boundaries was unnecessary and that the different peoples should simply learn to live peacefully alongside one another, but eventually he was forced to put his mark to a boundary agreement though he did so under protest.[2] His people were becoming impatient and in spite of his wish for peace there were limits to the restraint he could impose on them without compromising his authority. Thus when Warden, with the support of the Rolong, attacked Moletsane in retaliation for a raid he had made on Sikonyela, the Basuto assisted the Taung in a counter-raid which seized three thousand head of cattle from the Rolong chief, Moroka. Moshesh still tried to keep the peace and returned two thousand of the stolen cattle, but his people's exasperation grew greater when Warden attacked two other vassals of their chief, the Phuthi of Morosi and the Thembu. Warden had invited Moshesh's brother, Poshuli, to take part in this campaign without his overlord's consent and it seemed as if he was trying to undermine the authority of the paramount and create a blood feud between the Basuto and their vassals. Moshesh wrote in strong but

1 See Theal: *Basutoland Records*, vol. I, pp. 294–360.
2 Ibid., pp. 281–4, 286–91, 294.

balanced terms complaining against this conduct[1] but he received a stern reply. He could no longer keep his people fully in hand and fighting broke out in several areas. Warden then determined to humble the Basuto chief, sent him an ultimatum demanding a large fine in cattle for his action against the Rolong and prepared to invade Basutoland.

Moshesh warned the Boer farmers that they would be exposing their families and property to danger if they accompanied the expedition and very few of them answered the call. Warden's forces were far too small for the task and he underestimated the fighting force of the Basuto and had an exaggerated opinion of the Rolong and Griquas. Together with these allies he began the fighting, even before the ultimatum had expired, by attacking the hill Viervoet near Mekuatling. The Basuto and Taung offered combined opposition. They feigned a retreat at first and left a herd of cattle as a bait for the Rolong. Then, when their enemy had dispersed to round up the booty, they attacked in force. The Rolong were completely routed and the small number of British troops forced to retreat. Warden fell back on Thaba Nchu and remained there on the defensive.

The Sovereignty was then given over to anarchy. Warden appealed for help but no troops could be sent from the Cape, which was engaged in another Frontier War. Natal despatched a contingent of Zulu but they merely added to the confusion, and the Boers and tribesmen who had assisted Warden were at the mercy of the Basuto. Moshesh wisely showed great restraint and little life was lost.

The outbreak of hostilities in the Sovereignty, together with the war on the Eastern Frontier, had brought the whole of Sir Harry Smith's policy into question. The British Government sought to disentangle itself from responsibilities north of the Orange River and a commission was sent out to investigate. Warden was replaced as Resident by Green, and Sir Harry Smith was also recalled to be replaced as Governor by Sir George Cathcart. A measure of order was restored to the Sovereignty but the underlying problems remained. Sikonyela was encouraged by British favour and supply of firearms to make a surprise attack on Thaba Bosiu, but Moshesh launched a violent counter-attack and the Tlokwa chief was lucky to escape with his life.[2] The new Governor felt that the treatment of Moshesh had been unwise and unfair but that the future stability of the Sovereignty required that the prestige of British arms be restored. He thus felt that the Basuto must be humbled before any

1 Theal: *Basutoland Records*, vol. I, pp. 360–1.
2 Lagden: *The Basutos*, vol. I, pp. 134–5, and Theal: *Basutoland Records*, vol. I, pp. 567–8.

other step could be taken. A force of British troops was assembled on Moshesh's borders and the chief was presented with an ultimatum demanding that a fine of ten thousand cattle be paid in three days. The chief had an interview with the Governor and pleaded for an extension of time, pointing out that it was difficult for him to force his people to surrender cattle and begging the Governor not to talk of war. Though 3,500 cattle were brought to Cathcart's camp on the third day he was not to be appeased and on 19 December 1852 he crossed the Caledon and began to advance directly towards Thaba Bosiu. On his way lay the Berea Mountain and there his troops captured large herds of cattle. As they were occupied in rounding them up the Basuto attacked and the British were driven back. Cathcart then decided to fall back to his camp on the Caledon to await reinforcements. Moshesh seized the opportunity to bring off his most famous diplomatic coup. A messenger was sent with a letter to the Governor which read:

> Your Excellency,
>
> This day you have fought against my people and taken much cattle. As the object for which you have come is to have a compensation for the Boers, I beg you will be satisfied with what you have taken. I entreat peace from you,—you have shown your power,—you have chastised,—let it be enough I pray you; and let me no longer be considered an enemy to the Queen. I will try all I can to keep my people in order in the future.[1]

Cathcart, in a difficult position, was glad to take the way out which the chief offered. The expedition was abandoned and the Basuto were left victorious.

By this time the British Government had determined to abandon its responsibilities in the Orange River Sovereignty and Sir George Clerk had been appointed to wind up its affairs. While he was engaged on this task the final struggle between Moshesh and Sikonyela took place. The Tlokwa had allied with a Korana leader, Gert Taaibosch, and made a number of raids on Basuto cattle. Moshesh appealed to Sir George but though he urged the Basuto to remain quiet he declined to intervene and in November 1853 Moshesh prepared for a major assault on the Tlokwa mountain. The attack was made before dawn and a complete surprise was achieved. One column stormed up the main entrance pass while others scrambled on one another's shoulders and succeeded in making their way up at other points. Before the Tlokwa realized the scale of the attack, the Basuto were in the heart of their stronghold. Sikonyela escaped by hiding in a cave and subsequently fled to seek

1 Theal: *Basutoland Records*, vol. I, p. 627.

protection from Clerk but the fighting power of the tribe was broken.[1] Moshesh offered to receive them into his kingdom and to reinstate Sikonyela if he would accept the paramountcy of the Basuto king. The majority of the tribe under the chief's brother, Mota, accepted, but Sikonyela himself refused. With a handful of followers he accepted the offer of a position in the north-eastern corner of the Cape Colony and settled in the Herschel district where he died in 1856.[2]

The incorporation of the Tlokwa was the culmination of the process of agglomeration set in motion by the invasions of Mpangazita and Matiwane on the highveld. The dreaded Mantatee horde, born out of the same conditions as the Basuto nation and a rival focus of attraction to lesser peoples, had disappeared as an independent entity. The only major people in the Basutoland area who were left outside Moshesh's kingdom were the Rolong, but in their case the attitude of the Wesleyan Missionary Society prevented their being absorbed. In subsequent years other small groups were driven into Basutoland and incorporated in the kingdom, but the phase of gathering tribes together was virtually complete. The task which occupied the rest of Moshesh's life and those of his successors was to maintain, in face of white pressure, the unity of the state he had constructed.

In view of Moshesh's recent victory over British forces, the Boers of Transorangia were understandably reluctant to venture on independence but Sir George Clerk brushed protests aside. He found a committee that was prepared to agree to dis-annexation and in 1852 concluded the Bloemfontein Convention with its members. Under this agreement the Boers were to become an independent republic known as the Orange Free State. They were given a free hand to deal as they pleased with their non-European neighbours and the British undertook to sell them arms and ammunition, but to prevent the Bantu from enjoying access to gunpowder. In the haste of withdrawal the problem of frontiers between Basuto and Boer was left unresolved. Moshesh was given the impression that war had cancelled all previous agreements and the Warden line was abolished, but the Boers believed that the old arrangement still stood.

In spite of goodwill on both sides at first, relations soon deteriorated and in 1858 the first Free State/Basuto war broke out. The Boers, like the British, underestimated their adversary and though they were victorious in the first few engagements they suffered considerable losses. When they reached Thaba Bosiu they found themselves face to face with the whole of Moshesh's army and realized that it was impossible to assault the fortress in the face of such opposition. They heard that

1 Theal: *Basutoland Records*, vol. II, pp. 76–8. 2 Ibid., pp. 82–5, 96–7, 216.

the Basuto were devastating the Free State behind their backs. The Boers abruptly broke up their camp and dispersed. President Boshoff was forced to sue for peace and was fortunate that Governor Grey agreed to act as arbitrator. A new frontier line was established which gave some benefit to the Basuto but it was far from satisfactory to Moshesh, and the sources of future conflict remained.

Population on both sides of the frontier was increasing. The Boers sought to expel Basuto whose homes had been left on their side of the frontier. Moshesh on the other hand refused to withdraw his people or abandon claims to territory beyond the boundary line. In addition neither side possessed the means of law enforcement to maintain peaceful conditions on their borders. The Boers constantly demanded that Moshesh should take firm measures against stock theft but Jan Letelle, a chief who had been excluded from Basutoland by the boundary, was stealing cattle from the Basuto on a large scale and was openly encouraged by white traders who made quick profits from buying up his stock. In 1866 war broke out again but by this time the white population of the Orange Free State had increased considerably and the Boers were led by an energetic and capable president, J. H. Brand. In Basutoland Moshesh was growing old and the weakness of a bureaucracy of 'royals' showed itself. His sons were quarrelling over the succession and their divisions weakened the entire state.

The Boers were unable to capture Thaba Bosiu but they adopted a policy of destroying all the crops and reducing the Basuto to starvation. They were so successful that Moshesh was forced to agree to a treaty which ceded nearly all the fertile land of Basutoland to the Orange Free State, but signing the treaty was only a device to gain time for his subjects to reap a harvest. The Basuto did not abandon the ceded territory and the first Boers who entered the area to occupy farms they had acquired from the Free State Government were killed. The commandos reassembled and the war began again. The Boers were still unable to capture Thaba Bosiu but they wore down Basuto resistance by a campaign of attrition. The Basuto people were on the verge of disintegrating but Moshesh was able to make use of missionary influence in seeking British protection. Wodehouse, then Governor at the Cape, feared that if the Basuto were dispersed, instability would spread to the Eastern Frontier and exceeded his instructions by proclaiming Basutoland annexed to the Crown in 1868. The Boers, too exhausted by the long war to envisage continuing hostilities, were forced to surrender most of their recent conquests. Moshesh died a few months later, happy that his people had been saved from disintegration.

The work of Moshesh was still far from secure. None of his sons, in spite of their education in the Cape Colony, possessed the statesmanship of their great father and external pressure might easily reveal the deep divisions within Basuto society. The supreme test of Moshesh's work came in 1880. In 1879 the British Government had handed the administration of Basutoland over to the Cape Colony and the Cape Prime Minister, Sprigg, procured an act requiring all Bantu to surrender their guns. This aroused the utmost hostility in Basutoland where memories of white encroachment were still so vivid. In 1880 the War of the Guns broke out and after two years of fighting it ended without any decisive result. The Cape, recognizing its failure, handed Basutoland back to the Imperial Government. The country was in a desperate condition, for different chiefs had fought on opposite sides and recognized no common authority. In this trying period the good sense of the Basuto people, the traditions of unity under Moshesh and fear of renewed white encroachment eventually triumphed over the forces of division. The unity of Basutoland had survived and the nation is now about to celebrate its independence.

Moshesh in 1854

8 The Career of Sebetwane and the History of the Kololo

WHILE one consequence of the Mfecane in Transorangia was the gathering together of many different peoples under the authority of Moshesh, another was the migration of a powerful Sotho group out of the area of conflict on a tremendous journey to the flood plains of the upper Zambesi. The core of this migratory horde was made up of two tribes both belonging to the Fokeng group and its hero was the remarkable military leader and statesman, Sebetwane.

The Fokeng of Patsa had grazed their herds near Moletsane's Taung in the neighbourhood of Kurutlele when they were struck by the invasion of Mma Ntatisi and the Tlokwa. Deprived of their cattle they fled across the Vaal and joined forces with another Fokeng tribe. In the course of their flight the chief of the Patsa group was killed by a lion. The young and energetic prince, Sebetwane, took his place and soon established his ascendancy over both sections of the Fokeng.

As the disturbed conditions in their home country showed no signs of improving, Sebetwane and his followers determined to set out to find a new home where they could live in peace. Their most immediate need was cattle to replace the herds lost to the Tlokwa and, attracted by rumours of the great amounts of stock in the possession of the Tlapin, they turned their steps westward towards Dithakong. Chastened by witnessing the effects of the Griquas' guns and renamed the Kololo after their successful battle with the Phuting,[1] they took a northward path through the territory of the Tswana tribe. Moving up to the Molopo River the Kololo attacked and defeated the northern branch of the Rolong near Khunwana and then passed on into the present Marico district. This was the domain of the Hurutshe whose capital, Kaditshwane, had recently been sacked by the Phuting. The Hurutshe made an attempt to resist this new invasion but their forces broke before the Kololo onslaught and their chief was killed.[2]

1 See above, Chapter 6, p. 95.
2 E. Smith: 'Sebetwane and the Makololo', *African Studies*, vol. 15, no. 2, 1956, pp. 49–74. Schapera: *Ditirafalo tsa Merafe ya Batswana*, p. 41.

At this time Sebetwane was joined by Moletsane who had followed in his tracks. The two chiefs entered into an alliance for a time, devastating the Hurutshe country and raiding the Kgatla near the confluence of the Api and Crocodile Rivers. The association of the two warrior chiefs was short-lived, for they were attacked by the Ndebele regiments who

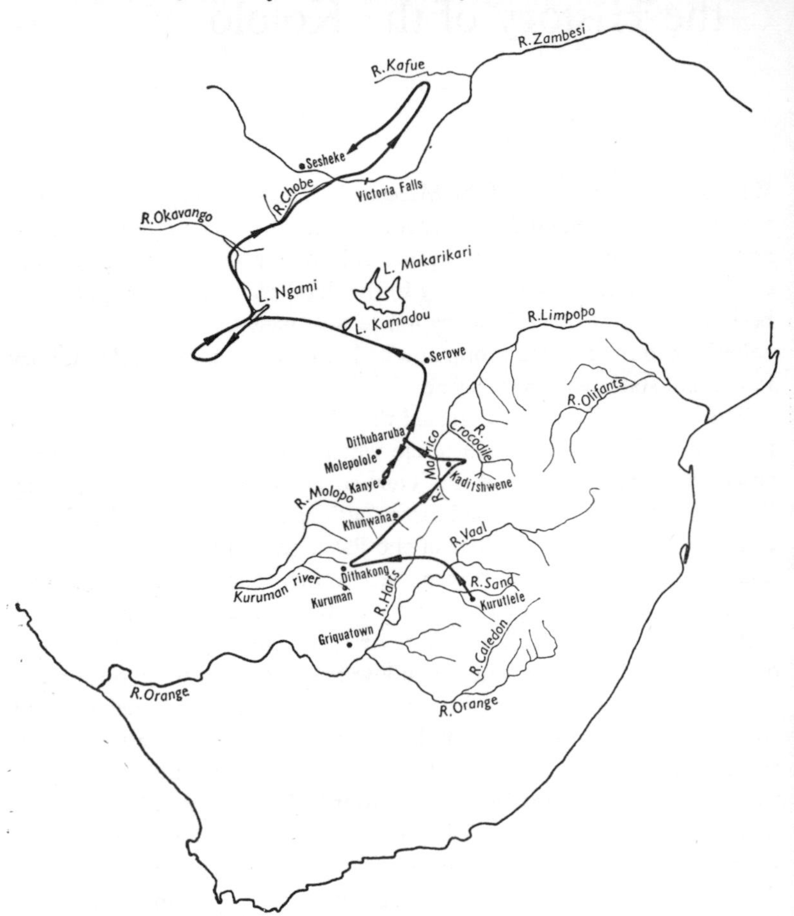

Approximate route of the Kololo under Sebetwane

regarded them as intruding on their own raiding preserves. According to Sebetwane's account, the Ndebele attacked them twice in the course of his wanderings in Bechuanaland and Moletsane stated that it was an Ndebele attack which forced him to turn back towards Maquassie.[1] After the conflict with the Ndebele, the Kololo continued north-west

1 Livingstone: *Missionary Travels and Researches*, p. 85. Theal: *Basutoland Records*, vol. I, pp. 517–32.

into the area of the modern Bechuanaland Protectorate. The first to feel their onslaught were the Tlokwa.[1] Next the Kwena, settled at Dithubaruba, were attacked. The Kwena were divided against one another in a succession dispute and one party invited the aid of the formidable invaders. Surrounding the Kwena town by night Sebetwane achieved a complete surprise. Those of the Kwena who avoided the spears of the attackers fled in panic. The Kololo made themselves masters of the town and captured one of the princes, Sechele.[2] He was carried by the Kololo to the Ngwato country and Sebetwane seems to have wished to adopt the lad as a son, but Sechele's mother was too weary to accompany the Kololo on their advance. Sechele expressed a desire to return home and was released with a gift of nine cattle.

The conquest of the Kwena involved the Kololo in conflict with their more powerful neighbours, the Ngwaketsi. The defeated Kwena faction hastened to summon the aid of this tribe. The Ngwaketsi had long been the most powerful of the Tswana tribes. [When the southern Tswana had been thrown into confusion by the depredations of the Korana, aided by the guns of Jan Bloem, the Ngwaketsi were the only tribe to offer effective resistance. In 1798–99 they had beaten off an attack by the notorious outlaw on their capital on the hill of Kanye. Bloem himself was killed or died shortly afterwards leaving his half-caste son of the same name to carry on the family tradition. After this the Ngwaketsi were left strictly alone.] In August 1824 Moffat visited them and estimated the following of their chief, Makaba, at 70,000.

Makaba did not hesitate to answer the Kwena appeal. Augmenting his own following with contingents from the Kwena, Hurutshe and the Kgatla he prepared for a massive onslaught on the common enemy. The battle took place near Melita but the numbers of the allied forces were no match for the battle experience of the Kololo and the leadership of Sebetwane. 'Placing his men in front and the women behind the cattle . . .' Sebetwane '. . . routed the whole of his enemies at one blow.'[3] Makaba himself was killed and the Kololo occupied his town. Soon

1 E. Smith, op. cit. The existence of this tribe of the Tlokwa contributed to the belief that Mma Ntatisi had taken part in the battle of Dithakong. The Bechuanaland Tlokwa, however, are only remotely related to their namesakes in Basutoland and do not recognize the same totem animal.

2 Sechele was afterwards to become famous as Livingstone's first convert. Differing versions of the relationship between Sechele and Sebetwane are to be found in Livingstone's *Missionary Travels and Researches*, pp. 14–15, and in his *Family Letters*. The version given here is that of a letter by Livingstone to Robert Moffat in 1849. See the discussion of this point by Schapera: *David Livingstone's Family Letters, 1841–1856*, p. 43 and footnote. See also A. Sillery: *Sechele*.

3 D. Livingstone: *Missionary Travels and Researches*, p. 84. E. Smith, op. cit., identifies Melita with modern Makolontwana.

afterwards, however, they returned to the Kwena capital, Dithubaruba. In this encounter Sebetwane, advancing too close to the enemy, received the wound which was to be responsible for his death twenty-seven years later.

Though the Ngwaketsi had been defeated they had not been dispersed and under their new chief, Sebego, they began to prepare for a counter-attack. In 1826 they gained an unexpected reinforcement when two English traders, Bain and Biddulph, arrived in their town. On their way the traders had crossed the Melita battlefield and found it '. . . literally strewed with human skulls'.[1] The young chief set about at once trying to persuade the newcomers to support his people in a war of revenge with their guns. They resisted as long as they could but eventually, under threat of force, agreed to accompany the expedition. The Ngwaketsi plan was to surround the enemy town by night and make a surprise attack at dawn. Filled with the ardour of revenge and chastened by their earlier defeat the Ngwaketsi marched quickly and silently, preserving the most perfect discipline. As they approached the hostile encampment each section was given its position and battle instructions. Then at daybreak Sebego delivered a moving oration and the signal for attack was given. As the Ngwaketsi charged, the Kololo were thrown into complete confusion and the panic was increased by the traders firing their guns. The Kololo fled completely routed leaving their cattle, the spoils of so much fighting, in the hands of the victors.[2]

After this dramatic reversal of fortune Sebetwane moved on and raided the Ngwato at Serowe. The Ngwato at this juncture fatally weakened their forces by trying to recoup their losses by a raid into modern Southern Rhodesia. The raid ended disastrously for they were defeated by the Kalanga, and the heroic Mangwato chief, Kgari, and four of his brothers were killed. Then the Kololo attacked again and the Ngwato were completely overwhelmed. Abandoning their cattle to the enemy they fled across the Kalahari to take refuge for a time with their relatives, the Tawana of Lake Ngami.[3] Sebetwane and the Kololo

1 *Journals of Andrew Geddes Bain*, p. 51.

2 For an eye-witness account of this battle see *Journals of Andrew Geddes Bain*, pp. 52–71. Bain insists that he and Biddulph merely fired their guns into the air. Livingstone who had only heard Sebetwane's account probably criticized the two traders too harshly when he described the incident as '. . . one of those unrecorded attacks by white men, in which murder is committed and materials laid up in the conscience for a future judgment'. D. Livingstone, *Missionary Travels and Researches*, p. 85.

3 J. Mackenzie: *Ten Years North of the Orange River*, pp. 358–9, gives an account of the disastrous raid to the north. E. Smith, op. cit., suggests that the date of the second Kololo attack and the flight of the Ngwato was probably 1829.

followed their fleeing enemies but not knowing the tracks across the desert they lost their way. They had captured a guide but he took the first opportunity to give them the slip. Travelling at night to cover the distance between waterholes before the heat of the day they lost direction in the dark and 'After marching till morning and going as they thought right, they found themselves on the trail of the day before'.[1] By this time the cattle were desperate with thirst. They stampeded and finding their way by natural instinct, went back to the homes of their original owners. The Kololo were once more reduced to severe straits but shortly afterwards they encountered the Tlatli in the neighbourhood of Lake Kamadou and seized their cattle. After settling there for a short while the Kololo moved off again westward and reached the vicinity of Lake Ngami where they defeated the Tawana.

While at Lake Ngami Sebetwane decided to try to establish contact with whites whom he had heard were to be found further to the west. His experience of the effects of Griqua guns at Dithakong, and the alarm caused by those of Biddulph and Bain, made him feel that only the possession of firearms could give him peace and security. The rumours he had heard probably concerned the Portuguese in Angola. In pursuit of this ambition Sebetwane led his people westward across the desert country as far as the present Ghansi district of South-west Africa, and possibly beyond.[2] On this expedition the lack of water caused the loss of most of their cattle. The Bushmen were hostile and kept up constant attacks with their poisoned arrows. One of Sebetwane's sons was killed and he decided to abandon the attempt to reach the coast. Returning to Lake Ngami Sebetwane moved off once more in search of cattle. Passing northward to the Chobe River he attacked the Tawana once again in the new town they had established after their first defeat. Moremi, the Tawana chief, had recently died of smallpox. The Kololo conquered his people and ruled over them for a time. The Tawana soon broke away, however, and fled back to their original home near Lake Ngami.

Finding the vicinity of the Chobe unhealthy, Sebetwane moved his people once more to the north and after an arduous journey reached the southern bank of the Zambesi. The shores of the river at this point were dominated by the Tonga, who lived on islands in the river. They often took advantage of their position as the only ferrymen to trap their passengers on uninhabited islets and leaving them to starve. They

1 D. Livingstone: *Missionary Travels and Researches*, p. 85.

2 E. Smith, op. cit., believes that he may have reached the dried-up bed of the Otjiombonde River as Andersson in 1853 found a number of abandoned wells in the sandy river-bed along the route from Ghansi. Andersson: *Lake Ngami*, p. 380.

would then take possession of all their victims' goods and use their skulls to decorate the huts of their chiefs. Sebetwane, however, took the wise precaution of forcing the chief of the Tonga to sit in the same canoe as himself and kept him there till all his people and cattle were safely across.[1] News of the coming of Sebetwane and his invading horde united the tribes of the northern bank of the Zambesi in self-defence. The Kololo were met near the Victoria Falls by '. . . an immense army collected to make trophies of the Kololo skulls; but instead of succeeding in this they gave him good excuse for conquering them, and capturing so many cattle that his people were quite incapable of taking any note of the sheep and goats'.[2] After this decisive victory the Kololo made their home in the highlands near the Kafue. This was excellent pastoral country to which they afterwards always looked back with regret.

Their settlement in this new home, however, took place at the very time when Mzilikazi, driven from the Transvaal by the Boers, was also wandering near the Zambesi in search of a new home. The Ndebele ran into the Kololo and an indecisive conflict took place. In the first attack the Ndebele captured Sebetwane's women and cattle but in a counter-attack the Kololo won them back again. A second Ndebele assault was beaten off and the two groups then parted company, Sebetwane moving westward up the Zambesi and Mzilikazi south-east in search of the main body of his people.[3] Sebetwane's decision to move up the Zambesi after the Ndebele attack was undertaken partly in pursuit of his aim to establish contact with white men and provide himself with the firearms which would give him peace, but also in response to the advice of a local Bantu prophet. This man, Tlapane, used to work himself into the characteristic ecstatic state of 'spirit possession' when he would make utterances believed to be of divine inspiration. According to the account given by Livingstone, 'Tlapane, pointing eastwards, said, "There, Sebituane, I behold a fire: shun it; it is a fire which may scorch thee." . . . Then turning to the west, he said, "I see a city and a nation of black men—men of the water; their cattle are red; thine own tribe, Sebituane, is perishing, and will all be consumed; thou wilt govern black men, and, when thy warriors have captured red cattle, let not the owners be killed; they are thy future tribe—they are thy city." . . .'[4]

1 D. Livingstone: *Missionary Travels and Researches*, p. 86.
2 Ibid.
3 See below, Chapter 9, p. 147.
4 D. Livingstone, op. cit., p. 87. The reference to black men alludes to the Zambesi people who are considerably darker than the southern Sotho, who have some admixture of Khoisan blood. The correspondence between the prophecy and Sebetwane's future policy is so close that one may suspect an element of myth in the story.

As they moved up the river the Kololo entered the Barotseland flood plain through the gap of Kataba. The Barotse plain is flooded annually leaving only a number of hillocks unsubmerged as islands. In the dry season the floods recede, leaving a wide plain intersected by numerous waterways. This annual cycle has led the inhabitants to develop a special pattern of life. In the dry season they live on the plain and cultivate the rich alluvium. As the waters begin to rise they retire to villages on the islands and live largely by fishing. This annual change is accompanied by much ritual and is initiated each year by the ceremonial movement of the Lozi king and his court from the dry season to the flood season capital.[1]

The plain was flooded at the time when the Kololo arrived and the Lozi army came by canoe to attack the invaders, but the Kololo feigned a retreat and enticed their enemies to pursue them far from their boats. Sebetwane and his men then turned on their opponents and routed them completely. The Lozi kingdom was not in a position to offer united opposition to the Kololo as it was internally divided by a succession dispute. As soon as the dry season came Sebetwane began a systematic conquest of Barotseland. This extended over three or four years, during which time the Kololo made themselves familiar with the new environment and the use of canoes. Gradually the whole of the Lozi kingdom was brought under control but a number of refugees succeeded in escaping up the Leambye River with some members of the royal lineage and maintaining their independence. During Sebetwane's lifetime this small refugee group was no serious threat to the Kololo kingdom, but it kept alive the sense of Lozi independence and by preserving the old dynasty made possible the revolution which was ultimately to destroy the Kololo state.

While Sebetwane was consolidating his new kingdom he was faced by three attacks from Nguni-speaking groups coming from the east. The first of these consisted of the followers of Nxaba. This hardened warrior had left northern Zululand shortly after Shaka's defeat of the Ndwandwe and travelled northward into modern Portuguese East Africa in association with the Maseko Ngoni. After their conflict with Soshangane, Nxaba and the Maseko parted company. Nxaba moved westward through modern Rhodesia while the Maseko continued north into Tanganyika.[2] Nxaba and his group of seasoned fighters now irrupted unexpectedly into the Barotse plain. Their military abilities, however, were no match for the superior tactical skill of Sebetwane and

1 Gluckman, 'The Lozi', in *Seven Tribes of British Central Africa*. The name Barotse is a corruption of (Ba) Lozi.

2 See above, Chapter 5, p. 65.

the knowledge which the Kololo had gained of the amphibious terrain. The followers of Nxaba were lured into a barren area where they were soon cut off by the rising water. Nxaba saw his men decimated by starvation and accepted the offer of a group of Lozi to save him with their canoes. The Lozi, however, were secretly in alliance with Sebetwane and treacherously drowned Nxaba in the Zambesi.[1]

A more serious threat to the Kololo was posed by the Ndebele. Mzilikazi did not forget the partial defeat he had suffered during his flight from the Transvaal and on two occasions he sent his regiments to Barotseland to destroy Sebetwane. The first Ndebele expedition was at a grave disadvantage for lack of canoes. They did not carry much in the way of food supplies but expected to maintain themselves by capturing cattle and grain on their way. By the time they had made their way into the Barotse plain they were already in desperate straits and Sebetwane took advantage of this to lure them into a trap. 'Sebituane placed some goats on one of the large islands of the Zambesi, as a bait to the warriors, and some men in canoes to co-operate in the manœuvre. When they were all ferried over to the island, the canoes were removed, and the Matabele found themselves completely in a trap, being perfectly unable to swim.'[2] The Kololo waited until starvation had so weakened their enemies that they were unable to fight. They then crossed over to the island, killing all the adults and adopting some of the young shield-bearers into their tribe.

This check did not put an end to the Ndebele threat. A much larger force was assembled, and this time the regiments were supplied with canoes which were laboriously carried on their long march. The Ndebele also sought to gain the alliance of the peoples along the Zambesi and on its islands. A combined assault on the Kololo was planned. Sebetwane, however, succeeded in dealing with his enemies separately. His people had by then become thoroughly familiar with the use of canoes and he had won the loyalty of most of the Lozi. He was thus able to muster a large canoe fleet and with this he gave battle to the river peoples at Upa and completely defeated them. The battle, though victorious, almost ended in a disaster for Sebetwane's canoe was overturned and he narrowly escaped drowning. After this victory Sebetwane was free to deal with the main Ndebele force. His tactics were aimed at reducing them to starvation by withdrawing his people and their food supplies on to the islands, while his canoe fleet with its superior skill and knowledge of the waters prevented the enemy from using the canoes they had brought with them. His plan proved perfectly success-

1 Bryant: *Olden Times*, pp. 471–2, and E. Smith, op. cit.
2 D. Livingstone: *Missionary Travels and Researches*, p. 88.

ful. 'After some time in this way, Sebituane went in a canoe towards them, and addressing them by an interpreter, asked why they wished to kill him; he had never attacked them, never harmed their chief: "Au!" he continued, "the guilt is on your side."'[1] The Ndebele did not deign to reply and the regiments set off for home. Only a few survivors managed to get back. They arrived in a starving condition.[2]

The Ndebele attack had shown the danger of an invader gaining the support of the riverain peoples. Sebetwane decided to punish them for their assistance to his enemies and to extend his kingdom to bring them under his authority. Transporting his warriors by canoe he was able to storm their island fastnesses and established his rule as far as the Victoria Falls.

Once the Ndebele threat had been removed Sebetwane was free to consolidate the kingdom he had conquered. Like Moshesh he did not employ the age-regiment system for this purpose. During the long march northward from Dithakong small numbers of captives had been taken by the Kololo from the tribes with whom they fought, but as these were few and belonged to groups whose culture was basically similar to that of the main body, their absorption did not pose any serious problem. With the conquest of the Lozi, however, a much more difficult situation was created. The great mass of conquered peoples whom the Kololo referred to as Kalaka not only spoke languages quite different from that of their conquerors but were sharply differentiated from them in culture, for they belonged to the Central Bantu with a matrilineal family system quite different from that of their conquerors. Sebetwane, however, had the breadth of imagination to realize that the stability of his conquests depended on attaching the loyalty of the subject peoples to himself. He discouraged the Kololo from adopting the attitudes of a dominant aristocracy and consciously strove to fuse the two groups into a single people. Though many Kololo were appointed as local chiefs, indigenous headmen were also often confirmed in their positions over their own people. Sebetwane himself married wives from the local people and took their leaders into his confidence. His policy of fusion was embodied in the decree that 'all are children of the chief'.[3] During his lifetime this policy met with remarkable success. The Lozi and even the river peoples adopted the name Kololo and took pride in the daring military exploits with which it was associated.[4]

1 Ibid., p. 88.
2 R. Moffat, *Matabele Journals*, pp. 233, 239–40.
3 D. Livingstone: *Missionary Travels and Researches*, p. 197.
4 The porters whom Livingstone took down the Zambesi came mainly from the conquered peoples but this did not prevent them from feeling a pride amounting to arrogance in being Kololo.

In spite of the considerable success of Sebetwane's attempts to amalgamate the conquered peoples with his own, some disquieting signs could be seen even in his lifetime. The southern Sotho, coming from a malaria-free climate, had less resistance to the disease than the indigenous peoples of the Barotse plain. The central core of the new state thus tended to dwindle rapidly and in 1851 Sebetwane moved his capital from the centre of the flood plain to higher ground at Linyanti. In the same year Mambari traders from Angola, who had previously attempted unsuccessfully to open trade with the Lozi kingdom, introduced the Slave Trade into his domains. This, however, remained on a small scale at first. When Livingstone first visited the Kololo in 1851 their kingdom seemed to be firmly established and likely to survive as a permanent institution. Sebetwane, in spite of his long and arduous adventures, was still in full vigour and appeared at the height of his powers. He was delighted to hear of the arrival of white men with whom he had long sought to establish contact. He hastened to meet the explorer and long before dawn he came to sit at Livingstone's camp-fire and told him the story of his long wanderings and many battles. Livingstone was very impressed by the personality of the chief and his reputation for bravery. He compared the account of his adventures to the 'Commentaries' of Caesar. Yet in spite of his warlike career Sebetwane did not revel in fighting for its own sake. His migration, with its long series of wars and battles, had been forced upon him by the needs of survival, and the wise and gentle policy he adopted towards the conquered Lozi gives a better picture of his character than the bare record of his numerous campaigns. As Livingstone remarked, 'He had lived a life of war, yet no one apparently desired peace more than he did.'[1] The year of Livingstone's visit was, however, a tragic one for the Kololo. The wound which Sebetwane had suffered in his first battle with the Ngwaketsi twenty-seven years earlier and which had apparently healed, reopened. The chief fell into a fever and quickly passed away.[2]

Before his death Sebetwane had decided to install his favourite daughter Mamochisane in his place instead of his son, Sekeletu. His choice may have been influenced by the matrilineal customs of the Lozi but the strongly patriarchal and patrilineal principles of the original Kololo culture created a serious problem. According to southern Sotho tradition a married woman was under the authority of her husband and if Mamochisane were to marry she could no longer rule. Sebetwane

1 D. Livingstone: *Missionary Travels and Researches*, p. 86.

2 According to a Kololo tradition this was caused by Sebetwane falling off Livingstone's horse, which he had insisted on riding. See E. Smith, op. cit. Livingstone's account contains no mention of this and he remained on good terms with Sebetwane's successor and the Kololo people.

had therefore suggested that she should not marry but take any men she liked as lovers. Mamochisane, however, found this situation intolerable, for the other women mocked at her calling her lover her wife. Thus when Sebetwane died she refused to accept the succession. The problem was further complicated by another member of the family, Mpepe, who argued that Sekeletu was not the legal son of Sebetwane as his mother had previously been married to another chief. Sekeletu therefore tried to persuade his sister to retain the throne while he would act as war leader. A great *pitso* was held which lasted for three days and eventually Mamochisane stood up and bursting into tears said to her brother, 'I have been a chief only because my father wished it. I always would have preferred to be married and have a family like other women. You, Sekeletu, must be chief and build up your father's house.'[1]

The man on whom the chieftaincy was thus unwillingly thrust turned out to be an unfortunate choice. He lacked his father's imagination and the statesmanship which was able to bridge the gulf between peoples of different culture. He contracted leprosy and the development of this unfamiliar and incurable disease produced in his naturally suspicious temperament a morbid obsession with the idea that he was bewitched. His suspicions fell first on the subject peoples whose foreign ways were naturally regarded as mysterious and evil. He thus reversed the wise policy which Sebetwane had pursued. He married only Kololo wives, created only Kololo chiefs and surrounded himself with advisers drawn from his own tribal group. With this example from their chief, his Kololo subjects naturally took advantage of their opportunity to arrogate to themselves the position of an exploiting aristocracy subsisting on tribute wrung from the subject peoples. Livingstone noticed that the older Kololo still went out to farm but the younger ones, accustomed to domineering over the subject groups, were disinclined to work of any kind and expected their subjects to do all the manual labour.

Sekeletu's suspicions were not confined to his non-Kololo subjects. He was even more afraid of leading members of his own group who might have pretensions to succeed him. Many of the more important men were put to death and Sekeletu eventually withdrew almost entirely from public life, refusing to see any but a small group of favourites.[2] Thus he inevitably lost control over the kingdom. His subordinate chiefs did as they pleased without reference to his authority and the riverain peoples regained their independence.[3] Sekeletu's rule became so unpopular that when he ordered the execution of a man who had

1 D. Livingstone: *Missionary Travels and Researches*, p. 179.
2 David and Charles Livingstone: *Expedition to the Zambesi*, p. 272.
3 Ibid.

openly defied his authority the spectators jeered at the executioners, threatening them with a similar fate.[1]

As the subject peoples became increasingly disaffected the refugee group who had fled up the Leambye River were provided with the opportunity to win back the loyalty of the subject Lozi to their old dynasty. Messengers were sent with the object of seducing the Lozi from their loyalty to the Kololo king. Shortly before Livingstone's visit in 1860 a considerable rebellion took place and the rebels succeeded in escaping to rejoin the heir to the old Lozi line, Masiku. On their way they killed a man in order to create a blood feud between Masiku and the Kololo.[2]

While these disturbing events were taking place the numbers of the Kololo nucleus continued to decline. Malaria took its toll and Sekeletu recognized that the salvation of his people lay in returning to the Kafue highlands, but fear of the Ndebele prevented the move being made. By 1860 disintegration had gone so far that leading Kololo told Livingstone they feared the tribe was breaking up.[3] Four years later the blow fell. When Sekeletu died the Kololo, instead of combining their forces, weakened themselves in a succession dispute. The majority of the tribe was opposed to Mpololo, Sekeletu's uncle, acting as regent. He was defeated and killed. His followers fled to the neighbourhood of Lake Ngami. This was the signal for a violent Lozi insurrection which assumed the form of a national revolution under the leadership of Sipopa, successor to Masiku. All the male Kololo who fell into the hands of the insurgents were put to death, though the women were kept as wives for the chief men. A small remnant of the Kololo escaped to take refuge with the Tawana of Lake Ngami.

In Barotseland itself the short reign of Sipopa was followed by a long period of turbulent politics until the great Lozi ruler, Lewanika, finally succeeded in consolidating his authority and reconstituting the kingdom under indigenous rule. Though the Kololo kingdom had completely collapsed the short period of Kololo rule left a permanent mark on Lozi society. The patrilineal descent pattern of the conquerors permanently altered the matrilineal customs of earlier times to a bilateral descent pattern. The Kololo language had gained such a hold that even to this day the Lozi speak a tongue which belongs to the southern Sotho language group. The strength and extent of Lewanika's rule also reflected the centralizing consequences of the Kololo conquest which must be regarded as largely responsible for the fact that the Lozi kingdom remains today a powerful bloc within the new state of Zambia.

1 David and Charles Livingstone: *Expedition to the Zambesi*, p. 292.
2 Ibid., p. 273. 3 Ibid., p. 266.

The Kololo Kingdoms of the Shire River

Though the Kololo empire collapsed a strange freak of fortune ensured that the Kololo name should appear again in African history, this time on the banks of the Shire River. When Livingstone first visited Sebetwane he was so impressed by the character of the chief that he made his kingdom the base for his journeys to Angola and down the Zambesi. For these expeditions he recruited Kololo porters and in 1860 he made an expedition up the Zambesi to Barotseland to return them to their homes. Sixteen of them, however, preferred to remain behind with the local wives they had married in a small village on the Shire River. They retained a few guns they had acquired from the missionary and a few English words.[1] Partly as a result of their association with Livingstone but also in reaction to the situation in which they found themselves, they were strongly opposed to the Slave Trade and became the champions of the local people against slave raiders. Most important of all, their pride in the warlike reputation of the Kololo gave them tremendous self-confidence, and their experience of an extensive state organization helped them to organize the local people for defence. Conditions in the Shire Valley were such as to set a premium on leadership. Slave-raiding by the Portuguese and their agents and by the expanding Yao had thrown the ill-organized Nganja into chaos and despair. The establishment of the Maseko Ngoni on the Kirk Highlands to the west of the Shire River and the frequent raids of their regiments completed the picture of havoc and destruction. The Kololo in these circumstances were able to offer a measure of security. They gradually brought the Nganja of the entire Shire Valley under their control, together with considerable numbers of Yao refugees, to form a state in which they constituted a ruling aristocracy. After defeating the existing Nganja chiefs and establishing their authority, the two strongest personalities among the Kololo, Molokwa and Kasisi, divided the conquered territory between themselves. They distributed the other Kololo at strategic points along the river to act as chiefs over the subject people. Mindful of their association with Livingstone, the Kololo welcomed the Livingstonia Mission and their aid made it possible for the expedition's vessel to be transported to Lake Nyasa. By this time their dependants amounted to thousands and most of the Shire Valley was under their control.[2]

The strength of the Kololo political organization, their possession of guns and the good relationships they established with the Yao gave them

1 They used the English greeting 'Good morning, sir' as a mark of distinction. Young: *Nyassa*, pp. 172–3.
2 Young, op. cit., p. 36.

immunity from attacks from the east, but they were threatened by serious danger from two other directions—the Portuguese in the south and the Ngoni in the west. The Kololo were strong enough to repel the Portuguese slave-raiding parties and prevented the extension of Portuguese influence up the Shire. The Ngoni were a more serious threat. Not only did they raid as far as the banks of the river but in 1875 they crossed it and began to devastate the Yao villages to the east.[1] Kasisi, who united the Kololo under his command after the death of Molokwa, took determined action to deal with the danger. The Kololo were gathered together on the eastern bank and all the fords of the upper river were protected by stockaded villages.[2] These measures could not hold back the superior military force of the Ngoni indefinitely and in 1884 they terrorized the Kololo chief, guarding one of the fords, into allowing them to pass. They devastated the Shire Highlands until the Blantyre missionaries persuaded them to retire but they did not make a major attack on the Kololo themselves.

Situated as they were along the strategic link between the Zambesi and Lake Nyasa the Kololo were inevitably caught up in the process of European imperial competition in Africa. The Portuguese were infuriated by British attempts to seize the territory which they had long regarded as falling vaguely under their sovereignty and in 1889 the Serpa Pinto expedition tried to force its way through the Kololo towards the lake. The Kololo, however, hastily signed treaties with the British and Johnston's ultimatum ensured that they would make part of present-day Nyasaland. The new administration, however, in spite of the historic association of the Kololo with the British, proved little more sympathetic to them than the Portuguese might have been expected to be. Their pretensions to a continuing measure of independence were forcibly suppressed and their territory was brought under strict control. The brief period in which the companions of Livingstone played an important part in African history had come to an end. Their work had, however, ensured the survival of the Nganja who now form the bulk of the population in the Shire Valley. Some of their descendants still rule as chiefs among these people, from whom they cannot now be distinguished.

1 See above, Chapter 5, p. 78.
2 See W. T. Rangeley, 'The Makololo', *Nyasaland Journal*.

9 Mzilikazi and the Ndebele

One of the smaller Nguni-speaking tribes which was caught up in the struggles of rival groups which preceded the emergence of the Zulu was the Khumalo. Unable to maintain their independence under their chief, Mashobane, they accepted the suzerainty of Zwide, but when the rivalry between the Ndwandwe and the Mthethwa broke into open war and Dingiswayo walked into Zwide's trap the Khumalo were suspected of intrigue with the enemy. Mashobane was summoned to Zwide's court and put to death. The leadership of the Khumalo then devolved upon the young prince, Mzilikazi. Much of his childhood had been spent at Zwide's court and on his father's death the Ndwandwe overlord had sufficient confidence in the young man to place him in his father's position.

By nature Mzilikazi seems to have been a peaceable, even gentle soul. Moffat, who met him first in 1829, describes him as '... rather below the middle size, lusty, has rather a pleasing and soft countenance and is exceedingly affable in his manners. His voice is soft and feminine and cheerfulness predominates in him. He does not appear to be passionate ...'[1] He was also physically athletic and brave in the face of danger. In battle he was often in the front line and his body was marked by several scars from enemy spears. He was highly intelligent, shrewd and observing and was capable of following an argument even when he appeared to be paying no attention. An able general, he was quick to adopt new tactics and to see the advantages of new weapons. A born leader of men, he knew how to mingle clemency with severity, to keep his followers under firm control and to win the allegiance of men whose tribes and families he had destroyed. Through a life of almost continuous warfare, he survived to die peacefully of old age leaving as his legacy a new people made up of many different elements, the Ndebele.

In the circumstances in which he was placed, ruling a people organized on Zulu military lines, he could not afford to leave his warriors idle. Living, as he came to do, far from his original home, surrounded by alien peoples, he could not afford to tolerate any affront or challenge to

1 Moffat: *Matabele Journals*, ed. Wallis, vol. I, p. 29.

his supremacy. Thus he came to earn the reputation of one of the most savage destroyers of human life in the history of South Africa: a tyrant who wallowed in blood and rejoiced in the smoke of burning villages. The massacre of some of the first Boer trekkers to enter the Transvaal by Ndebele regiments has helped to strengthen his reputation as a monster of cruelty.

Yet the records of those who met and knew him give a very different picture. His outward pride and self-confidence were largely bravado concealing a deep sense of insecurity. In spite of his wide conquests he was deeply conscious of the weakness of his military position and far from being the ruthless enemy of the whites he was very anxious to establish good relations with them. European visitors found a ready welcome at his court and he was eager to enter into alliance with the Cape Government which he hoped might be able to restrain the marauding activities of the half-castes on his borders. The attack on the Boer trekking parties was an unfortunate mistake. The Boers entering his territory unannounced were taken for a hostile Griqua invasion.[1]

It was not only in the military sense that Mzilikazi felt insecure. The loss of his father while he was still a youth left him with a deep sense of emotional deprivation. When he met Moffat he found in the stern and uncompromising attitude of the pioneer missionary the qualities of a father-figure. 'He added that, as his father was dead, Molimo had raised or, more literally, made for him another father in myself, and in future he would call me Machobane.'[2] Mzilikazi indulged the missionary in every way he could and could hardly bear to be separated from him. There is something almost pathetic in the deep devotion of the war chief of the Ndebele for the missionary of Kuruman—a friendship between two men with superficially so little in common, that survived the passage of time and the vicissitudes of war to end only with the death of the Ndebele king. The paradox of Mzilikazi's life and character is well brought out by John Mackenzie, who knew him in his old age. After describing the fearful destruction caused by the Ndebele regiments he remarks: 'But as a matter of fact the master spirit animating and regulating all these movements was personally averse to pain and suffering. Even his oxen Moselekatse did not permit to be lashed severely by the long whip of the wagon driver; his men were allowed to beat them only with green wands cut from the bushes in the forest.'[3]

Though he had been established by Zwide in his father's place, Mzilikazi had every reason to fear that the jealousy of his overlord would not

1 See below, p. 145.
2 Moffat: *Matabele Journals*, vol. I, p. 16.
3 J. Mackenzie: *Ten Years North of the Orange River*, pp. 310–11.

leave him long untouched and at the first opportunity he transferred his allegiance to Shaka. His qualities of courage and intelligence soon gained him the favour of his new leader. In his case Shaka made an exception to his normal rule that military command was entrusted to commoners. Mzilikazi was made a regimental *induna* and furthermore the regiment he commanded appears to have consisted largely of members of his own tribe. This may have been because the Khumalo joined the Zulu at an early stage in the development of the kingdom. They came as a consolidated group voluntarily offering their allegiance rather than as a defeated tribe. This arrangement produced a serious weakness in the Zulu state, for Mzilikazi could command the loyalty of his followers not only as the commander appointed by the king but also by virtue of his hereditary position. The possibility of secession was inherent in the situation.

About 1821 the rupture came. Whether Mzilikazi resented his subordinate position or whether he feared the jealousy of Shaka he determined to make a bid for independence. He had been sent to conduct a raid against a Sotho tribe to the north-west of Zululand and had returned with a large booty of cattle, but instead of despatching them to his overlord he kept them for himself. This action amounted to a direct denial of Shaka's political authority. Messengers were sent to demand the cattle but Mzilikazi turned them away and cut off their ostrich-feather plumes as a token of defiance. It was an open declaration of war. The Zulu regiments marched at once against the rebellious chief. Taking advantage of a strong hill position the Khumalo beat off the first assault but a second more determined effort followed and Mzilikazi's defensive position was stormed. He and his followers saved themselves by flight and slipped across the escarpment onto the interior plateau.

There Mzilikazi and his small band of warriors found themselves surrounded by the far more numerous Sotho-speaking tribes. In spite of their small numbers, the military discipline and Zulu fighting tactics of Mzilikazi's men gave them an immense advantage over their potential enemies who were still accustomed to the mild warfare of the pre-Shaka period. Smashing all opposition to their passage, Mzilikazi and the Ndebele cut a path northward to escape the reach of Shaka's vengeance. About 1824 they reached the upper Oliphant's River where they built a settlement and halted for a while. This settlement was called, appropriately enough, Eku Pumeleni (the resting place). From this headquarters Mzilikazi sent his regiments on far-flung raids capturing cattle, destroying towns and bringing back women and children to reinforce his fighting stock. One expedition went as far west as the

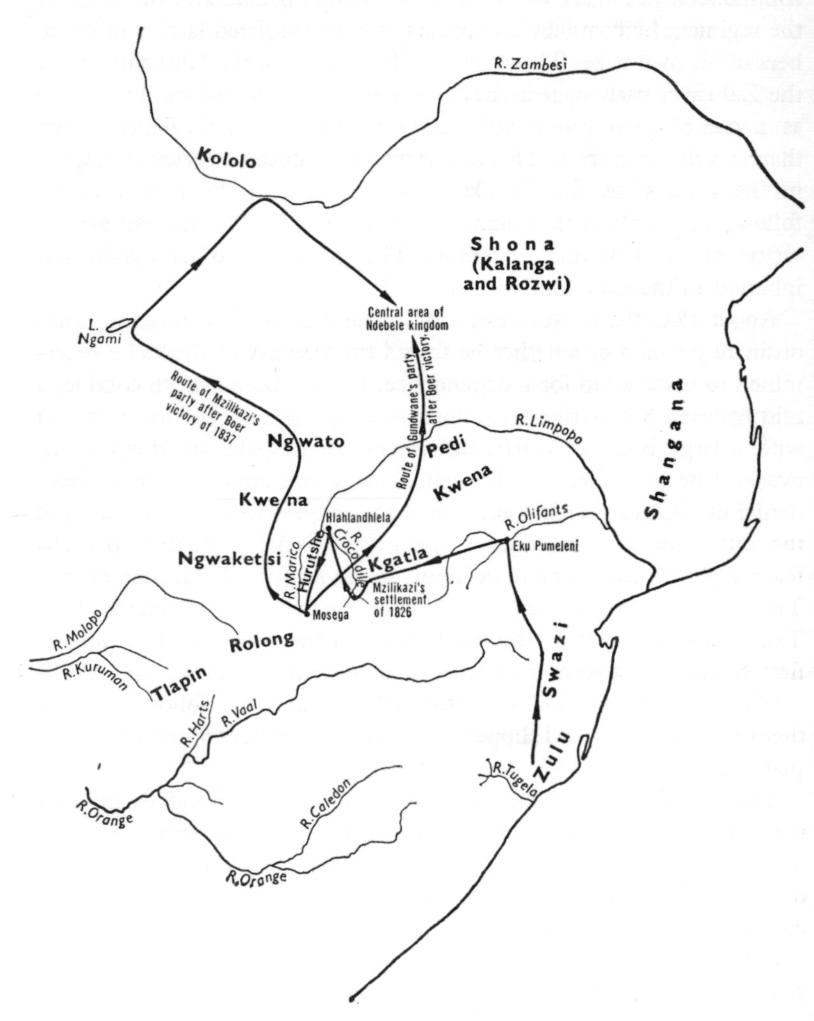

Approximate route of the Ndebele under Mzilikazi

Tswana country where it attacked two other marauders, Moletsane and Sebetwane.[1] The Sotho of the north-eastern Transvaal suffered most at this period. On the open plains no tribe could stand before him. In the Zoutpansberg range, however, the northern Sotho found a natural defensive terrain not dissimilar from the Basuto mountain massif. Here the Pedi tribe, taking refuge on inaccessible mountain-tops, beat off the Ndebele regiments with showers of stones and spears. Mzilikazi abandoned the attempt to storm their fastnesses for some time and the Pedi danced for joy hurling insults at the Ndebele and singing in triumph. 'It sleeps, it is tired, is the evil beast. Its roars trouble us no more.'[2] Mzilikazi's stay in Eku Pumeleni was not entirely satisfactory. Not only did the Pedi foil him but the position was too close to Zululand to be permanently secure from Shaka's regiments. The area could not provide adequate grazing for the immense herds which had come into his possession and the situation was made worse by a severe drought in the summer of 1824–25.[3] So in 1825 the temporary headquarters were abandoned and the Ndebele moved westward into the central Transvaal.

They first settled near the junction of the Apies and Vaal Rivers but soon afterwards moved to more suitable ground near the eastern edge of the Magaliesberg range not far from modern Pretoria. The area then knew a relatively dense Bantu population, belonging mainly to branches of the Kwena, concentrated in settlements of substantial size. Huts of a more solid type than those of the east-coast Bantu were built and the lower courses of the walls as well as the cattle enclosures were often constructed of stone. The density of the population and its settled way of life can be seen in Moffat's account of his journey to meet the Ndebele king in 1829. Travelling towards the Ndebele settlement from Kuruman he found himself on a wide plain dotted with small chains of mountains and conical hills, '. . . along the bases of which lay the ruins of innumerable towns, some of amazing extent. . . . The ruined towns exhibited signs of immense labour and perseverance, every fence being composed of stones, averaging five or six feet high, raised apparently without either mortar, lime, or hammer.'[4]

The arrival of the Ndebele brought the era of peaceful development among the northern Sotho to a sudden and violent end. Between 1825 and 1834 the Ndebele regiments devastated the central and northern Transvaal. The Kwena in particular were fearfully decimated. Captured

1 See above, Chapter 6, p. 96, and Chapter 8, p. 116.
2 Bryant: *Olden Times*, p. 427.
3 Ibid., p. 425. Andrew Smith confirms that shortage of water was the cause of the abandonment of the settlement. *Andrew Smith's Diary*, vol. II, p. 101.
4 Moffat: *Matabele Journals*, vol. I, p. 8.

towns were set on fire, the inhabitants butchered and the herds seized to increase the vast stock at the king's disposal. Captured women and children were incorporated with the Ndebele and came to identify themselves with their conquerors. The population of large areas was virtually exterminated. Early in 1829 McLuckie and Schoon, two traders from the Cape, entered the Ndebele domains from the south-west and visited Mzilikazi. McLuckie later told a friend that for six weeks of his journey he saw no human beings or any sign of human life except the burnt ruins of towns and skeletons.[1] Archbell and Moffat, who met Mzilikazi together at the end of 1829 but had approached his kingdom by different routes, both confirm that the Ndebele headquarters were surrounded by a vast extent of virtually depopulated country. To such a state of desolation had the plains of the Transvaal been reduced that lions and other wild beasts roamed about at will and on the edges of Mzilikazi's domain Moffat found a few wretched Kwena living in huts built on the branches of trees to avoid the lions which prowled about by night underneath.

The extent of this depopulation should not be exaggerated. There can be no doubt that some of the original population survived in inaccessible places unseen by travellers on their journeys. After the departure of the Ndebele, population would no doubt have grown up once again, yet as late as 1835, three years after Mzilikazi had moved his capital westward to the Hurutshe country, Andrew Smith could say of the country round the previous Ndebele settlement, 'The population here at one time must have been very great; now not a single inhabitant to be seen. The whole of the tract over which we have travelled since leaving the kraal where Masalacatzie was residing might be thickly colonized.'[2] In the course of these devastating campaigns the Pedi of the northern Transvaal were not forgotten. Mzilikazi's regiments, now reinforced by many newly incorporated recruits, succeeded in storming their mountain strongholds and many captives were seized and forced to take part in building Mzilikazi's chief military town, Em Hlahlandhlela, as a penance for the insults they had hurled at the mighty bull elephant.

At the settlement in the central Transvaal the Ndebele state crystallized along the lines on which it was subsequently to develop. The regimental system of the Zulu was retained, each regiment being accommodated in a special military settlement under the command of an *induna*. As in the case of the Zulu each of these military towns was regarded as a section of the royal household and contained some of Mzilikazi's wives. In the case of the Ndebele, however, the army and the civilian

1 Tabler: *The Far Interior*, p. 188.
2 *Andrew Smith's Diary*, vol. II, p. 87.

population could not be distinguished from one another. The whole group were immigrants living by force of arms in an alien country. There was thus no hierarchy of territorial chiefs separate from that of the military *indunas*. The regimental headquarters constituted the territorial divisions of the tribe as a whole.

The young men remained permanently in the military settlements and were not allowed to marry. After a regiment had distinguished itself in battle, however, its members were given the right to wear the head-ring of manhood and lead a family life. They were settled in small villages scattered around the military towns and they and their families were responsible for herding the cattle and performing the agricultural work of the community. Nevertheless they were still regarded as members of their regiment and could be called up for active service in times of war. Mzilikazi's army thus consisted of two sections—a permanent standing force of young men known as *machaha* and a reserve of older married men who were only mobilized in times of emergency or for major campaigns.[1] Captive boys were often given to their captors to serve as weapon-bearers but when they grew older they were incorporated in the regiments. They were regarded very much as inferiors by the true Nguni-speaking Ndebele, who ordered them '. . . about like dogs and if they wish any peace or favour they are necessitated to supplicate young Matabeli in a most humiliating manner, . . . and give utterance to the most endearing and at the same time the most submissive expressions such as Baba, kosi etc.'[2] Nevertheless as they fought alongside the true Ndebele in the regiments they came to develop a sense of pride and loyalty to their new community and the contempt to which they were subject encouraged the rapid adoption of the Nguni language and the culture of the dominant class.

The age-regiment system amongst the Ndebele implied other features typical of the Zulu system. Power was highly centralized and was exercised through a commoner bureaucracy of *indunas* rather than through a hierarchy of traditional chiefs. Members of the royal lineage did indeed enjoy a privileged aristocratic status and were known as *numzana* but they exercised less effective power than the *indunas*.[3] As in the Zulu system, the warriors received their arms from the chief and were fed from the products of the royal herds. These were inflated to enormous proportions by a long series of successful wars. Private individuals could own cattle as well as the king but even in these cases their use was regulated by Mzilikazi and no one could slaughter a beast without his consent.[4]

1 Ibid., p. 67. 2 Ibid., pp. 138–9. 3 Ibid., p. 79.
4 Moffat: *Matabele Journals*, vol. I, p. 25.

Mzilikazi does not seem to have practised Shaka's system of maintaining a vast harem of concubines but a large proportion of the marriageable girls were regarded as wards of the king. He gave them to warriors as a mark of favour and collected the marriage dowry for them.[1] Both Moffat and Archbell were impressed by the concentration of power in Mzilikazi's hands. As Moffat put it, 'The government of the Matabele is tyrannical in the strictest sense of the word. All the people as well as what they possess, are considered Moselekatse's. His word is law, and he has only to lift his finger and his order is promptly carried into execution.'[2] Archbell adds that '. . . he has obtained such authority among his People that their very senses are influenced by him; so that nothing delights his People that does not delight him and if he is well pleased his people are in exstacy'.[3] Nevertheless he was always careful to preserve traditional constitutional forms. When important trials took place they were conducted publicly in the cattle enclosure. Thorough discussion was allowed and only after everyone had had his say would the king retire with his principal advisers to consider his verdict.[4] His following at this time was estimated by Archbell at sixty thousand, spread out over an area of about two hundred square miles. From every corner of this territory messengers were constantly appearing before the king to inform him of the latest news.

At this settlement Mzilikazi received unexpected reinforcements of Nguni-speaking people from his homeland. After the defeat of Sikhunyane in 1826 and the final break-up of the Ndwandwe, some of his followers joined the Ndebele while others went to swell the ranks of Soshangane. Then after the defeat of the Hlubi by the Ngwane in Transorangia, Mehlomakhulu led a large body of Hlubi refugees into the Transvaal. They were met by an Ndebele regiment and conducted to the king who received them gladly and intended to incorporate them with his own following. Mehlomakhulu was in high favour at first with Mzilikazi but after some time he began to fear that his popularity with the people and his strong position as the leader of a powerful group of followers would excite the jealousy of his overlord. He succeeded in escaping with his followers and fled to the south-east, hotly pursued by the Ndebele. Fortunately his pursuers were involved in conflict with the Ngwane and Mehlomakhulu escaped over the Drakensberg to enter the seething cauldron of tribal warfare in northern Pondoland.

In spite of Mzilikazi's apparent military and political strength his

1 Moffat: *Matabele Journals*, vol. I, p. 26. This system was maintained after the Ndebele move to modern Southern Rhodesia. See Mackenzie: *Ten Years North of the Orange River*, p. 329.
2 Moffat: *Matabele Journals*, vol. I, p. 24.
3 Archbell to Secretaries, Wesleyan Missionary Society, Platberg, 31 Dec. 1829, M.M.S. 1829/37.
4 Moffat: *Matabele Journals*, vol. I, pp. 93–4.

position in his new home was very insecure. The conqueror of so many tribes was conscious that a single battle might dissipate his following like smoke. Danger faced him on two fronts. To the south were groups of Hottentots and half-caste banditti. Among these were the scattered clans of the Korana and in particular the Springbok clan led by Jan Bloem, the half-caste son of the notorious German outlaw. There were also bands of dissident Griquas who had broken away from the main body in protest against Waterboer's refusal to tolerate cattle-raiding. The numbers of these plundering bands were small, but firearms and horses gave them a strength out of proportion to their numbers. By employing the tactics adopted by the Griquas at the battle of Dithakong they could prove more than a match for the Ndebele regiments and defeat forces far larger than themselves. Their small numbers made it difficult for them to press a victory home, but if they associated themselves with Bantu allies the Ndebele kingdom might be completely destroyed. This possibility was ever present as tribes reduced to poverty by the Ndebele and other predatory groups were naturally ready to participate in an assault on the common enemy.

To the east an even greater danger threatened from the regiments of the Zulu themselves. The death of Shaka in 1828 and the succession of Dingane increased, rather than diminished, the threat from this quarter. The new ruler was personally inclined to peaceful pursuits but the regimental system could not be disbanded and the revolt of Nqeto[1] forcibly illustrated the need to keep the warriors occupied in external wars if they were to be prevented from venting their energies in civil strife. The old quarrel with Mzilikazi offered Dingane an excellent opportunity to employ his regiments on a task worthy of their mettle and at a distance from his own rather unsteady seat of power.

The first serious attack on the Ndebele position came in 1829. A number of minor raids on Ndebele outposts had excited the cupidity of the Korana. An Ndebele raiding party which seized some of Moletsane's cattle encouraged him to seek revenge and when the Korana chief, Haip, who had also suffered from an Ndebele plundering party, went to seek his alliance he offered his full support.[2] The old quarrel between the Taung and the Rolong which had been eased by Hodgson's visit to Moletsane in 1827 was now completely forgotten and the two tribes made common cause against Mzilikazi. Jan Bloem was persuaded to give his support to the expedition and the composite force set off on a campaign of plunder and revenge.

The Ndebele could not stand against the guns of the Korana and

1 See below, Chapter 10, p. 159.
2 *Andrew Smith's Diary*, vol. I, pp. 158, 378.

abandoned vast herds to the enemy. But with the capture of the cattle the momentum and coherence of the coalition was lost. No attempt at a systematic conquest was made and all attention was concentrated on conveying the captured cattle home. The Korana, over-confident at their easy victory, travelled by easy stages while Moletsane, more versed in the ways of the Ndebele, pushed on as hard as he could go. On the third or fourth night the Ndebele regiments caught up with the Korana, surrounded their camp and made a surprise attack at dawn. The careless Korana had taken no precautions and were caught off their guard. Some of them succeeded in escaping on their horses but they left a number of guns and the bulk of the cattle in the hands of the victors. The regiments then set off in pursuit of the Taung and Rolong but Moletsane had crossed the Vaal and the Orange before his enemy caught up with him.[1] This encounter, though it ended in an Ndebele victory, left a profound impression on the mind of Mzilikazi and his people. On Moffat's second journey to visit the king, he noticed that the story of the struggle with Jan Bloem featured prominently in the praises of the chief.[2] Though his military reputation had been strengthened Mzilikazi fully appreciated the difficulty of his situation. His regiments had been helpless against the Korana guns and victory had only been won by surprise. He now became most anxious to learn the use of the new weapons he had captured and to increase his supplies of guns and horses. It was for this reason that he took steps to get in contact with the whites.[3]

These new contacts did little to alter the exposed military situation in which Mzilikazi found himself. The year after Moffat's visit the Ndebele king was faced by an attack of the Zulu army. The Ndebele, though more than a match for the less organized Sotho-speaking tribes, had not the discipline and coherence of the Zulu themselves, but the Zulu force constituted only a part of the Zulu army and was far from home in unfamiliar country. Mzilikazi was fighting for survival with all his available forces on their home ground. Thus the struggle ended without any decisive victory on either side. The Zulu retreated taking with them a considerable number of Ndebele cattle.

Hardly had the danger from the Zulu receded than the Ndebele were attacked again from the south. The idea of an alliance between the

1 P. Becker: *Path of Blood*, p. 89.

2 Moffat: *Matabele Journals*, vol. I, pp. 89–90.

3 His purpose was made clear during the visit of Schoon and McLuckie. It also lay behind his embassy to Kuruman and his reception of Moffat and Archbell at the end of 1829. See Tabler: *The Far Interior*, p. 188. Also Archbell to Secretaries, Wesleyan Missionary Society, 31 Dec. 1829, M.M.S. 1829/37.

Bantu enemies of Mzilikazi and the Koranas and Griquas with their firearms was renewed. The initiative in forming this new coalition was taken by the old half-caste leader, Barend-Barends. Dissatisfied with the rule of Waterboer and his missionary advisers, he had withdrawn to his own settlement at Boetsap. He did not, however, become one of the lawless Bergenaars but remained on reasonably good terms with the missionaries. He had taken part in the battle of Dithakong and in 1829 he accompanied Archbell on his visit to Mzilikazi. His experiences on this journey had made him horrified at the devastation committed by the Ndebele and at the same time brought to his notice the vast herds in Mzilikazi's keeping. During this expedition he had met Pilane, chief of the Kgatla, who urged him to assist in a campaign against Mzilikazi. These impressions combined in the mind of the old leader to form a grandiose vision. He began to see himself as the man chosen by destiny to liberate the country from the Ndebele scourge and restore it to its original owners. Griquas and Koranas of many different groups flocked to join the projected expedition which was reinforced by contingents of the Taung, Rolong and many other Tswana tribes. Eventually a thousand armed horsemen were assembled together with a much larger number of Bantu allies and the great host set out, followed by a long train of wagons carrying ammunition and provisions. A camp was made at the site of the old Rolong capital, Maquassie. There Barend-Barends explained the purpose of the campaign. The expedition was not to cease until the Ndebele had been completely defeated. Captured cattle were to be returned to their original owners. Then the fighting men set off, leaving their old leader to await their victorious return.

The Barend-Barends commando was a force which might well have defeated the Ndebele even if these had been able to oppose it with their full strength, but in fact the bulk of Mzilikazi's regiments were away on an expedition to raid the Ngwato. Only the married men remained to oppose the coalition forces. The Griqua-led attack met little opposition. One or two cattle posts were taken at the first onslaught then the Ndebele began to fly in all directions. Great herds of cattle were taken and with a little determination the object of the campaign could have been achieved. But even before the commando reached the Ndebele dissension had begun to appear in its ranks. The grand project of old Barend-Barends had little appeal to the lawless vagabonds who made up the bulk of the force and regarded the expedition as nothing more than a cattle raid on an unusually large scale.[1] The idea of distributing the spoils to their original owners was an especial source of disagreement. Once the cattle were in their hands all thought of the original

1 *Andrew Smith's Diary*, vol. I, pp. 381–4.

plan was at once abandoned. Everyone struggled to round up cattle for himself and instead of following the retreating Ndebele the commando hastened to withdraw with its spoils. In spite of the lessons of the earlier disaster, the instructions of Barend-Barends, and the advice of some captured women who warned them that the older men who were the only force then present at the Ndebele capital specialized in night attacks, the Griquas made the same elementary mistake that had caused the downfall of Jan Bloem's party. While still only a few days' journey from the Ndebele settlement they camped on open ground near a small hill, taking no precautions against surprise attack. One of the leaders, Gert Hoogman, did indeed point out the need to keep a watch and said that he expected an Ndebele attack that night but so elated were the majority at their easy victory that they treated the possibility with contempt. A member of the Heemraad, Jan Pienaar, said, 'Answer how shall the Caffers come; the Caffers do not fight, how then shall they come to night?'[1] Nothing more was said and then they went to sleep with no one placed to watch.

Once again the Ndebele regiments silently surrounded their sleeping foes. Then shortly before dawn while the moonlight was still resting on the hills they seized their spears and charged. One of the Griquas saw them when they were still at about two hundred yards and shouted to his companions who leapt for their guns but by this time the Ndebele were almost upon them screaming and beating their shields. The Taung and Rolong were the first to feel the brunt of the Ndebele attack. Fleeing in panic they burst in among the Griquas with such force that many had the guns forced out of their hands. All organized resistance was impossible and the only hope was flight, but the Ndebele were upon them and only about three hundred managed to get away to bring the news of the disaster to old Barend-Barends.[2]

To recoup his losses Mzilikazi then sent a strong expedition to chastise Moletsane and the Taung. This force passed on to reach the Basuto capital at Thaba Bosigo but the attempt to storm the mountain was defeated and on the receipt of a conciliatory gift of cattle from Moshesh the regiments withdrew home.

This sanguinary defeat marked a turning point in the history of relations between the Ndebele and the half-caste peoples. These now tended to turn their attention eastward to the Basuto of Moshesh and many of them drifted across Transorangia to settle in and near Basutoland. The

1 *Andrew Smith's Diary*, vol. I, p. 384.
2 A contemporary account of the Barend-Barends commando can be found in *Andrew Smith's Diary*, vol. I, pp. 381–4. See also Becker: *Path of Blood*, pp. 139–43.

Ndebele were not left entirely alone but no great expedition like that of Barend-Barends was organized. It was not only the Koranas and Griquas who were affected by this disaster. Moletsane had lost all but a fraction of his following and it was after this débâcle that he wandered eastward to settle first with Adam Kok at Philippolis and later to move on to Basutoland.[1]

From Mzilikazi's point of view there was no room for complacency. He had only been saved from complete defeat by lack of resolve on the part of his enemies and only their almost incredible fecklessness had enabled him to retrieve his initial defeat. Though the commando had been broken up there were still groups of Korana and Griqua between the Orange and the Vaal who might be tempted to make a new attack upon him at any time. After these two attacks he began to think of moving his capital further to the west. There he would be further from the Zulu armies and closer to his friend Moffat at Kuruman. To clear the way his regiments began attacking the Tswana tribes in systematic fashion. The Ngwaketsi who had successfully survived the Kololo invasion now felt the full impact of the Ndebele regiments. In spite of their military renown they were completely routed and driven into the Kalahari and their position as the dominant Tswana tribe was destroyed for ever. The Kwena of Bechuanaland were also attacked and the Kgatla, whose chief had been instrumental in persuading Barend-Barends to form the great commando, were broken up.

Next the Ndebele turned their attention to the Hurutshe in the fertile Marico district which Mzilikazi desired as the site for his new capital. The Hurutshe had suffered much in the previous chain of disturbances. Their capital had been sacked by the Phuting and they had been plundered by the Taung and the Kololo but they still remained a numerous people and a few years of peace had enabled them to make good much of their earlier losses. The Ndebele move against the Hurutshe was delayed for some time because three missionaries of the Paris Evangelical Missionary Society, Rolland, Lemue and Pellissier, had established themselves at Mosega in 1832. Mzilikazi, anxious to maintain good relations with the whites and in particular not to offend Moffat, was placed in a quandary. He did his best to persuade the Frenchmen to transfer their field of operations to his own people. Pellissier was summoned to the capital and given a hearty reception. He noted the chief's agreeable manner but did not feel at home with him as Moffat had done. He found the intense concentration of authority in the ruler's hands offensive. He was appalled by the frequent executions and was suspicious of Mzilikazi's intentions. When the Ndebele king tried to keep him

1 See above, Chapter 6, p. 98.

from returning to Mosega and insisted on his helping to clean the captured firearms his disenchantment was complete. The idea of opening a mission with the Ndebele was postponed and the missionaries remained at Mosega.[1]

Mzilikazi's impatience with the missionaries and his desire to move further to the west were greatly increased by a second Zulu attack. Once again the regiments of the two greatest Bantu military powers met in the open field. In the first encounter the regiments of older men broke before the Zulu advance, but Mzilikazi then threw the *machaha* into the fight and succeeded in holding his enemy to a stalemate. Both sides broke off the fight with one accord and the Zulu retired taking with them numbers of Ndebele cattle, destroying many outlying cattle posts as they went.[2] [Some time later, after establishing himself in his new position in the Marico valley, Mzilikazi punished the older regiments for cowardice. He ordered them back to barracks to live separated from their families until they had purged their guilt.[3]]

The Hurutshe then gave Mzilikazi a perfect *casus belli*. A group of Ndebele envoys were seized and put to death on suspicion of being spies. There could be no doubt that a full-scale Ndebele attack was imminent and when another embassy arrived with orders for the missionaries to proceed at once to Mzilikazi's capital they decided to withdraw from the station. The Ndebele then began to move into the Marico district. Mokgatla, the Hurutshe chief, rather than risk an engagement, fled with the bulk of his followers to the south-east, leaving his town deserted. He was subsequently encountered by the French missionaries near the Harts River with about a hundred of his followers in a starving condition. They attempted to persuade him to bring his followers to the new station which they had opened with Moffat's advice at Motito on the outskirts of Waterboer's domains. Mokgatla, who had tried in vain to persuade Barend-Barends to undertake another commando, at first agreed but subsequently he met Jan Bloem who promised to give his support to such a venture. Only about fifty of the Hurutshe followed the missionaries to Motito. The others with Jan Bloem made yet another attack on the Ndebele. Once again many cattle were captured but on this occasion also the party was ambushed on its

1 For Pellissier's account of this visit, see his letter of 12 May 1832, *Journal des Missions Évangéliques*, vol. VIII, pp. 5–19. It confirms the main outlines of Ndebele political and military organization described above.

2 Slightly different accounts are given of this encounter in the contemporary sources. See *Andrew Smith's Diary*, vol. II, p. 78. Extracts from the letters of Rolland and Pellissier: *Journal des Missions Évangéliques*, vol. VIII, pp. 97–111. And *Letters of the American Missionaries, 1835–1838*, Letter 35, p. 134.

3 *Andrew Smith's Diary*, vol. II, p. 79.

return. Many of the Koranas were killed and Bloem himself only just escaped as his horse was speared under him. A retaliatory expedition of Ndebele then attacked the Hurutshe at the Harts River but they were driven off with Korana aid.[1]

Though the Hurutshe chief had fled with many of his fighting men the majority of his people remained in the Marico district. Many of the young men were incorporated in the Ndebele regiments, but the rest of the population was allowed to live in its own villages alongside the Ndebele though in a subordinate capacity. On his second journey to visit Mzilikazi in 1835 Moffat, who had been told that nearly all the Hurutshe had been killed, noted that the report was false, '. . . for even here there are four or five towns, or rather villages, of Bahurutse, independent of those living farther [in the] interior. I rather think my words will prove true, that Moselekatse is not so bad as some think.'[2]

As the Ndebele moved in to settle in their new home, the lands they had previously occupied were left almost entirely uninhabited. The new settlement was planned and laid out in accordance with the principles of political and military organization which had taken shape in the central Transvaal. The chief settlement was set up in the fertile basin of Mosega and there Mzilikazi established barracks for several of his regiments. Sometimes as many as two or three thousand persons might be gathered there when the regiments were assembled for dancing or in preparation for an expedition.[3] In addition to this town two other military centres were established at strategic points—Tshwenyane and e-Gabeni. Each of these contained a section of Mzilikazi's household and was under the command of a chief *induna* with subordinates under him responsible for sub-divisions of the district. Discipline was maintained at a high standard and the *indunas* who acted both as military and civil officials '. . . hold the country under a police of the strictest order'.[4] Each of the military commanders was responsible for guarding one section of the approaches to the Ndebele kingdom. Mzilikazi was particularly anxious to ward off any new attack by the Griquas and Koranas. Patrols were constantly maintained to the south-east to fall upon any attacking party and give advance warning of any hostile move.

In 1834 these regiments came upon a party of Griquas led by Peter Davids, one of Barend-Barends' lieutenants, who had unwisely trespassed on the Ndebele preserves to hunt elephants near the Vaal River. His wagons were seized together with two of his children, Willem and

1 See *Journal des Missions Évangéliques*, vol. X, pp. 5–30.
2 Moffat, *Matabele Journals*, vol. I, p. 70.
3 Letter Champion to Anderson, Ginani, 21 April 1837, *Letters of the American Missionaries*, no. 40, p. 161.
4 *Letters of the American Missionaries*, no. 35, p. 130.

Truey, and they were carried back to Mosega. In the same year Andrew Geddes Bain, on a trading journey into the Ndebele country, foolishly allowed himself to be accompanied by a party of Griquas who took the first opportunity to loot Ndebele cattle. In retaliation the regiments swooped on his wagons and the traveller was lucky to escape with the loss of all his property.[1]

In spite of his move to the new home Mzilikazi still felt far from secure. When Moffat, accompanied by Dr. Andrew Smith, visited him in 1835 they were eagerly welcomed. Mzilikazi's friendship and respect for his adopted father was still as strong as ever. He agreed at once to the idea of entering into a treaty with the British Government provided that the Governor would undertake to control his 'children' who had done the Ndebele so much harm. Two of his chief *indunas*, Mnombate and Mkalipi, travelled to Cape Town with Andrew Smith's returning expedition and a treaty of mutual friendship between the Ndebele and the British Government was signed. Moffat also gained the king's permission for a mission to be established with his people and by the end of 1835 two American missionaries, Lindley and Venables, had begun building their home in Mosega. Even so Mzilikazi still felt unsafe. Spies were sent out far to the north and brought reports of fertile land and fat cattle. Mzilikazi himself accompanied a raiding expedition in that direction and he was clearly contemplating a further move out of the range of Dingane's armies and the depredations of the Koranas and Griquas when circumstances precipitated his decision.[2]

Early in 1836 the first parties of the great Boer trek, those of Louis Trichardt and Jan van Rensburg, crossed the Vaal into Ndebele territory. These small groups passed unnoticed by Mzilikazi's regiments and moved on through the devastated country till they reached the Zoutpansberg. There the van Rensburgs were attacked and massacred by an unknown tribe, possibly a branch of the Pedi. Louis Trichardt made his painful way eastward to Delagoa Bay to establish contact with the Portuguese.[3] Later in the same year a number of other trekking parties crossed the Vaal. They included Hendrik Potgieter who had decided to spy out the land with a view to settlement together with the Erasmus,

1 *Journals of Andrew Geddes Bain*, pp. 144–5. In spite of his friendship for Moffat Mzilikazi in 1835 refused to return either Bain's wagons or the Griqua children, arguing that they were spoils of war justly taken in retaliation for Griqua depredation. The two Griqua children were taken to Southern Rhodesia. Permission for them to return was eventually given on Moffat's fifth visit.

2 *Letters of the American Missionaries*, no. 35, p. 140.

3 The journey was accomplished in face of almost superhuman difficulties but most of the expedition died of malaria at the Bay. The few survivors were eventually brought to Natal.

Liebenberg, Botha and Steyn families who had crossed the river on a hunting expedition. This concourse of wagons and peoples could not escape the attention of Mzilikazi's regiments. As the intruders came unannounced and from the direction from which Griqua attacks were to be expected they were naturally taken for a hostile invading party. That this was a genuine mistake and that the Ndebele had no bloodthirsty hatred for the whites is clear from the fact that at this very time Captain Cornwallis Harris, an Indian Army officer on leave, was received by Mzilikazi with all possible hospitality.[1] The regiments came down on the Boer wagons unexpectedly. The Erasmus and Liebenberg families were largely destroyed but the Bothas and Steyns succeeded in beating off the first attack. Then all the Boer survivors united under the leadership of Potgieter and prepared to defend themselves on a hill later known as Vegkop. Here the first major clash between the Ndebele and the Boers took place. The regiments charged the Boer laager in close formation but the Boers behind the barricade of wagons kept up such a devastating fire that the Ndebele were forced to withdraw taking the Boer cattle with them.

Mzilikazi had thus unwittingly involved himself in conflict with an enemy far more formidable than the Korana of Jan Bloem or the Griqua of Barend-Barends. In December 1836 the Boers were ready to make a counter-attack. Like the half-caste leaders before them, they allied with other enemies of Mzilikazi. The Griqua, Peter Davids, sent forty horsemen and six Koranas also joined the expedition which was reinforced by a contingent of Tlokwa despatched by the old robber chief, Sikonyela. On 2 January 1837 the commando fell on the Ndebele settlement at Mosega. A complete surprise was achieved and the Ndebele were entirely routed. The whole population fled northward and the regiments prepared to make a new stand at e-Gabeni.[2] The Boers then returned to their base near Thaba Nchu driving before them huge herds of cattle and taking with them the American missionaries who saw no point in staying now that the settlement at Mosega was destroyed and their own position compromised.

The news of the successful Boer raid on the Ndebele was gladly received by Dingane. It provided an excellent opportunity to renew his long-standing conflict with the Ndebele king and also perhaps to gratify

1 See C. Harris: *Wild Sports in South Africa.* It may also be pointed out that in 1834 Moshesh warned Andrew Smith not to enter Mzilikazi's territory from that direction as he would be mistaken for an enemy. *Andrew Smith's Diary*, vol. I, p. 118. The Boers unfortunately did not consult anyone before crossing the Vaal.

2 For accounts of the conflict between Ndebele and Boer see E. Walker: *The Great Trek*; also P. Becker, op. cit.

his new and potentially dangerous neighbours.[1] A Zulu army set off at once and a third battle between the two military states took place. As on the previous occasions no outright victory was gained but the Zulu seized a substantial loot of Ndebele cattle which they took back to their king.

In October 1837 the final blow fell. Potgieter, after quarrelling with Maritz and Retief about the destination of the Great Trek, decided to stake a definite claim to the wide lands of the Transvaal. He set out with a strong commando of over three hundred men for a decisive attack on the Ndebele. Again Mzilikazi was caught unawares. His regiments were helpless against fighters who used their horses to keep out of range while mowing down the warriors from a distance. In seven days of fighting his two remaining military towns, Tshwenyane and e-Gabeni, were captured and burnt and the whole Ndebele population streamed out of the Marico valley to the north. Potgieter proclaimed his title by right of conquest to all the lands previously ruled by Mzilikazi and the Boers began to settle in the wide areas which had been so conveniently cleared of their previous population by the spears of the Ndebele regiments.

Mzilikazi now decided to carry out the project he had been contemplating for some time of moving his people to a new site far to the north where the healthy uplands of modern Southern Rhodesia promised excellent pasture land. The difficulties of feeding such a huge host on the march made it desirable to divide his forces, and the fact that he would be moving through relatively unknown territory occupied by hostile tribes dictated such a measure as a wise precaution. The women and children with the remaining cattle were sent ahead in the protection of one section of the army under a chief *induna*, Gundwane Ndiwene. With this contingent travelled Kuluman,[2] the heir apparent to Mzilikazi's throne, and other princes of the royal blood including the future Lobengula. Mzilikazi himself with another section of the army and Magqekeni Sithole as its chief *induna*, stayed back to cover the rear. The two parties marched separately. Mzilikazi and his group took a westerly path raiding the Ngwato on their way and then passing northward through the fringes of the Kalahari. The other section took a more easterly route. It passed through territory in the northern Transvaal devastated by previous Ndebele raids. Then it crossed the Zoutpansberg range, forded the Limpopo and entered modern Southern Rhodesia. Still pressing northward it came at last to what seemed an

1 On the return of his expedition Dingane notified the Boers of its results. He offered to return to them cattle and sheep that had been seized by Mzilikazi and recaptured by his regiments.

2 The young prince had been given this name, a corruption of Kuruman, on the occasion of Moffat's first visit to Mzilikazi in 1829.

ideal place for settlement not far from the Matoppos range and there they built a settlement which they called Gibixhegu after Shaka's military town of that name.[1]

In the meantime Mzilikazi and his company had lost all contact with the other half of his people and struggled northward to the banks of the Zambesi. There he fell in with the Kololo of Sebetwane. The exact place of their encounter is not known but as the Kololo gave it as their reason for abandoning the desirable cattle country near the Kafue on the northern bank of the Zambesi, it is probable that the Ndebele regiments had crossed the river even if the king did not accompany them.[2] For once, under the leadership of Sebetwane, a Sotho army proved a match for the Ndebele. The two forces parted with both sides anxious to avoid a further contest. Mzilikazi turned his steps to the south while Sebetwane led his people westward to Barotseland.[3]

In the settlement at Gibixhegu the people waited for their king in vain. At last the *indunas* began to feel that something must be done to provide the community with a legal head. Some felt that Kuluman should be placed on the throne without delay but others urged the need to conduct further investigations to discover whether Mzilikazi was still alive and wished to rejoin his people. An embassy sent in search of Mzilikazi encountered him and his followers on the desert fringes of northern Bechuanaland. He was delighted to hear that the women and cattle were safe but furious at the news of the plan to establish his son in his stead. He set out at once to rejoin his people. On his march he found a site near the present town of Bulawayo where he decided to establish his new headquarters. Here he halted and sent to summon the *indunas* of Gibixhegu to answer for their treason. Five of the *indunas* together with the chief *induna*, Gundwane, were found guilty and executed on a hill which is still called 'the hill of the *indunas*'.[4] Orders

1 For accounts of the routes taken by the two armies, see N. Jones (Mhlaga-zanhlansi): *My Friend Kumalo*. P. Becker, op. cit., pp. 180–6. The general outline of events is confirmed by Moffat who visited Mzilikazi in his new home for the first time in 1854. *Matabele Journals*, vol. I, pp. 371–2.

2 Mzilikazi later told Moffat that he had abandoned an earlier intention of settling north of the Zambesi because of tsetse fly. It is possible that this defeat was the real reason which Mzilikazi did not wish to mention. Moffat: *Matabele Journals*, vol. I, p. 371.

3 See above, Chapter 8, p. 120.

4 Kumalo maintains that the *indunas* were not executed on the hill but merely tried there as the Ndebele regarded such hills as sacred. N. Jones, op. cit., pp. 13–16. This is difficult to accept as the Zulu certainly used hilltops as places of execution. Matiwane's Kop gained its name from the execution of the Ngwane chief and was later used as the execution ground of Retief and his followers. It is probable that the religious reverence for mountains comes from the later acceptance of the Mlimo cult associated with the Matoppos mountains.

were also given to execute the presumptuous heir Kuluman and two other royal princes, one of whom was Lobengula. The sentence against Kuluman was almost certainly carried out though rumours persisted that he had been sent to the south and still survived. In the case of Lobengula, however, the execution never took place. He was temporarily concealed from the angry monarch. Later when his anger had cooled the prince was shown to the king and won his favour thus surviving to become the second and last of the Ndebele kings. After the execution of the ringleaders, Gibixhegu was abandoned and a new royal capital, Inyati, was built near the scene of the *indunas*' execution.

In its new home the Ndebele kingdom rapidly recovered from the losses of war and grew stronger than ever before. The peoples of this area were ill organized to meet the new invaders. The Rozwi empire which had been established over the Kalanga inhabitants of the old Monomatapa kingdom had been shattered by the invasions of Zwangendaba and Nxaba. After the Ngoni regiments had hunted down the last Rozwi emperor and put him to death the kingdom had disintegrated. Divided into many small groups the Rozwi could not offer any co-ordinated resistance. The Kalanga, long accustomed to Rozwi dominance, were still less in a position to do so. Forced in desperation to defend themselves on inaccessible mountain-tops some of these peoples (now generally classed together as Shona) did give a good account of themselves but this amounted to no more than the survival of isolated pockets of resistance. There was no attempt at combination for defence nor any serious effort to dislodge the Ndebele from their new settlements. The fighting potential of the Shona had been further weakened and Mzilikazi's task made easier by the depredations of a section of Zwangendaba's army under the leadership of a women chief, Nyamazana. This warrior queen had refused to cross the Zambesi with her following. She and her followers now joined forces with the Ndebele. She became one of Mzilikazi's queens and her people were absorbed into the Ndebele regiments.[1]

In Southern Rhodesia the Ndebele state went through the final stages of its evolution. The regimental pattern was retained and a series of military towns was established. Inyati, Mahlokohlokho and em Hlahlandhlela were the most important. At these the regiments were quartered and at strategic points outside the central area of the kingdom smaller posts were established to keep a watch on the frontiers and as cattle posts. Because in the Ndebele system the army and the state were identical the military towns came to play a different role from that which they performed in the Zulu system. As the older men

1 N. Jones, op. cit.

remained members of their regiments on marriage and were still attached to the military centre where their regiments had been barracked, the military towns came to constitute permanent territorial divisions of the state. Instead of youths from every section of the people being gathered together in a single regiment, membership of a military settlement became hereditary. Only when increase of population and the needs of war dictated the formation of new regiments did the system operate in the original way. On such occasions the king would gather youths from all the regimental towns, form them into a new regiment and establish them in a settlement of their own. In time this would in turn become a permanent territorial division and the children of the first group of warriors would belong to it from birth.[1]

Thus the Ndebele system evolved differently both from the original Zulu model and from the Ngoni system. To some extent the evolution had taken the form of a return to the territorial system of pre-Shakan society but with great modifications. The basis of the Ndebele system remained a military one and the effective authorities over the different sections of the tribe were not persons of chiefly descent but commoner *indunas* chosen for their military abilities. They might act as a check on the action of the ruler to some extent but far less than territorial rulers of the royal blood. They could not, like royal chiefs, organize secession. Thus in spite of the development of territorial divisions within the state, power still remained concentrated in the hands of the monarch. The unity of the kingdom was ensured and no process of sub-division took place similar to that which arose from the development of artificial lineage systems in Ngoni society. Tensions between the different sections would reveal themselves in a struggle over the succession but not in a division of the state.

Within this system there also developed what might be called a class system. The development of this could be seen in its early stages when the Ndebele were still in the Transvaal. Its basis was the perfectly natural one that prestige attached first to those who belonged to the parent Nguni group from which the Ndebele had developed and then to those with the longest record of incorporation. The American missionaries at Mosega had noticed that 'The tribes whom he first subjugated are now almost incorporated with his original followers, using their language and to all appearance holding a rank not far below them; while the tribes more recently conquered occupy a more servile station.'[2] With the move to Southern Rhodesia this class structure crystallized into a three-tier system. The highest class was made up of the descendants of

1 See A. Hughes: *Kin, Caste and Nation amongst the Rhodesian Ndebele.*
2 *Letters of the American Missionaries*, no. 35, p. 129.

the original Nguni warriors, the repositories of tribal tradition and the purity of language and culture. As in the case of the Ngoni they were known as the 'zansi'. Next in prestige came the descendants of the numerous different tribes of Sotho and Tswana stock incorporated during the period spent in the Transvaal. They were known as the 'enhla'. Lowest in the hierarchy came the latest recruits of all, persons descended from the Shona tribes incorporated in the final period of the kingdom's development. These class groupings were jealously preserved. Marriages between persons of different classes were strongly disapproved. Between 'zansi' and the lowest group they were almost unknown but even between 'zansi' and 'enhla' they were remarkably infrequent.[1] Though they were regarded as so important, these class divisions were essentially matters of prestige rather than economic divisions. The newly conquered peoples were subjected to a considerable amount of bullying. Yet as they acquired the Ndebele language and proved themselves in war their position came to approximate to that of anyone else. They might even be appointed to military commands. In spite of the class system even the newly conquered Shona soon came to think of themselves as Ndebele and to take pride in their identification with the conquering people.

The chief function of the class system, apart from gratifying the pride of the upper classes, was to keep alive the prestige of the original Nguni language and hold up the traditional culture from the south as a standard for imitation. This may be partly the reason why the language of the conquerors succeeded in imposing itself on all the diverse peoples incorporated in the Ndebele state. In contrast to what occurred amongst the Ngoni, Sindebele is now almost universally spoken by those who consider themselves Ndebele and the original Shona languages have virtually disappeared amongst them. The success of the Ndebele state in welding so many different peoples into a political unit and imposing on them a single linguistic and cultural pattern is the more remarkable because of the short period of independent existence of the kingdom and also because in conquering the Shona Mzilikazi did not attempt to force all of them into the regimental pattern.

Many captive youths were so incorporated. When first taken they were given to the captors to serve as weapon-bearers and cattle-herders but when they grew older they would go to Mzilikazi and present a petition. 'We are men, O King; we are no longer boys; give us cattle to herd and to defend.'[2] If the king approved he would entrust a num-

1 On this subject see Hughes: *Kin, Caste and Nation amongst the Rhodesian Ndebele.*

2 Mackenzie, op. cit., pp. 327–9.

ber of cattle to their keeping and appoint an experienced *induna* who would choose a place for a new military settlement and train them as Ndebele soldiers. In addition to those who were incorporated in this way, however, others continued to live in villages loosely attached to the Ndebele military towns. On his fourth journey to visit Mzilikazi in 1857 Moffat noticed 'Many of that people [the Mashonas] live among the Matabele and, besides numbers who are living as servants and youths amalgamated with the Matabele, there are many towns or villages where they are permitted to live in their own way, but muster for public service when called on. . . .'[1] Yet even these groups who were associated with the Ndebele state rather than fully a part of it, have for the most part come to regard themselves as Ndebele and to adopt their language and culture.[2] The process was not entirely one-way. The Ndebele were also influenced by the culture of the conquered peoples. In particular they adopted the Mlimo cult of the Shona which was associated with the Matoppos Mountains. Mzilikazi himself, and Lobengula after him, treated the priests of this cult with the utmost respect and placed a great deal of confidence in their prophecies.

This fusion of cultures and peoples was confined to the central area of the Ndebele kingdom (roughly the area of the present Matabeleland districts of Southern Rhodesia). Outside this area there extended a loose zone of Ndebele influence. To the south this stretched as far as the north-eastern corner of the present Bechuanaland Protectorate. In the early days of the Ndebele in Southern Rhodesia the Ngwato tribe of Bechuanaland had acknowledged Mzilikazi's paramountcy and taxes were collected for the Ndebele king every year, but after some time they rebelled and regained their independence.[3] To the north, Ndebele authority extended to the Zambesi River and to the east their suzerainty extended roughly as far as the boundary of present Portuguese East Africa. Outside the central area Mzilikazi asked no more than that his authority should be recognized and tribute in cattle paid on demand. From time to time great raiding parties of Ndebele would pass through the land battening on the cattle of the inhabitants and massacring any considered to be recalcitrant. It was undoubtedly a cruel and sanguinary system but it was based on principles which were easily understood. It made no demands on the labour of the Shona and Ndebele overlordship generated no deep sense of personal humiliation. Ngwato who fell within the southern portion of Mzilikazi's kingdom seemed to Moffat in 1854 '. . . to be happy and fat. They speak favourably of Moselekatse

1 Moffat: *Matabele Journals*, vol. II, p. 154.
2 See Hughes, op. cit.
3 Mackenzie, op. cit., pp. 359–60.

and seem quite shocked at the very idea of his rule being compared to the tyranny of the Dutch Boer.'[1]

Mzilikazi's rule in his new home was generally prosperous. His regiments passed through the Shona country until they reached the limits of the territory raided by Soshangane. A rough-and-ready agreement to respect a boundary was made between the two conquering rulers and eventually the alliance was reinforced by a dynastic marriage between Gungunyana and one of Lobengula's daughters.

In 1847, however, the Ndebele were temporarily alarmed by a renewed Boer attack. Hendrik Potgieter organized a commando with the avowed object of recovering three Boer children believed to have been taken from the wagons of the Liebenbergs in 1836. The raiding party penetrated into Ndebele territory and seized large numbers of cattle. An Ndebele regiment which tried to prevent them was driven off and the Boers began to retire with their loot. The Ndebele then employed the tactics they had previously used against Jan Bloem and Barend-Barends. They waited until the Boers camped for the night and then crept up silently on the camp. Wiser than the Koranas and Griquas, the Boers had taken the precaution of camping on a hill away from the cattle which were left in the keeping of a group of Pedi who had accompanied the expedition. Before it was light the regiment swept down on the Pedi massacring them all and driving the cattle away.[2] Potgieter then made a lightning raid on Mzilikazi's chief settlement but he found it abandoned and the Boers then turned their horses homeward. The failure of this expedition deterred the Transvaal Boers from further attacks on the Ndebele and in 1852 a treaty between them and Mzilikazi was made which opened the way for Boer hunters to enter Ndebele territory.

The other major enemy with whom Mzilikazi grappled in this period was Sebetwane and the Kololo. He could not forget the partial defeat he had experienced near the Zambesi. Two expeditions were sent up the river to fall on the Kololo, but both ended in complete failure. A more serious danger to the Ndebele kingdom was the insidious infiltration of white travellers, traders and missionaries which prepared the way for Rhodes and the British South Africa Company. In spite of his defeat by the Boers Mzilikazi remained anxious to maintain his contacts with friendly whites and in particular to see Moffat again. In 1854 his wish

1 Moffat: *Matabele Journals*, vol. I, p. 213. Ndebele rule was to seem preferable to that of the British South Africa Company also, as was demonstrated in the Shona rebellion. On this subject see P. Mason: *The Birth of a Dilemma*.

2 Moffat visited the spot where this encounter took place in 1854. He estimated that the bones of between one and two hundred of the Boers' Bantu allies lay in the valley. *Matabele Journals*, vol. I, p. 225.

was fulfilled and the old missionary found that the affection which the Ndebele king felt for him had lost none of its force. Moffat returned again in 1857, and for the last time in 1860. Under his persuasion Mzilikazi even agreed to allow missionaries to settle among his people though he was not unnaturally suspicious after the desertion of the American missionaries from Mosega.

In the last years of Mzilikazi's reign hunters and traders flocked to his kingdom. The king did his best to keep control of the ivory trade which he regarded as a royal monopoly. He also established an elementary quarantine system at the frontier post near present Plumtree to prevent the spread of cattle diseases.[1] In 1867 Henry Hartly and Karl Mauch, prospecting in abandoned Bantu mine workings, found gold in the Tati district on the borders of Ndebele and Ngwato territory. This was to be followed by a flood of white visitors but by this time Mzilikazi had lost effective control of affairs.

The Ndebele king had been ill for many years. When Moffat visited him in 1854 he was shocked at his condition: '. . . the vigorous active and nimble monarch of the Matabele, now aged, sitting on a skin, with feet lame, unable to walk or even to stand.'[2] When Moffat entered Mzilikazi took him by the hand and pulled his cloak over his head to hide his tears. The king was to live for a further fourteen years but his complaint grew worse. He was excessively fat and troubled with swellings in the feet which gave him constant pain. Moffat believed that it was caused by drinking too much millet beer and certainly Mzilikazi turned increasingly to drink as an escape from his sufferings. He also grew fearfully restless and his last years were spent travelling almost continuously from settlement to settlement in a wagon which Moffat had given him. Yet even in the last years of his life he did not lose the devoted loyalty of his subjects nor his capacity for leadership. Indeed the greater confidence resulting from relative military security enabled him sometimes to indulge the finer aspects of his character which had been suppressed in the struggles of earlier years. Though his people adored him almost as a god he never became intoxicated with their praises. Moffat recounts how on one occasion a subject chief was brought before him on the charge of allowing the Potgieter raiding party to pass without offering resistance. Instead of grovelling before the ruler the culprit stood up to him and told him that as the destroyer of so much human life he wished him dead and would have liked the Boers to have killed him. Instead of ordering his instant execution Mzilikazi said, 'You have spoken what your heart feels: go in peace. You shall [not] die, but

1 See G. Tabler: *The Far Interior.*
2 Moffat: *Matabele Journals*, vol. I, p. 229.

live while I live; only in future let me know when any strangers approach your district.'[1] In 1868 the old king, worn out with his long affliction and the subject of delusions and hallucinations, finally passed away.

The death of their king threw the Ndebele into confusion. While the question of the succession was undecided the *indunas* maintained law and order. The issue was complicated by the fact that rumours of the survival of Kuluman somewhere in South Africa persisted. He was thought to have been identified in the person of a groom working for Sir Theophilus Shepstone, who did his best to keep the rumour alive as a means of gaining influence over the Ndebele tribe. An Ndebele embassy was sent to Natal to seek for the prince but it returned with a negative report and the majority of the *indunas* then placed Lobengula on the throne. The Zwangendaba regiment, however, refused to recognize the new king and insisted that a further search should be made for Kuluman. Lobengula tried to win them over at first but as they remained obstinate he had to resort to force. A bitter civil war was fought but eventually the Zwangendaba regiment was overpowered and Lobengula established firmly on the throne.[2] By this time the forces of advancing colonialism were closing in. Rumours of mineral wealth in his kingdom persisted although the Tati goldfields proved a disappointment. The discovery of the Maxim gun had made the Ndebele fighting methods, so carefully perfected, hopelessly anachronistic. In 1893 the Maxim guns of the British South Africa Company brought the Ndebele kingdom to an end. Lobengula died a refugee and in the Ndebele rebellion of 1896 the regimental system was used in war for the last time. After their final defeat the Ndebele lost much of their lands and the regimental towns were broken up. Since then they have been increasingly affected by European education and the demands of white society. Many have taken service on white farms or in the mines of Southern Rhodesia and South Africa to supplement the returns of the inadequate agricultural resources of their remaining land. Many have adopted Christianity and political attitudes are now directed towards modern ideas, the formation of political parties and the struggle for majority rule in Southern Rhodesia, but they have never ceased to feel themselves Ndebele. Even to this day it is said that every rural Ndebele knows to which regimental settlement he should belong and who are his rightful commanders. Through the period of white domination the pride of the Ndebele has been sustained by memories of their heroic age, 'before

1 Moffat: *Matabele Journals*, vol. I, p. 243.

2 For a detailed account of this episode in Ndebele history see R. Brown: 'The Ndebele Succession Crisis 1868–1877', *Historians in Tropical Africa* (Proceedings of the Leverhulme History Conference, 1960), pp. 159–75.

the white man spoiled the country', and these feelings helped to provide the emotional foundations on which a forward-looking African nationalism is based. So strongly did the personality of their founder chief impress itself upon them that the Southern Rhodesian mineworkers who go to South Africa are still known as *aba kwa Mzilikazi*.

10 The Devastation of Natal and the Flight to the South

THE first impact of the rise of the Zulu was felt in Natal with the violent passage of a powerful tribe dislodged from its home by Shaka's regiments.[1] The northern Thembu were attacked by the Zulu in their home on the Mzinyati River. In a bitter battle the Zulu took possession of the Thembu cattle though the Thembu were not completely routed. Under the leadership of Ngoza they set out for the south, crossed the Tugela and cut a path of destruction through the tribes of Natal. Turning inland near the Howick Falls they crossed the upper waters of the Umzimkulu into Nomansland. Then they turned towards the sea again and poured into northern Pondoland. Faku, the Pondo chief, did his best to avoid an open conflict at first. He received them with a good grace and allowed them to settle on a portion of the Pondo tribal lands. By about 1822–23, however, the proximity of this rapacious band of invaders was proving intolerable. Faku launched a surprise attack. Ngoza was killed and the Thembu were broken up. Some drifted northward towards their old home and offered their submission to Shaka, who settled them on the lands from which the Ndwandwe had been driven. Others remained to be incorporated among the Pondo.

The sudden eruption of the Thembu into Natal began a process of tribal movement and disruption similar to that of the Hlubi and Ngwane in Transorangia. The Wushe, one of the most powerful tribes encountered by the Thembu on their flight to the south, threw in their lot with the invaders after an initial defeat and followed them for some time on their career of warfare and plunder. When the Thembu turned inland near the Howick Falls, however, the Wushe, under Madikane, broke away and thus became an independent predatory band.

1 The following account is based on Bryant: *Olden Times* and *History of the Zulu*. His reconstruction was founded largely on oral traditions which cannot be expected to be entirely reliable with reference to such a complicated and confused situation. I have made use of contemporary evidence where possible to supplement and correct Bryant's account but complete accuracy is probably impossible.

It was not long, however, before they were caught up by yet another group. The Cunu under Macingwane, like the Thembu before them, found the neighbourhood of the Zulu intolerable. Defeated but not seriously weakened they poured across the Tugela and took a course nearer the coast than Ngoza, devastating the tribes who still retained their cattle.[1] Macingwane and Madikane joined forces for a time but they soon separated again.

This second wave of devastation threw all the Natal tribes into chaos. Banding themselves together in desperation a group of tribes comprising the Dunges, the Nyamvini, the Fuzes, the Tlangwini, the Memela and the Bhele, under the leadership of a number of chiefs of whom Mdingi of the Bhele was the most outstanding, abandoned their homes and followed the general move to the south. Struggling with tribes in their way they were defeated by Madikane and in turn defeated Macingwane. Gradually the unwieldy confederation broke up. Some turned back to the north but the bulk of them under the leadership of Mdingi continued on their southward march and poured into Nomansland closely followed by Madikane who fought fiercely with them. About 1822 a Zulu raiding expedition encountered Macingwane in central Natal and completely defeated him. The Cunu were broken up and the remnants of their tribe struggled back to Zululand where they were incorporated with the Zulu.

Behind the struggling mass of fugitives came the Zulu regiments themselves. Once Shaka had established himself in power, annual raiding expeditions were sent to Natal which gradually extended the scope of their activities southward.[2] In 1823–24 a major Zulu expedition was launched. The regiments passed through the whole of Natal completing the desolation of the country and the destruction of any remaining tribal groups. They then went on to attack Faku and seized much of his cattle. The Pondo leader wisely restrained his people from engaging in any major battle with the Zulu. He offered his submission to Shaka and retained the fighting strength of his tribe virtually intact.[3]

In the neighbourhood of the Pondo intolerable conditions of overcrowding developed which found their outlet in almost continuous struggles between rival groups. The main conflict was between the group led by Mdingi made up mainly of Bhele, Memela and Tlangwini and the followers of Madikane who had also been recruited from many different tribal groups. (This composite body was later given the name

1 Bryant: *Olden Times*, p. 267, denies that the Cunu were attacked by the Zulu but Fynn: *Diary*, pp. 16–17, makes it clear that there was at least one battle.
2 See Bryant: *History of the Zulu*.
3 Fynn saw the regiments returning from this great campaign soon after his arrival in Natal. *Diary*, pp. 16–17.

Bhaca.) In an attempt to break out of the cramped conditions of northern Pondoland Madikane led a raid to the south into Thembu territory (namely that of the southern Thembu who lived between the Pondo and Xhosa, and not the northern Thembu of Ngoza). The Thembu appealed for help to the senior branch of the Xhosa and their combined forces inflicted a severe defeat on the invaders. Shortly after this Madikane was killed in conflict with the Bhele and in 1826 Mdingi succeeded in a daring coup which might have been expected to crush his rivals for ever. He surrounded the huts of Madikane's successor and setting them on fire, burned his greatest enemy to death.

This blow did not, however, produce the expected result, for the Bhaca found a brilliant new leader in a young chief named Ncapayi. The new chief rapidly rallied his peoples' morale but hostilities were suspended for a time as all took refuge from Shaka's great expedition of 1828. Hardly had Shaka's regiments withdrawn than the two sides engaged in a major clash. The Bhele were now strengthened by an unexpected reinforcement. The young Hlubi leader, Mehlomakhulu, after breaking away from Mzilikazi, crossed the Drakensberg and entered Nomansland. He settled alongside Mdingi and allied with him for an attack on Ncapayi. The numbers of the allied forces were, however, no substitute for the military skill of the young chief. They suffered a total defeat and their leaders parted to follow different paths. Mehlomakhulu and the Hlubi recrossed the Drakensberg to take refuge in Basutoland. Mdingi fled south into Thembuland hotly followed by the army of the Bhaca. On their way the pursuing forces met the Thembu, defeated them and killed their paramount chief, Gubencuka, but Ncapayi then turned back leaving Mdingi to his fate. He settled with his followers as Fingos amongst the Thembu but others of the same tribe remained in Nomansland and still constitute an important tribal group in the Mount Frere district.

Ncapayi had thus emerged supreme amongst the emigrant groups but his power was still not equal to that of Faku. This chief was the key to the whole situation. He is not usually thought of amongst the great Bantu figures of this period but he deserves to be considered one of the most outstanding leaders of the *Mfecane*. By his diplomacy and military skill he held his people together in the face of wave after wave of invasion, dealt with all his enemies one by one and prevented the tide of disturbance from flowing on down the coast.

Missionary and travellers' accounts give little impression of his personality. Andrew Smith, who formed a more favourable judgement than most, describes him as of middling stature with a stoop rather like an English dandy. 'His whole appearance indicates a superiority, and I think if a person not knowing him were to meet him they would consider him more than common.'[1] He kept the governance of his people very much in his own hands and had a capacity for taking quick decisions. He was also very frank and would tell stories even against himself. He had real respect for only one member of his tribe, a commoner *induna* who had distinguished himself in war. This man was allowed to criticize Faku's policy and when he did so the chief took it in good part. His rule was generally mild. He rarely employed the death penalty except for witchcraft and throughout his long reign he always retained the loyalty of his subjects. In face of the series of invasions from the north his policy was to avoid conflict wherever possible, to achieve his ends by playing off one enemy against another and to fight only on his own chosen ground when he was sure of victory. After his first conflict with the Thembu he managed to avoid a major clash with the other groups. He also survived two Zulu invasions though he lost a great deal of his cattle in the process and when he was first met by missionaries in 1828 his people were living almost entirely by agriculture.[2]

It was, however, after the death of Shaka that Faku faced his greatest trial. The Qwabe tribe was one of the largest to be incorporated in the Zulu kingdom. It had been conquered early in Shaka's rise to power and its chief, Nqeto, was highly favoured. Like Mzilikazi, he became a favourite *induna*, leading regiments largely composed of his own people. On Shaka's death Dingane attempted to destroy or render powerless all who had been closely associated with his predecessor and might resent his assassination. Nqeto, feeling his life in danger and taking advantage of the temporary relaxation of military discipline which followed Dingane's succession, gathered his people together and offered defiance to the new king. Regiments sent to destroy him were repulsed and Nqeto, taking a great herd of the royal cattle, fled through Natal determined to put as great a distance as possible between himself and the Zulu.

This new invasion was far more dangerous than those which had preceded it, for the Qwabe, like the Ndebele, were a break-away section of the Zulu army, battle-trained in its fierce discipline. After traversing the deserted lands of Natal, Nqeto established himself between the Umzimkulu and Umzimvubu Rivers in part of the Pondo territory from which Faku had withdrawn his people. The raids of the Qwabe excited the hostility of their new neighbours and early in 1829 a Dutch deserter, Klaas Lochenburg, who had lived for more than twenty years amongst

1 *Andrew Smith and Natal*, p. 108.
2 Letter, Shaw to Secretaries, Wesleyan Missionary Society (containing his Journal for 1828), Wesleyville, 10 June 1829, M.M.S. 1829/18.

the southern Nguni tribes, organized a raiding expedition against them. Gathering a body of Pondo warriors he set off with the combined purpose of avenging their wrongs and seizing a handsome loot. The approach of this party became known to the Qwabe in advance and the regiments drew themselves up on a hill to await the attack. Hardly had Lochenburg fired the first shot than the regiments charged down the hill. Lacking the fire power to halt the charge the raiding party was overwhelmed and Lochenburg, together with a Hottentot servant and most of the Pondo, was killed.[1] Shortly after this brush Nqeto received a visit from Farewell, who was travelling back overland to his trading post in Natal. Farewell was accompanied by two white companions, Walker and Thackwray. He was well received by Nqeto who had known him in Natal but the chief was anxious to persuade him not to continue his journey towards the Zulu. Nqeto wished to prevent goods being carried to his deadly enemy and probably felt that Farewell and his party would serve as spies. When Farewell refused to abandon his journey the attitude of the Qwabe began to change. The Hottentot servants tried to persuade Farewell to leave at once, but he was so confident of the friendship of the chief that he refused to hear of it. In the night the warriors fell on the sleeping party. The three white men were murdered and the wagons with their loads of trade goods fell into the Qwabe's hands. Some of the Hottentots escaped, however, to bring the news to the missionaries at Morley.[2]

Emboldened by this successful act of robbery Nqeto began preparations for a move further to the south. A series of raids was started which avoided the Pondo but sought to isolate them by destroying the smaller tribes all around them. The fires of burning villages could be seen from the mission station at Morley and the missionary judged it wisest to abandon the post for a time. The mission settlement was sacked and when he returned to the scene on 11 November he remarked, 'The extensive plains which a few days since were enlivened with herds of cattle now bore a dreary appearance and nothing seemed to enliven the monotonous scene but the occasional sound of the feathered inhabitants of the forest who seemed more cheerful than we. . . .'[3] In the meantime outwardly friendly relations were maintained between the Pondo and the Qwabe but both sides were waiting a favourable opportunity to commence the struggle. Faku sent messengers to the Thembu and

1 Samuel Young to Rev. G. Morley, Mount Coke, 26 Aug. 1829, M.M.S. 1829/22. S. Kay: *Travels and Researches in Caffraria*, pp. 384–5.

2 Shepstone to Secretaries, Wesleyan Missionary Society, Morley, 25 Oct. 1829, M.M.S. 1829/30.

3 Shepstone to Secretaries, Wesleyan Missionary Society, Mount Coke, 3 March 1830, M.M.S. 1830/14.

Xhosa with a view to co-ordinating defence. Nqeto sent frequent embassies to the Pondo to act as spies while he waited for his people to gather their corn. In the first days of December the Qwabe were ready and their regiments began a general advance.

Faku had had ample opportunity to study Zulu military tactics in Shaka's two invasions of his territory. He realized that if the enemy were able to deploy their forces in orderly formation their discipline and fighting methods would easily outweigh the superior numbers of the Pondo. He therefore planned to surprise them on difficult terrain where numbers could win the day before the Qwabe could consolidate their ranks. He allowed them to take his first cattle posts without resistance but he posted a strong contingent of his men near the ford over the Umzimvubu River to fall on the enemy on their return. He then massed his people on the heights overlooking the river. The slope to the river-bank was dotted with mimosa trees and Faku waited until the Qwabe, confident that the Pondo would not dare to oppose them, passed along this strip of land in a disorderly mass. The Pondo then made a charge. A desperate hand-to-hand struggle took place among the thorn trees and the Qwabe, unable to form into ranks, fell one by one to the more numerous Pondo. Some were driven into the river, others broke away and made for the ford. Here they were met again by the Pondo who had been hiding in the tall grass and a second massacre took place as they struggled to make their escape across the river.[1] Nqeto with a few survivors made his escape and gathering up the cattle, fled inland towards the Bhaca. Faku prevented his victorious army from following in their tracks and seizing the cattle as he knew that they were legally the property of Dingane and to touch them would be to invite another Zulu invasion. Ncapayi, however, had no such scruples. He fell upon the retreating Qwabe, killing Nqeto and most of his following. When Dingane heard of Faku's victory he sent messengers to congratulate him and to ask him to ensure the return of the cattle. Two Zulu expeditions were sent against the Bhaca for this purpose but Ncapayi succeeded in eluding them.

The destruction of the Qwabe left Faku and Ncapayi the only substantial Bantu powers in the Pondoland area. The danger of a complete collapse of the southern Nguni had passed but it was not long before another danger appeared. The emigration of the Boers to Natal and their successful conflict with Dingane changed the whole situation along

1 There are two accounts of this battle by contemporaries. They agree on the main outlines of Faku's tactics but differ slightly on points of detail. Shrewsbury to Secretaries, Wesleyan Missionary Society, Graham's Town, 16 April 1830, M.M.S. 1830/15. Kay: *Travels and Researches in Caffraria*, pp. 392–4.

the coastal corridor. From the overcrowded lands of Pondoland an ever-increasing migration back to Natal took place. From Zululand also many who were dissatisfied with the rule of Dingane poured into Natal. This was essentially a question of temporarily displaced persons returning to their homes, but to the Boers who had won Natal at the cost of many lives it was an unwanted and dangerous invasion. Conscious of their small numbers and the difficulty of controlling large numbers of Bantu on isolated farms they sought for some means to prevent them settling down permanently.

In addition they were faced with an internal problem of their own. In the first flush of victory over Dingane, titles to land were distributed with considerable laxity. Soon there was not enough for newcomers who still poured in from the Cape. The same was true with regard to cattle. The losses which the Boers had suffered were amply restored by the reparations levied on Mpande but certain individuals secured such a large share of the spoil that many were left without enough to provide a livelihood. The weak government of the Republic, always in danger of being overthrown by a popular coup, was not able to ensure a more equitable distribution of available resources.[1] The only answer seemed to lie in further territorial expansion and in squeezing more cattle from the neighbouring tribes. The Swazi were faced with demands on the grounds that those they had seized when they killed Dingane belonged to the Boers by right of conquest, and in the south the theft of some cattle by Bushmen said to be under the authority of Ncapayi was made the excuse for an expedition against that chief. Great herds of cattle were seized and a number of the Bhaca killed.

To this move Faku gave at least indirect support but he himself was soon thoroughly alarmed for the Boers were openly planning to seize the land between the Umzimkulu and Umzimvubu which he had temporarily abandoned as a reserve into which the great mass of newly returned Bantu could be thrust. Fortunately for the Pondo this threat was not fulfilled. The British Government was worried at the danger to its eastern borders of this southward pressure from the Natal Republic. It was anxious at rumours that the Natalians might persuade a foreign power to occupy Port Natal. Under pressure from philanthropic bodies which were moved by missionary criticism of Boer behaviour in general and the raid on Ncapayi in particular, it gave permission to the Governor at the Cape to take effective action. Faku was declared an *amicus* of the Colony and a small force was sent to protect him against the threat of Boer expansion. This force soon moved on to Port Natal, thus beginning the process which led to British annexation.

1 See E. Walker: *The Great Trek.*

The end of the immediate threat from the Boers left Faku and Ncapayi face to face. Neither was anxious for a struggle and they attempted to consolidate their alliance by a dynastic marriage. Ncapayi married one of Faku's daughters but the attempt to avoid conflict between two such powerful groups differing in culture and living in close proximity in an area which left little room for population expansion proved impossible. They were drawn into war by their followers. Ncapayi was out-generalled by Faku and killed, though his tribe still constitutes an important group in Pondoland.[1] The Pondo had thus succeeded in eliminating all their most important enemies and retaining their original position. They were faced with yet another problem when Grey persuaded the Griquas of Adam Kok to abandon their lands in the Orange Free State which were under increasing pressure from the Boers and trek to Nomansland to establish a 'wall of iron' between the Basuto and the coast tribes. The Griquas achieved this great trek and, in spite of appalling difficulties, established a Griqua Republic in what thereafter came to be called Griqualand East. This new state flourished for a time and even proposed to issue its own currency, but under the pressure of Bantu constantly migrating into it and the temptations held before the Griquas by canteen keepers from the Cape, it crumbled and collapsed.[2]

By the end of Faku's long reign European colonialism was creeping up the coast. The ever-increasing volume of traffic passing through his territory on its way from the Cape to Natal meant that the European authorities were bound to take a close interest in the situation of his tribe. During his lifetime the Pondo had become closely bound up with the economy of white South Africa and it was not long before white authority was formally extended over the tribe. When the old chief finally passed away he left behind him a tribe which had successfully survived many hazards and which still remains one of the most important ethnic groups in South Africa.[3]

1 For a recent study of this group see Hammond-Tooke: *Bhaca Society*.
2 The tragic history of the last Griqua Republic is described by Halford, *The Griquas of Griqualand*.
3 For a recent study of the Pondo, see M. Hunter: *Reaction to Conquest*.

11 The History of the Fingo People

THOUGH the refugees from Shaka's regiments did not succeed in breaking through the line of the Pondo and disorganizing the southern Nguni tribes, many of them penetrated into the territory of these tribes in small homeless groups. Having lost all their cattle they were forced to beg for food (Uku Fenguza) from which they were given the name Mfengu (Fingo).

Amongst these groups one of the largest consisted of the remnants of the composite Ngwane and Hlubi army led by Matiwane. After his defeat by British forces in 1828 some followed him on his flight to Dingane and later, under his son Zikhale, the Ngwane tribe was reconstituted. The majority, however, settled down in their new homes and constitute an important section of the modern Fingo people.

In addition to these there were numerous other refugees who poured out of Natal. Mdingi and the Bhele, after their defeat by Ncapayi, were one of the largest of these but there were innumerable smaller parties derived from many different tribes. Even before the coming of Matiwane their numbers were very considerable. When the Wesleyan mission with Hintza, chief of the senior branch of the Xhosa, was opened in 1827 W. Shaw reported, 'In the immediate vicinity of the spot selected are a number of villages formed by Africans of several distinct nations, who in consequence of war and commotions in the interior, have been scattered and driven from their native countries and have sought refuge in the country of Hintza. He has received them kindly and allowed them to settle among his people. They are known among the Caffers under the general name of Amafengoo, they are however of many different nations, some of them from the neighbourhood of the Portuguese settlements on the East Coast but all speak the Caffer language, with various degrees of difference, as to the pronunciation.'[1] Still further up the coast Shrewsbury at Butterworth reported in July 1827 that the number of Fingo had so increased around that station

1 W. Shaw to Secretaries, Wesleyan Missionary Society, Wesleyville, 19 June 1827, M.M.S. 1827/17.

that '. . . they cannot be fewer than from 5 to 6,000 souls within a few miles round Butterworth.'[1] Some of these fugitives continued as far as the colonial frontiers and took service with the farmers around Grahamstown but the majority settled amongst the Pondo, Thembu, or Xhosa of the Transkei.

The chiefs, anxious to increase their following in relation to their rivals, received them well. As the fugitives were without any means of support the chiefs provided for them by placing them in charge of sections of the royal herds. This was in accordance with a recognized Bantu procedure under which the persons to whom such cattle were entrusted could use the milk but would not acquire rights of ownership in the cattle themselves. At first this arrangement was welcomed by the Fingo as it saved them from starvation but once they became established and recovered their self-confidence they began to resent the situation in which they were placed. Not only were cattle needed if marriages were to be contracted in the traditional way but the ownership of cattle was one of the most important marks of prestige in Bantu society. Without cattle of their own the Fingo felt themselves no more than unpaid herdsmen to the Xhosa chiefs. These chiefs, indeed, frowned on attempts by the newcomers to acquire cattle of their own by service with the whites or trade for they feared that if the Fingo had their cattle it would be difficult to distinguish these from those belonging to the royal herds and the way would be open for these latter to be stolen. In addition to this grievance the Fingo resented the attitude of the host tribes who tended to look down on them for their outlandish pronunciation and commonly referred to them as dogs. They thus came to feel themselves an oppressed minority and were eager for any opportunity to throw off the yoke.

If there had been no external influences at work the Fingo would ultimately have lost their separate identity and this did happen to a considerable extent with those who settled amongst the Pondo, but the activities of the missionaries amongst the tribes provided a stimulus to resistance. Their devotion to the traditional culture having been shaken by the events of the *Mfecane*, the Fingo found in the new way of life preached by the missionaries a channel through which to express their social revolt. Thus the missionaries were surprised and delighted by a rapidly increasing crop of converts from the Fingo people, to whom they ascribed virtues superior to those of the southern Nguni tribes. The chiefs who understood the cause for this movement did their best to persuade the missionaries not to accept Fingo converts and even

1 J. Shrewsbury to Secretaries, Wesleyan Missionary Society, Butterworth, 12 July 1827, M.M.S. 1827/19.

threatened to close the stations.[1] The result of this situation was to make the missionaries the champions of the Fingo cause.

The intrusion of so many newcomers into a territory already overcrowded as a result of the advance of the white frontier increased tension between the Bantu and the Colony. Some slight relief of pressure was gained when Macomo and other followers of Gaika were allowed to return to the neutral strip between the Fish and the Keiskamma, but the situation of these groups remained precarious. Colonial land-hunger and the irritation of cattle thefts led to ever-more insistent demands that the Bantu be driven still further back. The expulsion of Macomo from the neutral strip, the failure of D'Urban to follow up Philip's negotiations with the chiefs, signs of military preparations in Grahamstown, and finally the sufferings of a prolonged drought brought about the sudden outbreak of war in 1834. Colonial troops retaliating against the invasion of the Colony went beyond the territory of the Gaikas to interrogate the Gcaleka chief, Hintza, who was accused of receiving stolen cattle. With the unfortunate shooting of Hintza, both major branches of the Xhosa tribe became involved in a war which had spread from the frontier to the Transkei.

When British troops entered the Transkei the Fingo saw an opportunity to shake off the bonds of subordination to the Xhosa and seize the cattle they had herded for so long. They thronged to the British camp and begged to be placed under British protection. Sir Benjamin D'Urban saw in this an opportunity to weaken the Xhosa and he was moved by the humanitarian desire to protect these pro-Christian, pro-British Bantu from the vengeance which would certainly fall upon them. He acceded to their request, declared the Fingo to be British subjects and offered them land for settlement near the frontier, which would be taken from the Xhosa as a punishment for their invasion of the Colony. A great Fingo trek[2] then took place and they were resettled in the old neutral strip where they were to be protected by a new fort at Peddie. At first it was intended to drive the Xhosa out of all the lands between the frontier and the Kei River leaving this new province (Queen Adelaide Province) to be occupied by white settlers and the Fingo only The determined resistance of the Xhosa, however, finally convinced D'Urban that this was impracticable and missionary pressure led to the complete reversal of the original policy and the abandonment of Queen Adelaide Province. The Fingo thus found themselves living in close proximity to the tribe they had betrayed and whose cattle they had

1 Ayliff and Whiteside: *History of the Abambo*, pp. 20–2.
2 A contemporary description is given by Ayliff and Whiteside, op. cit., pp. 27–34.

stolen. The natural hostility of the Xhosa towards the Fingo was made even worse by the fact that the Fingo were settled on lands for which the Xhosa had fought so long. In these circumstances conflict could not be avoided and the British commitment to defend the Fingo kept the border areas in a state of tension for many years. As a result, the association between the Fingo and the British was strengthened and hostility between the former and the Xhosa was maintained.

Because of their early association with the missionaries, their alliance with the British and the degree to which traditional ways had been undermined by the *Mfecane*, the Fingo adopted western ideas much more rapidly than their more settled neighbours. New agricultural techniques were readily accepted and the figures for school attendance were very much greater than amongst other tribes. The Fingo locations were often held up as a model illustrating the possibilities of African development. The possibilities of economic development were, however, limited by the extent of land at their disposal. The area of their settlement formed part of the region in which Grey's unhappy experiment in mixed settlement was tried. It is now one of the most heavily eroded, overcrowded and poverty-stricken areas in South Africa.

Though the Fingo adapted themselves to European ways they suffered equally with their neighbours from the general pattern of colour discrimination. This has led to the more highly educated among them seeking to identify themselves with the language and traditions of the Xhosa. Because of the high degree of education amongst the Fingo they have provided many political leaders for African political movements of the Cape Province. Some of the greatest scholars of Xhosa language and culture have also come from this group.[1] Today, under the increasing pressure of white society, the delayed process of amalgamation of the northern peoples with the Xhosa is finally reaching fulfilment. Differences of language have almost disappeared, though occasional tricks of pronunciation still sometimes betray Fingo origin. Xhosa and Fingo intermarry and live alongside one another in many different occupations. Nevertheless, in the countryside the distinction between them and their neighbours still persists. The Xhosa sing war songs aimed against the Fingo and the old men recall the conflicts of earlier times. The Fingo, like refugee groups throughout the world, sing melancholy songs of their lost homeland. They look back to the lands beyond the Tugela and to their sufferings as a subject people forced to serve their Xhosa overlords.

1 The Jabavu family is a good example of this. An account of their background is given by N. Jabavu in *The Ochre People*.

12 The Mfecane in the History of Southern and East-Central Africa

UNTIL very recently African societies were generally thought of as static and stagnant, changing, if at all, with infinite slowness and needing the impact of outside influences to break out of the ossified shell of countless years of tradition. In accordance with this view the development of modern Africa was believed to be the result of European enterprise acting on passive material. The African patiently acquiesced or dumbly resisted but did not make any positive contribution to the pattern of the future. With the spread of the process of decolonization new historical perspectives are being adopted, for not only are African historians coming forward to write about their own peoples but the utilitarian motive of the need to understand the political attitudes and behaviour of the inhabitants of the newly independent African states as well as other considerations has led scholars throughout the world to interest themselves in the development of African societies rather than just the activities of Europeans on the continent. Nevertheless, there is still a tendency to concentrate on the reaction of Africans to European activities rather than on developments internal to African societies themselves. There are many obvious reasons for this but amongst them is the persistence of the view that African societies had no record of significant autonomous development and therefore no history, or none that is of importance as a guide to the understanding of the contemporary world.

The study of the Mfecane clearly shows the superficiality of this view. For it was essentially a process of social, political and military change internal to African society and taking place with explosive rapidity. This revolution not only produced catastrophic consequences at the time but has left a profound imprint on the demographic pattern of Southern and Central Africa. It also brought into existence peoples who still define their identity by reference to the leaders and the wars of the Mfecane. They include two distinct African Nations as well as others included in wider political groupings.

It is sometimes argued that the whole process was a direct or indirect reaction to European activities at the Cape. The chance acquaintanceship of Dingiswayo with the ill-fated white traveller has sometimes been invoked as the basic cause of the military revolution in Zululand. It was even suggested by Sir Theophilus Shepstone that Dingiswayo had visited the Cape and was inspired to introduce his military reforms by witnessing the drill of British troops.[1] Not only, however, is there no shred of evidence to suggest that the Mthethwa chief ever visited the Colony but the changes which took place in political and military organization under his rule and that of Shaka can be fully explained in terms of the modification of existing Bantu institutions. They show no distinctive resemblance to European patterns. The fact that the use of an age-regiment system appeared more or less simultaneously amongst a number of northern Nguni tribes suggests that it was a natural reaction to changing conditions and makes it doubtful whether Dingiswayo should be regarded as the sole originator.

Another more plausible argument is that it was the expansion of the Cape Colony, the frontier clashes with the Xhosa and the resulting closure of the Bantu migration route to the south which was the ultimate cause of the Mfecane. On this hypothesis a wave of compression swept back from the Fish River area to produce the conditions of overcrowding in Zululand which in turn generated the military revolution.[2] The attraction of this hypothesis lies more in its neat simplicity and the way that it relates widely separate developments in a common framework of explanation than in any evidence adduced to support it. If the closing of the frontier was the real cause of the explosion it is surprising that it should not have taken place in the immediate hinterland of the frontier where the evidence shows that there was severe overcrowding but rather at a distance of hundreds of miles. This is especially odd as there were places between the two points where population pressure was relatively low (e.g. the area referred to as Nomansland which received very large numbers of refugees during the Mfecane period).

The assumption of action at a distance would only be plausible if it were not possible to explain the situation in terms of more local conditions. In fact, however, such an explanation is perfectly possible. The area of Zululand and Natal is a fairly narrow strip between the escarpment and the sea. It is known to have supported a considerable Bantu population at least as early as the sixteenth century. The healthiness of the climate and the fertility of the soil, taken together with the marriage customs of the Bantu which aimed at conserving the reproductive

1 Bird: *Annals of Natal*, vol. I, p. 163.
2 This interpretation is adopted by Oliver and Fage: *A Short History of Africa.*

powers of every female (i.e. the custom of marrying widows to their husbands' brothers or encouraging them to live with other men called seed-raisers to bring up children in the dead men's names) suggest the probability of a rapid population increase. Examination of tribal histories and the rapid process of tribal multiplication which they exemplify, shows that all over Bantu South Africa population was in fact expanding at a very rapid rate. The only outlet for such expansion in the Zululand area was either onto the interior plateau to the west or southward down the coastal strip. Some westward movement onto the plateau undoubtedly did take place and accounts for the existence of numerous tribes of Nguni origin amongst the Sotho peoples of the Transvaal (the Transvaal Ndebele who appear to have established themselves on the plateau before the Mfecane). But migration out of the rich coastlands onto the plateau with its icy winters and its population of alien Sotho-speaking tribes would only be undertaken with reluctance. So far as southward migration was concerned the Zululand tribes were faced with a great bloc of peoples in Natal and the Transkei lying between them and the unoccupied country. Whether the frontier at the Fish River were open or closed would not alter the fact that before reaching it one would have to cut a path through the intervening peoples. The idea that the peoples of the coastal corridor could be shunted about without difficulty to provide room for any population increase so long as expansion at the extreme south was possible, ignores natural human inertia and the attachment of tribes to familiar places and the graves of their ancestors. It seems unlikely therefore that events on the eastern frontier of the Cape Colony had any very significant effect on the developments in Zululand. These can most probably be accounted for in terms of developments entirely internal to Bantu society, namely, the emergence of a pocket of high population pressure in Zululand and cultural contact between the Sotho and Nguni-speaking peoples in the area where the escarpment loses its sharp linear character.

The essential features of this revolution in its centre of origin were the adaptation of the initiation ceremonies to military purposes and the creation of a permanent standing army organized in age-regiments. This was a reaction to conditions of frequent and severe warfare and was probably stimulated by contact with the rudimentary age-regiment system of the Sotho peoples. It implied much greater internal unity within tribes, as the age-regiments made up of youths from all parts of the tribal territory took the place of the territorial chieftaincies as the immediate foci of political loyalty. It also went with a greater concentration of power in the hands of the ruler. As the balance of power which had given meaning to the traditional system of consultation disappeared, true despotism began to emerge. This in turn was associated with an administrative change of vital importance. There was a transition from a bureaucracy of 'royals' to a situation in which effective administrative authority passed into the hands of the class of commoner *indunas* personally chosen by the ruler and dependent on him.

This change involves a principle which can be seen in any human society developing in the direction of greater political centralization and more active government. It can be paralleled in the transition from feudal to bureaucratic administration which marks the emergence of the modern European state. It can also be seen in the history of many African kingdoms. In Bornu a change of this general type took place between the break-away of the Bulala and the reign of Mai Idris Alooma and was one of the main reasons for the relative stability of the kingdom. In the Oyo empire the same principle is seen in the Alafin's administrative hierarchy of slaves and eunuchs. In Buganda the power of the Kabaka depended on the fact that the highest officials were commoners, personally appointed by him and transferable at will from post to post, district to district. In Ethiopia the accounts of Alvarez show that the strength of government at the height of its powers depended on the same principle. Only in the Mfecane, however, can we see this transition in the administrative organization of an African people in its entirety.

As the rising pressure in Zululand forced various groups out of the area they took the basic pattern developed there to far-distant parts of the continent, modifying it in various ways in the light of circumstances. The Swazi who left the storm centre before the revolution reached its climax never developed the full Zulu-type military system but adopted a form of organization half-way between it and the traditional system of the Sotho tribes. They also did not develop the highly centralized system of government which was typical of the Zulu. The traditional checks and balances were retained in, for example, the relationship between the king and the Queen Mother and under Sotho influence they even evolved in the direction of increased democracy. The Ngoni combined the age-regiment system with the development of greatly expanded quasi-lineage groupings. This led to an ambivalence in their societies. The military system operated in the direction of centralization and the increased power and prestige of kings, but the growth of lineages encouraged decentralization and fragmentation.

The Ndebele, being a break-away section of the Zulu themselves, naturally reflected the details of the parent system most closely. The regimental system in its full development, the emergence of an *induna* bureaucracy, the immense concentration of power in the hands of the king, even the system of making a large proportion of the marriageable girls wards of the king can be seen in Mzilikazi's kingdom. Nevertheless circumstances brought important changes. The Zulu age-regiments constituted an army within a society. They included only a section of the population. There was always a civil administrative system alongside the military. The Ndebele, however, arose out of a secession of part of the army. For them state and army were identical and the military towns were the divisions of the whole people. Hence the tendency for the regiments to take on a permanent hereditary character and lose their original nature as age groupings to become territorial administrative divisions with the *indunas* coming to fulfil the role of territorial chiefs in the pre-*Mfecane* tribal system.

The growth of militarism and strong government typical of the Zulu-type states went with important changes of a moral order. They were inevitably accompanied by a greatly increased sense of discipline. Travellers who visited the Zulu or the Ndebele invariably noticed the contrast between them and their neighbours. The unrestrained curiosity, unashamed begging for gifts and the frequent petty thefts of which European visitors to Southern Bantu peoples complained, were almost unknown. Instead there was an attitude of haughty reserve and quiet dignity. This was accompanied by an indifference to human life and suffering, particularly with regard to persons outside the group, and a transference of loyalties from the family and clan to the state.

Probably the most striking political change brought about by the *Mfecane* is the change from the small clan-based tribe to the large kingdom uniting peoples of diverse tribal origin. All the Zulu-type kingdoms could be said to constitute experiments in multitribal nation-building. Shaka succeeded in the space of ten years in uniting the members of many different tribes and inspiring them with a sense of unity which still survives. Mzilikazi incorporated members not only from different tribes but widely different language groups in his kingdom and so successfully won the loyalty of peoples he had conquered and whose relatives he had destroyed, that their descendants are proud to consider themselves Ndebele. But these achievements almost fade into insignificance when compared with the success of the Ngoni. So rapid and massive was the intake of new members in their case that different branches of the original stock now speak languages which are mutually unintelligible. Yet in spite of the fact that the recruits came from peoples of radically different cultures, a recognizable Ngoni polity persisted. In their case one could almost say that it was not a group of people that moved but a system of political and military organization which passed through widely varying human material (almost but not quite, for the relatively tiny number of the original Nguni nucleus who accompanied the migration played a disproportionately important part in maintaining cultural cohesion).

With the exception of the Shangana whose kingdom was destroyed by the Portuguese, all these different groups succeeded in creating a sense of common identity amongst the peoples they brought together which has lasted until today. They did this in spite of the fact that all of them, with the exception of the Zulu, developed some form of internal class system. This is most obvious amongst the Ndebele with their three-tier system but it is also apparent amongst the Ngoni and to a lesser extent among the Swazi. The system of class distinctions was taken very seriously and greatly affected intermarriage between different sections of the communities concerned, but it was primarily a matter of social standing and prestige rather than of economic differentiation. In spite of this system it was possible for men of low social standing to rise to positions of power by their abilities and through distinguished service to the community. Thus the growth of class systems did not mean that newly incorporated peoples felt permanently debarred from full participation in the life of the community and prospects of high position within it. On the other hand the class system and the restriction of intermarriage associated with it helped to preserve the original culture from being diluted to vanishing point and at the same time fostered cultural cohesion by according prestige to the 'zansi' and their culture.

The Zulu-type states, however, are only one series of multitribal kingdoms which grew up as a result of the Mfecane. Numerous other peoples in South and Central Africa developed stronger and wider political systems as a reaction to conditions of strife and turmoil. In some cases new multitribal kingdoms were built up, like the Basuto kingdom of Moshesh, Mirambo's empire in Tanganyika or the Kololo kingdoms of the Shire valley. Sometimes existing tribes were expanded and their political systems strengthened as with the Ngwato or the Pedi of the northern Transvaal. Sometimes Zulu-type methods were borrowed as by the Hehe of Tanganyika; more often, traditional methods of political organization were employed and simply expanded to cover wider areas and larger numbers. The traditional Southern Bantu tribal system was flexible enough to allow of the expansion of the tribe to incorporate new groups and Moshesh was able to build a viable multitribal nation with these means alone.

One of the most striking features of the Mfecane is indeed the very general success which attended the numerous and different attempts at forming political units out of originally separate peoples. It suggests that the task of instilling a sense of political unity into peoples of different language and culture in a limited time, the task which faces every political leader in the newly independent African countries, is not so difficult as pessimists tend to maintain. The most striking example of failure in the Mfecane period, namely, the collapse of the Kololo kingdom in Barotseland, is also instructive in this regard. The causes of the catastrophe are plain. Apart from the steady numerical decline of the aristocratic nucleus in the fever-ridden flood plain of the upper Zambesi, the misrule of Sekeletu, his reversal of his father's wise policy of treating the conquered peoples as sons of the chief and the attempt of the true Kololo to arrogate to themselves the position of an exploiting aristocracy, brought about the disaster. Under Sebetwane, integration was proceeding to such an extent that the river peoples were already priding themselves on being Kololo. Even though this tendency was subsequently reversed and the state overthrown in a Lozi revolution, the short period of the empire's existence was sufficient to implant the Southern Sotho language of the Kololo (as well as other aspects of their culture) permanently in the alien soil of the upper Zambesi valley.

Though the Mfecane was essentially a process of political change, its most immediately obvious character is that of a holocaust of wars and migrations. It permanently modified the ethnic map of much of Bantu Africa and thereby played an important part in establishing the framework of political and cultural life in a number of modern African states. The establishment of the Ndebele in Southern Rhodesia and of the Ngoni in Malawi, Zambia and Tanganyika are obvious examples. The concentration of the southern Sotho around the Basutoland mountains and the establishment of the Swazi in their present homeland are others. In addition to these there were innumerable lesser instances of tribal displacement, less important individually perhaps but amounting, when taken together, to a revolutionary demographic change of profound significance. The general tendency produced by the havoc and destruction of the Mfecane wars was for the distribution of population to become more concentrated. Areas which offered good defensive features acquired dense populations often out of proportion to their agricultural potential. Other areas too open to offer protection against Zulu, Ndebele or Ngoni regiments were virtually deserted, even though they were naturally rich and fertile.

The pattern can be seen most clearly in South Africa where the effects were most severe and permanent. The rich and lovely land of Natal which had previously sustained a heavy Bantu population suffered the brunt of the military campaigns of the Zulu. Devastated from end to end by bands of refugees flying from the wrath of Shaka, it was visited annually by the Zulu regiments themselves until it was turned into a veritable solitude. The travellers and traders on whose reports we rely in reconstructing a picture of the situation, did not visit every nook and corner of the country. In view of the conditions of insecurity it is probable that survivors who remained in the land concealed themselves in inaccessible situations where they would be likely to have escaped notice. It is also not improbable that the European visitors to the area indulged in a certain amount of exaggeration on the subject of depopulation. Nevertheless, even when allowance is made for these possibilities, it is clear that Natal suffered a catastrophic decline of population, the bulk of its inhabitants being driven south to crowd into Nomansland and northern Pondoland or to settle down as Mfengu (Fingo) in the Transkei. The small remnant that remained had lost all their cattle and were too afraid of attracting attention to themselves to do much farming. On his first journey from Natal to Pondoland in 1824, Fynn '. . . witnessed very awful scenes, six thousand unhappy beings, having scarcely a human appearance, were scattered over this country, feeding on every description of animal, and driven by their hungry cravings in many instances to devour their fellows'.[1] A large proportion of these survivors gathered around the English traders at the Port, benefiting from the immunity which Shaka, and Dingane after him, accorded to the white men and their followers. In the aftermath of Shaka's assassination there may have been a small amount of migration back into Natal from the overcrowded areas to the south but not on a scale sufficient to alter the general picture. When Andrew Smith and his party passed through Natal on their way to visit Dingane in 1832 they found very few people after leaving the Pondo until they reached Port Natal.[2]

In Transorangia the devastations of the Hlubi, Ngwane and Tlokwa, and the Ndebele raids from across the Vaal together with the depredations of the Griquas, produced a similar result. The plains of what is now the Orange Free State were almost deserted, while population clustered round the skirts of the Basutoland mountains under the protection of Moshesh. In 1833 the Wesleyan missionary Archbell travelled eastward from his mission station at Platberg for twelve days through depopulated country, hardly seeing a single human being until he reached a Basuto outpost at Thaba Nchu.[3]

In the Transvaal the Ndebele regiments reduced the population of wide areas to a fraction of its former size. The ruins of previous settlements which Moffat saw on his journeys to visit Mzilikazi testify to the

1 Fynn: *Diary*, p. 22. 2 *Andrew Smith and Natal*, p. 29.
3 Archbell to Secretaries, Wesleyan Missionary Society, Platberg, 2 Sept. 1833, M.M S. 1833/28.

scale of the destruction and all the travellers' accounts agree in describing the deserted state of vast areas of fertile land.

In the north of the Transvaal the Zoutpansberg mountains offered some of the defensive advantages of the Basutoland area and there was a tendency for population to congregate there. Thus the Pedi, in spite of their defeat by the Ndebele, were able to retain their identity and to profit from the situation by building up a powerful kingdom which was later to defy the Transvaal Republic and precipitate the British annexation of 1877. On the fringes of the Kalahari also a considerable population was able to survive though it suffered fearfully, first from the invasion of Sebetwane and his Kololo and later from Ndebele raids. There the tendency was for the larger tribes to be swollen by refugees from weaker groups and for a greater premium to be placed on leadership than was traditional amongst the most democratic of the Southern Bantu peoples.

The immediate effect of the Mfecane in South Africa was therefore a drastic reduction of population in Natal, much of the Orange Free State and large areas in the Transvaal, while the neighbourhood of Basutoland and of the Zoutpansberg mountains became unnaturally crowded. In Bechuanaland, population maintained itself in spite of severe sufferings and the peoples of the coastal corridor between the Cape frontier and the borders of Natal were relatively unaffected (thanks to the successful defensive tactics of Faku, the Pondo ruler) though they had to accommodate numerous Fingo refugees. These displacements were essentially temporary in character. Loss of life must have been frightful, but with a rapid rate of population increase it would be restored in a few generations. Tribes which had fled from their homelands were awaiting the advent of peaceful conditions to return to them. (This is illustrated by the massive immigration of Bantu back into Natal after the Boer defeat of Dingane.) There can be little doubt that the demographic pattern would have readjusted itself again if events had not occurred which tended to crystallize the situation.

The growth of population and consequent land hunger which provided the dynamic force behind the Bantu expansion to the south and the explosion of the *Mfecane* operated with even greater force in the settler community of the Cape Colony. The white settlers' expectation of a standard of living considerably higher than the subsistence level enjoyed by the Bantu tribesmen and the economics of farming in South Africa at that period meant that a ranch of 6,000 acres was the minimum viable unit for white cattle farmers. As population grew very fast and the economic structure of society offered little alternative means of livelihood to the white settler, the frontiers of the Colony tended to expand rapidly with each generation. The tiny settlement on the Cape Peninsula established in 1652 grew so fast that by the beginning of the nineteenth century its eastern frontier had reached the Fish River and settlers were already speaking of pressing forward to the Koonap and the Kat. The natural line of advance lay along the line of greater rainfall up the east coast, but the determined resistance of the Xhosa tribesmen dammed up expansion in that direction and deflected some of the advance northward to the Orange River. By the second decade of the nineteenth century farmers were beginning to cross it and graze their cattle, even if only temporarily, alongside those of the Griqua in southern Transorangia. Meanwhile, as the pace of expansion failed to keep pace with growing population, land hunger in the Colony became more severe. Dissatisfaction with the British Government's policies, particularly with regard to the treatment of non-European labour, legal distinctions between the races and relations with the border tribes, also grew as that Government became increasingly influenced by the wave of humanitarian feeling which accompanied the Anti-Slavery movement. An upheaval of some kind could be expected but the form which it took depended as much on events within Bantu society as on the internal development of the settler community.

Missionary enthusiasm had led to the establishment of stations with tribes well beyond the colonial frontier and the economic circumstances of the Cape urged the more adventurous and the less scrupulous to seek their fortunes in trading ventures amongst the interior tribes. So many white traders were living with the east-coast tribes beyond the colonial frontier in 1832 that the price of commodities was very little higher than in the Colony.[1] This penumbra of missionaries, traders and scallywags provided a natural information network which kept people within the Colony informed of events in the interior. Hardly had the English traders established themselves in Natal for example than they began to urge that it be made a colony. Overland connection between Port Natal and the Cape through Pondoland and the Transkei was soon established and traders and travellers passed up and down bringing news of the rich land lying desolate in the interior. After the assassination of Shaka, pressure from the traders for the establishment of a colony was increased and in 1832 the Governor at the Cape sent Dr. Andrew Smith on a journey of exploration to Natal with secret instructions to investigate the potentialities of the place from the point of view of colonization and to ascertain the true wishes of Dingane.

Andrew Smith's expedition was accompanied by a number of Europeans. One of these, a lad named Hermanus Bury, the son of an English

1 *Andrew Smith and Natal*, p. 15.

father and a Dutch mother, was so excited by what he saw of Natal that he exclaimed, 'Almighty! I have never in my life seen such a fine place. I shall never again reside in the Colony if the English Government makes this a Drosdy.'[1] On the return of Smith's expedition an account was published in the *Grahamstown Journal* and on the 20th January a public meeting was held in Cape Town (previously advertised in English and Dutch in the *South African Commercial Advertiser* and the *Zuid Afrikaan*) to consider the question of establishing a settlement in Natal. The chairman, Cloete, in moving a resolution urging the Government to take steps for the establishment of a colony described Natal as 'depopulated by massacre for 200 miles;—or occupied if at all, by a few miserable wretches who find a scanty supply of roots and herbs in a country of vast extent,—inexhaustible in natural resources,—covered with rills of water, and demanding only the labours of the husbandman to call forth the choicest bounties of nature in rich abundance.'[2]

The situation in Transorangia and the Transvaal also came to be known in the Cape Colony. Missionaries on their journeys to collect supplies or recuperate their health could be expected to pass on a good deal of news and the farmers who took their cattle across the Orange River must have gathered information about events in the interior. In 1826 the Ordinance prohibiting trading expeditions north of the colonial boundaries was repealed and in the same year Andrew Geddes Bain took advantage of this to lead a trading party out of the colony amongst the Tswana tribes. It was in the course of this trip that he took part in the battle between the Ngwaketsi and the Kololo. In 1829 McLuckie and Schoon penetrated into the Transvaal and became the first white men to visit Mzilikazi. An account of their travels was published by J. C. Chase in the *South African Quarterly Journal*, who concluded by rejoicing that '. . . our stock of information regarding this quarter is likely to be speedily increased as two expeditions are now traversing those interesting regions'.[3] By 1834 interest in the Cape about the commercial prospects of the northern hinterland had reached such a pitch that a society for the exploration of the interior was formed in Cape Town and Dr. Andrew Smith was commissioned to lead an expedition to the territory of the Ndebele and beyond. On his visit to Mzilikazi he insisted on visiting parts of the king's domains outside the area of immediate settlement. The Ndebele evinced considerable reluctance,

1 *Andrew Smith and Natal*, p. 5.
2 Ibid., p. 147.
3 J. C. Chase, 'Substance of the Journal of two Trading Travellers and of the Communications of a Missionary', *South African Quarterly Journal*, vol. I, 1829, pp. 403–7.

for they feared that the result of his visit might be that white people would come and settle there, but they allowed him to visit the neighbourhood of their earlier capital Mhlahlandhlela (near present Pretoria) and he noted that there was wide land suitable for colonization.[1]

In 1834 also, as dissatisfaction in the Colony reached fever-pitch, men began to speak openly of secession; of migration into the interior to find new lands where they could govern themselves without interference from the British Government with its detestable belief in the equality of races and away from the ever-recurring strife with Bantu tribesmen which made life on the Eastern Frontier difficult and dangerous. As a first step three small parties (*commissie trekke*) were sent out to investigate the true position in the interior. One went to Natal, another into the Transvaal and a third to South-west Africa. When they returned the third party gave an adverse report but the other two were optimistic, especially the Natal group who were almost delirious with enthusiasm.

By this time the situation had altered. The perennial tension along the Eastern Frontier, aggravated by the influx of numerous homeless Mfengu amongst the overcrowded frontier tribes, had burst out in another war. D'Urban's sweeping annexation of the whole area between the frontier and the Kei River as Queen Adelaide Province and his declared intention to drive the Bantu out of it for ever and give it out for white settlement, delighted the settlers. It looked as if the expansion of the Colony would follow the natural geographic line. But the desperate resistance of the Xhosa tribesmen forced Harry Smith, who was in command of military operations, to conclude that it was militarily impossible to carry out the programme of expulsion. The plan would have to be modified and meanwhile missionary and philanthropic opinion turned on D'Urban and his policy with such force that his entire scheme was abandoned and Queen Adelaide Province handed back to the tribes.

This was the signal for the pent-up pressure in the Colony to release itself in the Great Trek, which passed northward through Transorangia, skirting the heavily populated kingdom of Moshesh, to pour into Natal and the Transvaal. The resulting distribution of peoples, the white settlements in Natal, the Orange Free State and the Transvaal, the solid bloc of Bantu occupation in the Transkei and Basutoland, the Bantu hold on Zululand and Swaziland and the relatively undisturbed Bantu settlement in the Zoutpansberg area and Bechuanaland were the result not of the action of white force on passive material but of a complex reaction between settler and Bantu societies. It was as much the work of Shaka and Moshesh as of Pretorius and Retief.

1 *Andrew Smith's Diary*, vol. II, p. 87.

The pattern established at the time of the Great Trek was subsequently modified by the further expansion of white landowning from the new nuclei, and the whole demographic map of South Africa has been further revolutionized by the consequences of mining and industrial development. Nevertheless, though the picture has been blurred, the battles and massacres of the Mfecane have left a permanent mark Not only do they account for the existence of the enclave African states, Basutoland, Swaziland and Bechuanaland, but also for the general distribution of white and Bantu landownership.

In Central Africa the picture is nothing like so clear, for the dislocations which resulted from the Mfecane merge into those produced by the Slave Trade and there was no pent-up settler population to pour into the gaps and solidify the situation. The evidence of Livingstone's travels as well as the accounts of other missionaries and travellers show that the sudden irruption of the Ngoni into East-Central Africa produced changes in population distribution comparable with those seen in South Africa. Some areas, like the shores on both sides of Lake Nyasa, offered refuge to a teeming population of overcrowded refugees while other areas, intrinsically more suitable for settlement, were wholly or partially abandoned. Here, as in South Africa, the Mfecane. contributed to the creation of conditions which invited white penetration albeit in a different form. To trace its effects on the peoples of Central Africa in detail would require a study in itself. It was a vital factor in the history of practically every major people between the Limpopo and the Great Lakes, the Congo watershed and the Indian Ocean.

A striking feature of the Mfecane is the quality of the leadership it called forth amongst the Bantu peoples. A whole dictionary of biography could be filled with accounts of the outstanding figures who emerged from this crucible of violent change. Many of them were men who demonstrated not only courage, powers of leadership and military skill but the capacity for original thought and action; the ability to devise or adopt new institutions and new techniques to solve new problems; the statesmanship to rise above a narrow tribal point of view. They demonstrated the capacity of the Bantu to respond to challenges and that the traditional tribal education had a far less cramping effect on the development of human personality than some have supposed.

The memory and traditions of the Mfecane have played and continue to play an important part in the lives of many Bantu peoples. For some it represents their heroic period and it is in terms of the leaders and events of those days that they define their unity and sense of identity. The Basuto still feel themselves the people of Moshesh; the Ndebele of

Mzilikazi. The Ngoni derive their sense of being a people from their historical traditions and seek to recapture the flavour of the past by relearning an Nguni language at any opportunity. This is true not only in the obvious cases of major peoples who owed their origin as corporate communities to the Mfecane but of many smaller and relatively obscure folk also; the Bhaca of the Transkei for example. For others the Mfecane is remembered as a dark period of suffering and defeat but which nevertheless helps to explain their internal institutions and their relations with their neighbours.

In the colonial period the traditions of the Mfecane have played an important part in determining psychological attitudes to white rule. It is no accident that the two greatest rebellions against white authority in the early phase of colonial rule should have broken out among the Ndebele and the Zulu or that the Ngoni should have played an active role in the Maji-Maji uprising against the Germans in Tanganyika. In more recent times the traditions of the Mfecane have retained their fascination largely because they provide a bulwark of self-respect, a shield against the crippling sense of inferiority encouraged by the authority structure of white-dominated society and the revolutionary pace of social and economic change produced by European technology. This development can be seen in the tendency of such groups as the Ngoni and the Ndebele to look back on the Mfecane as a golden age, ruined by white colonization. It can also be seen in the emergence at the high tide of the Ethiopian movement in South Africa of a Shaka Zulu church.[1] Thus in many subtle ways the traditions of the Mfecane help to keep a spirit of independence alive and to provide the basis on which Nationalist political movements are based. But though they serve this function they do not necessarily make for unity. The internal coherence of one people is often an obstacle to full co-operation with others, and the heroes of one group are not infrequently the villains of another. One thinks of the way that the Zulu sense of identity has sometimes been a factor of disunity in the African Nationalist movement in South Africa (Champion's break-away from the I.C.U. to form the I.C.U. lase Natal for example).[2] Political divisions in the Nationalist movement in Southern Rhodesia are also not unrelated to hostilities inherited from the Mfecane.

This is simply to demonstrate that to think of the role of the traditions of the period solely in terms of the confrontation of African Nationalism with European rule would be a gross oversimplification. Their role is much more complex than that for they underlie moral values and

1 Sundkler, *Bantu Prophets in South Africa*, p. 45.
2 See Roux: *Time Longer than Rope*, pp. 176–8.

character, as well as attitudes to authority in general and to relations between groups within, as well as across, the race barrier. Thus not only is the Mfecane a movement of fundamental importance in the past history of South and East-Central Africa but the victories and defeats, heroes and villains of the period, survive in memory as a potent force moulding moral, social and political attitudes in the contemporary world.

SOURCES

Unpublished Material

1. Material in the Archives of the Methodist Missionary Society, London.
   This is arranged in Files and Boxes. In most cases the file number is given but in one or two cases where the material did not come within the consecutive series I have referred to the Box reference.
2. Material in the Archivo Historico Ultramarina, Lisbon.
   The material is roughly sorted chronologically into boxes, *Caixa*, and bundles, *Maca*. There are also the *Codices* which are letterbooks kept by officers at Portuguese posts containing copies of correspondence despatched.

Published Material

ABRAHAM, D. P. — 'The Principality of Maungwe: Its History and Traditions', *Nada*, 28, 1951.

ALBERTO, M. S. — 'Os Angones os ultimos povos invasores da Angónia Portuguesa', *Moçambique*, 27, July–September 1941.

ANDERSSON, C. J. — *Lake Ngami*, London, 1856.

ARBOUSSET, REV. T. and DAUMAS, REV. F. — *Narrative of an exploratory tour to the north-east of the colony of the Cape of Good Hope*, Capetown, 1846.

ASHTON, H. — *The Basuto*, London, 1952.

AYLIFF, REV. J. and WHITESIDE, REV. J. — *History of the Abambo*, facsimile reprint of 1912 edition, Cape Town, 1962.

BACKHOUSE, J. — *A narrative of a visit to the Mauritius and South Africa*, London, 1844.

BAIN, A. G., edited LISTER, M. H. — *Journals of Andrew Geddes Bain*, Van Riebeeck Society, Cape Town, 1949.

BAINES, T. — *The gold regions of South Eastern Africa*, London, 1877.

BARNES, J. A. — *Marriage in a changing society* (Rhodes-Livingstone Papers, No. 20), Cape Town, 1951.

Politics in a changing society, London, 1954.

'Some aspects of political development among the Fort Jameson Ngoni', *African Studies*, vii, June 1948.

BAXTER, T. W. — 'The Angoni Rebellion and Mpeseni', *Northern Rhodesia Journal*, i, i, December 1950.

'More about Mpeseni', *Northern Rhodesia Journal*, ii, 6, 1955.

BECKER, P. — *Path of Blood*, London, 1962.

BEEMER, H. — 'The Development of the Military Organization in Swaziland', *Africa*, vol. X, no. 1, 1937.

BINNS, C. T. — *The last Zulu king*, London, 1963.

BIRD, J. — *The annals of Natal*, 2 vols., Pietermaritzburg, 1888.

BROADBENT, REV. S. — *A Narrative of the first introduction of Christianity amongst the Barolong Tribe*, London, 1865.

BROWN, R. — 'The Ndebele Succession Crisis, 1868–1877', in *Historians in Tropical Africa* (Proceedings of the Leverhulme History Conference, 1960), Salisbury, cyclostyled, 1962.

BRYANT, A. T. — *Olden times in Zululand and Natal*, London, 1929.

The Zulu People, Pietermaritzburg, 1949.

A history of the Zulu and neighbouring tribes, Cape Town, 1964.

BURTON, R. F. — *The Lake Regions of Central Africa*, London, 1860, 2 vols.

Lacerda's Journey to Cazembe in 1798, London, 1873.

CAMPBELL, J. — *Travels in South-Africa . . . (Second Journey)*, 2 vols., London, 1822.

CASALIS, REV. E. — *The Basutos*, London, 1861.

CHASE, J. C. — 'Substance of the journal of two trading travellers and of the communications of a missionary', *South African Quarterly Journal*, vol. 1, 1829.

CHIBAMBO, Y. M. — *My Ngoni of Nyasaland*, Africa's Own Library, 3, London, 1942.

COLSON, F. E. and GLUCKMAN, M., edited — *Seven tribes of British Central Africa*, London, 1951.

COOK, P. A. W. — 'History and Izibongo of the Swazi Chiefs', *Bantu Studies*, V, 2, 1931.

CRAWSHAY, R. — 'A journey in the Angoni country', *Geographical Journal*, iii, 1894.

CUVELIER, J. — *L'ancien Royaume du Congo*, Brussels, 1946.

DAVIS, C. S. — 'The Amandebele Habitat', *Nada*, 12, 1934.

DECLE, L. — *Three years in Savage Africa*, London, 1898.

DOYLE, D. — 'A Journey through Gazaland', *Proceedings of the Royal Geographical Society*, vol. XIII, new series.

DUBE, J. L., trans. BOXWELL, J. — *Jeqe the bodyservant of King Tshaka*, Lovedale Press, 1951.

EBNER, FR. E. — *History of the Wangoni* (cyclostyled), Songea, 1959.

ELLENBERGER, D. F. and MACGREGOR, J. C. — *History of the Basuto, ancient and modern*, London, 1912.

ELMSLIE, W. A. — *Among the Wild Ngoni*, Edinburgh, 1899.

ERSKINE, ST. VINCENT W. — 'Journey of Exploration to the Mouth of the River Limpopo', *Journal Royal Geographical Society*, 39, 1869.

FALLERS, L. A. — *Bantu Bureaucracy*, Cambridge, 1956.

FOÁ, É. — *Du Cap au Lac Nyassa*, Paris, 1897.

FRASER, D. — *The autobiography of an African*, London, 1925.

Winning a primitive people, London, 1914.

FURNEAUX, R. — *The Zulu War*, London, 1963.

FYNN, H., edited STUART, J. and MALCOLM, McK. D. — *The Diary of Henry Francis Fynn*, Pietermaritzburg, 1950.

GARDINER, CAPT. A. F. — *Narrative of a journey to the Zoolu Country*, London, 1836.

GENTHE, H. — 'A trip to Mpezeni's', *British Central Africa Gazette*, iv, 13, 1 August 1897.

GLUCKMAN, M. — 'The Kingdom of the Zulu', in Fortes and Evans Pritchard, edited, *African Political Systems*, London, 1940.

'Analysis of a social situation in modern Zululand' (Rhodes-Livingstone Papers, no. 28), Manchester, 1958, reprinted from *Bantu Studies*, xiv, 1940.

'The Lozi', in Colson and Gluckman, ed., *Seven Tribes of British Central Africa*, London, 1951.

GREENBERG, J. H. *The Languages of Africa*, Indiana, 1963.

GULLIVER, P. H. 'A History of the Songea Ngoni', *Tanganyika Notes and Records*, no. 41, December 1955.

HALFORD, S. J. *The Griquas of Griqualand*, Cape Town, 1941.

HALL, R. de Z. 'Angoni Raids in the Rufiji District', *Tanganyika Notes and Records*, 27, June 1949.

HAMMOND-TOOKE, W. D. *Tribes of the Mount Frere District, Bhaca society*, Cape Town, 1962.

HARRIS, CAPT. W. C. *The wild sports of Southern Africa*, London, 1839.

HARVEY, R. J. 'Mirambo, the Napoleon of Central Africa', *Tanganyika Notes and Records*, 28, January 1950.

HATCHELL, G. W. 'The Angoni of Tanganyika Territory', *Man*, xxxv, 1935, no. 73.

HLAZO, T. J. 'The Naming of the Hill "Intaba Yezinduna", Matabeleland', *Nada*, 12, 1934.

HODGSON, A. G. O. 'Notes on the Achewa and Angoni of the Dowa District of the Nyasaland Protectorate', *Journal of the Royal Anthropological Institute*, LXIII, 1933.

HOLDEN, W. C. *The past and future of the Kaffir races*, London, 1866.

HOLE, H. M. *Lobengula*, London, 1929.
The passing of the black Kings, London, 1932.

HOW, M. 'An Alibi for Mantatisi', *African Studies*, vol. 13, no. 2, 1954.

HUGHES, A. J. B. *Kin, Caste and Nation among the Rhodesian Ndebele* (Rhodes-Livingstone Papers, no. 25), Manchester, 1956.

HUNT, D. R. 'An Account of the Bapedi', *Bantu Studies*, v, 1931.

HUNTER, M. (WILSON) *Reaction to Conquest*, London, 1961.

ISAACS, NATHANIEL, edited HERMANN, L. *Travels and Adventures in Eastern Africa*, Van Riebeeck Society, Cape Town, 1936, 2 vols.

JABAVU, N. *The ochre people*, London, 1963.

JOHNSTON, K. 'Native Routes in East Africa from Dar-es-Salaam towards Lake Nyassa', *Proceedings of the Royal Geographical Society*, 1, 1879.

JONES, N. (MHLAGAZA-NHLANSI) — *My Friend Kumalo*, Salisbury, 1945.

Journal des Missions Évangéliques de Paris.

JUNOD, H. A. — *The life of a South African tribe*, London, 1927.

KAY, S. — *Travels and researches in Caffraria*, London, 1833.

KERR, W. M. — *The far interior*, 2 vols., London, 1886.

DE KIEWIET, C. W. — *British colonial policy and the South African Republics, 1848–1872*, London, 1929.

KOLLMAN, P. — *The Victoria Nyanza*, London, 1899.

KOTZÉ, D. J. edited — *Letters of the American missionaries, 1835–1838*, Van Riebeeck Society, Cape Town, 1950.

KUPER, H., HUGHES, A. J. B. and VAN VELSEN, J. — 'The Shona and Ndebele of Southern Rhodesia', in *Ethnographic Survey of Africa*, London, 1955.

KUPER, H. — *An African Aristocracy*, London, 1947.
'The Swazi', in Daryll Forde, edited, *Ethnographic Survey of Africa*, London, 1952.

LAGDEN, SIR G. Y. — *The Basutos*, 2 vols., London, 1909.

LANCASTER, D. G. — 'Tentative chronology of the Ngoni', *Journal of the Royal Anthropological Institute*, lxvii, 1937.

LANE-POOLE, E. H. — 'The date of the crossing of the Zambesi by the Ngoni', *Journal of the Africa Society*, xxix, April 1930.

LAWS, R. — *Reminiscences of Livingstonia*, Edinburgh, 1934.

LEWIS, D. G. — 'Lobengula's Regiments: Recruiting and Lobola', *Nada*, 33, 1956.
'The Battle of Zwangendaba', *Nada*, 33, 1956.

LICHTENSTEIN, M. H. K. — *Travels in Southern Africa*, 2 vols., Van Riebeeck Society, 1928, 1930.

LIENGME, G. — 'Un Potentat Africain: Goungounyane et son règne', *Bulletin de la Société Neuchateloise de Géographie*, 13, 1901.

LIVINGSTONE, DAVID and CHARLES — *Narrative of an expedition to the Zambesi and its tributaries*, London, 1865.

LIVINGSTONE, DAVID — *Missionary travels and researches in South Africa*, London, 1857.

LIVINGSTONE, DAVID, edited SCHAPERA, I. — *David Livingstone's Family Letters, 1841–1856*, 2 vols., London, 1959.
LIVINGSTONE, DAVID, edited WALLER, H. — *The last journals of David Livingstone*, 2 vols., London, 1874.
LIVINGSTONE, W. P. — *A Prince of Missionaries*, London, n.d.
Laws of Livingstonia, London, 1921.
MACGREGOR, J. C. — *Basuto Traditions*, Cape Town, 1905.
MACKENZIE, J. — *Ten years north of the Orange river*, Edinburgh, 1871.
MACMILLAN, W. — *Bantu, Boer and Briton*, Oxford, 1963.
MAPLES, CHAUNCY, edited MAPLES, E. — *Journals and papers of Chauncy Maples*, London, 1899.
MARAIS, J. S. — *Maynier and the First Boer Republic*, Cape Town, 1944.
MARWICK, B. A. — *The Swazi*, Cambridge, 1940.
MASON, P. — *The birth of a dilemma*, London, 1958.
(AL) MASUDI, trans. DE MEYNARD, C. B. and DE COURTEILLE, P. — *Les prairies d'or*, 9 vols., Paris, 1861–77.
MHLANGA, W. — 'The Story of Ngwaqazi', *Nada*, 25, 1948.
'The History of the Amatshangana', *Nada* 25, 1948.
MOFFAT, ROBERT — *Missionary labours and scenes in Southern Africa*, London, 1842.
MOFFAT, ROBERT, edited WALLIS, J. P. R. — *Matabele journals*, 2 vols., London, 1945.
MOFFAT, ROBERT, edited SCHAPERA, I. — *Apprenticeship at Kuruman*, London, 1951.
MOIR, F. L. M. — *After Livingstone*, London, 1923.
MONTEZ, C. — 'As invasoes dos Mangunis e dos Machanganas', *Moçambique*, 9–10, 1937.
MOODIE, D. C. F. — *The History of the battles and adventures of the British, the Boers and the Zulus*, Cape Town, 1888.
MSEBENZI, G., edited VAN WARMELO, N. J. — *History of Matiwane and the Amangwane Tribe*, Pretoria, 1938, Dept. of Native Affairs, Ethnological Publications, vii.
MURDOCK, G. P. — *Africa. Its peoples and their culture history*, New York, 1959.
MURRAY, A. C. — *Nyasaland en mijne ondervindingen aldaar*, Amsterdam, 1897.
OLIVER, R. and FAGE, J. D. — *A short history of Africa*, London, 1962.

OSWELL, W. E.	*William Cotton Oswell*, 2 vols., London, 1900.
OWEN, REV. F., edited SIR G. CORY	*Diary of Rev. Francis Owen*, Van Riebeeck Society, Cape Town, 1926.
OWEN, CAPT. W. F. W.	*Narrative of voyages to explore the shores of Africa, Arabia and Madagascar*, 2 vols., London, 1833.
POSSELT, F. W. T.	'Mzilikazi: the rise of the Amandebele', *Proceedings and Transactions of the Rhodesian Scientific Association*, xviii, pt. 1, July 1919.
PRELLER, G. S.	*Voortrekkermense*, 3 vols., Cape Town, 1920–25.
RANGELEY, W. H. J.	'The Makololo of Dr. Livingstone', *Nyasaland Journal*, 12, 1, January 1959.
	'Mtwalo', *Nyasaland Journal*, v, 1, January 1952.
READ, M.	'Tradition and prestige among the Ngoni', *Africa*, ix, 4 October 1936.
	'The Moral Code of the Ngoni and their former military state', *Africa*, xi, 1, 1938.
	'Songs of the Ngoni people', *Bantu Studies*, xi, 1 November 1937.
	The Ngoni of Nyasaland, London, 1956.
RITTER, E.	*Shaka Zulu*, London, 1955.
ROUX, E.	*Time Longer than Rope*, London, 1964.
SAMUELSON, R. C. A.	*Long Long Ago*, Durban, 1929.
SCHAPERA, I.	'The Tswana', in Daryll Forde, edited, *Ethnographic Survey of Africa*, London, 1953.
	Government and politics in tribal societies, London, 1956.
	The ethnic composition of Tswana tribes, London, 1952.
	Ditirafalo tsa Merafe ya Batswana, Lovedale, 1940.
SCHAPERA, I. edited	*The Bantu-speaking tribes of South Africa*, 4th edition, London, 1953.
	The Khoisan peoples of South Africa, London, 1930.
SHAW, W.	*Memoirs of Mrs. Anne Hodgson*, London, 1836.

SHAW, W. *The Story of my mission in South-eastern Africa*, London, 1860.

SILLERY, A. *Sechele*, Oxford, 1954.

SLASKI, J. 'Peoples of the Lower Luapula Valley', in *Ethnographic Survey of Africa*, London, 1951.

SOGA, J. H. *The South-eastern Bantu*, Johannesburg, 1930.

SMITH, ANDREW, edited KIRBY, P. R. *Andrew Smith and Natal*, the Van Riebeeck Society, Cape Town, 1955.

The Diary of Dr. Andrew Smith, 2 vols., Van Riebeeck Society, Cape Town, 1939.

SMITH, E. W. 'Sebetwane and the Makololo', *African Studies*, 15, 2, 1956.

The life and times of Daniel Lindley, London, 1949.

SPEKE, J. H. *Journal of the discovery of the source of the Nile*, London, 1863.

STANLEY, H. M. *Through the dark continent*, New York, 1878.

How I found Livingstone, New York, 1872.

STEEDMAN, A. *Wanderings and adventures in the interior of Southern Africa*, London, 1835, 2 vols.

STEVENSON-HAMILTON, J. *The low-veld: its wild life and its people*, London, 1929.

STOW, G. *The native races of South Africa*, London, 1905.

SUMMERS, R. 'The Military Doctrine of the Matabele', *Nada*, 32, 1955.

SUNDKLER, B. G. M. *Bantu prophets in South Africa*, London, 1961.

SWANN, A. J. *Fighting the slave-hunters in Central Africa*, London, 1910.

Swaziland Bluebooks.

TABLER, E. C. *The Far Interior*, Cape Town, 1955.

TAYLOR, G. A. 'The Matabele Head Ring and some Fragments of History', *Nada*, 3, 1925 (reprinted in 16, 1939).

TEW, M. 'Peoples of the Lake Nyasa Region', in Daryll Forde, edited, *Ethnographic Survey of Africa*, London, 1950.

THEAL, G. M. *Basutoland Records* (1883). Facsimile re-

production in 4 volumes, Struik, Cape Town, 1964.
History of South Africa since 1795, vols. 1 and 2, London, 1926, 1927. (Vols. v and vi of complete series.)
Records of South-Eastern Africa, vol. VIII, Cape Town, 1902.
The Portuguese in South Africa, Cape Town, 1896.

THOMPSON, J. *To the Central African lakes and back*, London, 1881, 2 vols.

THORNTON, R. W. *The Origin and History of the Basuto Pony*, Marika, 1936.

TOBIAS, P. 'Bushmen of the Kalahari', *Man*, March 1957.

TYLDEN, G. *The rise of the Basuto*, Cape Town, 1950.

WALKER, E. *A History of Southern Africa*, London, 1957.
The Great Trek, 4th edition, London, 1960.

WALTON, J. 'Villages of the Paramount Chiefs of Basutoland I: Butha Buthe', *Lesotho*, 1, 1959.
'Villages of the Paramount Chiefs of Basutoland II: Thaba Bosiu, the Mountain Fortress of Chief Moshesh', *Lesotho*, 2, 1960.

WARHURST, P. R. *Anglo-Portuguese Relations in South-Central Africa*, London, 1962.

WHITELEY, W. 'The Bemba and related peoples of Northern Rhodesia', in Daryll Forde, edited, *Ethnographic Survey of Africa*, London, 1951.

WIESE, C. 'Expedição portugueza a M'Pesene', *Boletim da Sociedade de Geographia de Lisboa*, x, 1891, and xi, 1892.

WILKERSON, G. J. *The Matabele Nation*, Manuscript in Central African Archives.

WILSON, G. H. *History of the Universities Mission to Central Africa*, U.M.C.A., 1936.

WILSON, M. 'The Early History of the Transkei and Ciskei', *African Studies*, 18, 4, 1959.

WINTERBOTTOM, J. M. 'A Note on the Angoni paramountcy', *Man*, xxxvii, 1937.

WOODS, G. G. B. 'Matabele History and Customs', *Nada*, 7, 1929.

'Extracts from Customs and History: Amandebele', *Nada*, 9, 1931.

YOUNG, E. D. *Nyassa*, London, 1877.

YOUNG, T. C. *Notes on the history of the Tumbuka-Kamanga peoples*, London, 1932.

'Tribal intermixture in Northern Nyasaland', *Journal Royal Anthropological Institute*, LXIII, 1933.

Index